D1605232

Energize the Network

ENERGIZE THE NETWORK

Distributed Computing Explained

MARK NORRIS
NEIL WINTON

Addison-Wesley

Harlow, England ● Reading, Massachussets ● Menlo Park, California ● New York
Don Mills, Ontario ● Amsterdam ● Bonn ● Sydney ● Singapore ● Tokyo
Madrid ● San Juan ● Milan ● Mexico City ● Seoul ● Taipei

© Addison Wesley Longman 1996

Addison Wesley Longman Limited
Edinburgh Gate
Harlow
Essex
CM20 2JE
England

and Associated Companies throughout the world.

The rights of Mark Norris and Neil Winton to be identified as authors of this Work has been asserted by them in accordance with the Copyright, Designs and Patents Act 1988.

All rights reserved. No part of this publication may be reproduced, stored in a retrieval system, or transmitted in any form or by any means, electronic, mechanical, photocopying, recording or otherwise, without the prior permission of the publisher or a licence permitting restricted copying in the United Kingdom issued by the Copyright Licensing Agency Ltd, 90 Tottenham Court Road, London W1P 9HE.

The programs in this book have been included for their instructional value. They have been tested with care but are not guaranteed for any particular purpose. The publisher does not offer any warranties or representations nor does it accept any liabilities with respect to the programs.

Many of the designations used by manufacturers and sellers to distinguish their products are claimed as trademarks. Addison Wesley Longman has made every attempt to supply trademark information about manufacturers and their products mentioned in this book. A list of the trademark designations and their owners appears on page xviii.

Cover designed by Designers & Partners, Oxford
and printed by The Riverside Printing Co. (Reading) Ltd
Typeset by Wyvern Typesetting Limited, Bristol
Printed and bound at the University Press, Cambridge

First printed 1996

ISBN 0–201–87738–4

British Library Cataloguing-in-Publication Data
A catalogue record for this book is available from the British Library.

Library of Congress Cataloging-in-Publication Data is available

To Libby, Rebecca and Benjamin, for constantly reminding me
that there are many more important things than writing a book –
but giving me the motivation to do so.

NDW

To Kate, Amy and Adam, whose concept of distribution
is different from mine, but no less interesting.

MTN

Contents

Preface   xi

A reader's guide to this book   xii

Acknowledgements   xv

About the authors   xvii

1 A distributed world   1

1.1 The dawn of the information age   3
1.2 Local knowledge, global presence   5
1.3 Anytime, anyplace, anywhere   7
1.4 The brave new world   11
1.5 About this book   15
1.6 Summary   16

2 Where are we now?   17

2.1 The seven ages of computing   18
2.2 Enterprise computing   30
2.3 Seven labours   33
2.4 Summary   37

3 The user's view   39

3.1 A window on the world   40
3.2 A World Wide Web   45
3.3 New horizons   46
3.4 Under the covers   48
3.5 Graunch and go   54
3.6 The shape of distributed systems   55
3.7 Summary   57

4 The big ideas   59

4.1 Transparency – smoke and mirrors?   61
4.2 Messaging – the electronic lifeblood   62
4.3 Clients, servers, peers, agents – what's in a name?   64
4.4 Partitioning – it will all end in tiers …   68
4.5 Objects – a rose by any other name   73
4.6 Parallelism – many hands make light work   81
4.7 Federation – peaceful co-existence   84
4.8 Who cares about distributed *processing* anyway?   85
4.9 Summary   86

5 Big ideas in practice   87

5.1 Remote procedure call – the distributed cover-all   88
5.2 Messaging – back to basics   103
5.3 Transactions and groups – coping with failure   114
5.4 Distributed objects – objects of desire   127
5.5 Necessary infrastructure – the supporting cast   140
5.6 Other technologies – the motley crew   150
5.7 Internet terminals and mobile code – the future of distributed
       computing?   155
5.8 Summary   158

6 Integration   161

6.1 Differentiation explained   162
6.2 Integration explained   165

6.3 The beleaguered user   169
6.4 The good citizen   179
6.5 Right next time   181
6.6 Making it happen   183
6.7 Legacy people   185
6.8 Summary   187

7   Common concerns   189

7.1 Security   189
7.2 Manageability   198
7.3 Performance   206
7.4 Reliability   207
7.5 Scalability   210
7.6 A cautionary tale   213
7.7 Summary   213

8   A route map   215

8.1 Architecture – the big picture   215
8.2 Rules of thumb   219
8.3 The people component   232
8.4 Summary   233

9   Metamorphosis   235

9.1 Great expectations   236
9.2 Sense and sensibility   238
9.3 A room with a view   239
9.4 Paradise lost   241
9.5 The master builder   243
9.6 Never-ending story   246

Appendix A Standards for distributed systems   **249**
               – who's who and who matters?

A.1 A little history   250
A.2 The key players   252

A.3 Standards strategy   262
A.4 How they work together   264
A.5 Summary   266

Glossary   267

References   299

Index   305

Preface

The information age is no longer a distant dream. The practical components that make it a reality are being deployed – now. Those who do not adapt to this new age will cease to compete, sooner rather than later. An appreciation of its challenges and opportunities is vital.

It is important not only to know what the issues are, but also what you can do about them and what is on offer to meet your needs. Where does technology help and how can you make it work in your environment?

This book has several unique features:

- It puts a wide range of networked systems issues into context. Rather than explaining the detail of one or two particular technologies, it explains why they have evolved, how they relate to one another and what the user needs to know to capitalize on them. The aim is to provide guidance and advice based on broad experience.

- It takes the pragmatic view of a complex area that has come to be dominated by technology, not always in the user's best interests. Care has been taken here to abstract from this technical complexity and make the topics covered accessible and relevant to real needs. The focus is on practical application rather than technology *per se*. This approach leads to an even-handed treatment with no supply or technology bias.

It is intended for a wide range of readers:

- Essential reading for those engaged in the purchase, planning, design and implementation of information-intensive systems. This book provides the broad understanding required to avoid expensive mistakes.

- A valuable professional updating guide for those who need to appreciate the practical subtleties of a complex subject – telecommunications engineers, system analysts and software designers, as well as business and information planners.

- A useful text for final year and postgraduate students in computer science, electrical engineering and telecommunications courses.

It seems likely that there will be few speed limits on information superhighways: and no turning back. Those who choose to stay in the lay-bys will be left behind very quickly. Those who choose to compete in the new age need to be aware of what lies ahead. Informed choices, taken now, will pay handsome dividends as complexity and choice (inevitably) rise. The end of the twentieth century is likely to be seen, in retrospect, as the 'adapt or atrophy' period for many organizations – this book can inform an exciting but perilous journey.

A reader's guide to this book

This book was really inspired by our wish to give a straightforward account of a subject often wrapped in baffling jargon and unnecessary complexity. We spent a long time ourselves making some sense of distributed systems and would like to spare others from this subtle form of torture. So we have tried our best to cater for a wide range of tastes by explaining both the technology and the impact of distributed systems. As far as possible, we have tried to avoid specifics – this is an area of technology that moves fast enough to make today's hot topic a faint memory tomorrow. There will be some products or technologies that we do not fully address. It is principles and basic ideas that will endure, however, and this is where we have tried to focus.

Different parts of the book will, no doubt, be more or less relevant to different people. Some parts have been written with the user in mind, others with the developer. To help you select a suitable path through the book, here is our summary of the joys that we think each chapter contains.

	Technical Content	Interest to Users	Interest to Developers
Chapter 1	★	★★★	★★★
Chapter 2	★	★★★★	★★
Chapter 3	★★	★★★★★	★
Chapter 4	★★★	★★★	★★★★
Chapter 5	★★★★★	★	★★★★★
Chapter 6	★★★★	★★★	★★★★
Chapter 7	★★★	★★★	★★★
Chapter 8	★★★	★★	★★★★
Chapter 9	★	★★★★	★★★
Appendix 1	★★★	★★	★★

To help those who prefer an occasional dip into a technical book, rather than a concerted attack, we have appended a fairly large glossary that should help get you through the more challenging sections.

Acknowledgements

The authors would like to thank a number of people whose help and cooperation has been invaluable. To those kind individuals who contributed ideas, advice, words, pictures and even volunteered (we use this word in its loosest sense) to review early drafts:

Professor Dave Bustard, Professor Richard Ennals, Peter Dadson, Dr Andy Herbert, Dr Allan Hudson, Ray Kent, Ray Lewis and his colleagues in the Systems Integration team, Steve West, John Wright, Steve Wright and all those involved in the first IEE distributed systems school.

Their observations, illustrative stories, guidance and constructive criticism have always been valuable and have done much to add authority, interest and balance to the final product.

Thanks are also due to our many friends and colleagues in the telecommunication and computing industries, standards bodies and professional organizations whose experience, advice and inside knowledge has been invaluable.

About the authors

Mark Norris has over 15 years' experience in software development, computer networks and telecommunications systems. Over this time he has managed dozens of projects to completion from the small to the multimillion pound, multi-site. He has worked for periods in Australia and Japan and currently manages BT's corporate information technology programme. He has published widely over the past 10 years with a number of books on software engineering, project management, telecommunications and network technologies. He lectures on network and computing issues, has contributed to reference works such as *Encarta* and is a fellow and active member of the IEE.

Neil Winton has worked in the computing industry for over 10 years. During this time he has been involved in a wide range of software development projects ranging from network management systems to a security-enhanced variant of UNIX. He has represented BT on international standards committees, particularly concerned with systems management. Neil's involvement with distributed systems stretches back more than five years and he has been responsible for the investigation and evaluation of a number of technologies. At present he is one of the main technical architects for the introduction of client/server technology into BT's operational support systems. In his (rare) spare time Neil is a passable tuba player but he tries not to mix this with distributed computing!

Trademark notice

ANSAware™, AnsaWeb™ are trademarks of APM
Apple Lisa™ is a trademark of Apple Computer, Inc.
Commodore PET™ is a trademark of Commodore
CompuServe™ is a trademark of CompuServe
DAIS™ is a trademark of ICL
DEC Microvax™, Decnet™ and ObjectBroker™ are trademarks of Digital Equipment Corporation
Eudora™ is a trademark of Qualcomm Incorporated
EZRPC™ is a trademark of Noble Net
HotJava™ and Java™ are trademarks of Sun Microsystems, Inc.
IPX™ and Netware™ are trademarks of Novell
Lan Manager™, Message Express™, MS-Mail™, MS-Word™ and MSDOS™ are trademarks and Windows®, Windows 95®, Windows for Workgroups® and Windows NT® are all registered trademarks of Microsoft Corporation
NewWave™ and ORBplus™ are trademarks of Hewlett Packard
NextStep™ is a trademark of Next
OMNI*Point*™ is a trademark of Network Management Forum
Oracle™ is a trademark of Oracle Corporation
Orbix™ is a trademark of Iona Technologies
Sybase™ is a trademark of Sybase Corporation
UNIX™ is a trademark of X/Open
Vines® is a registered trademark of Banyan Systems, Inc.

CHAPTER I

A distributed world

'The revolution will not be televised' – Gil Scott Heron

It should be obvious to most people that the quality of a communications infrastructure has a big impact on the well-being of a community. It is one of the biggest factors in determining where industry is placed, how competitive it is and how much profit it makes. Closer to home, most people's quality of life depends, to some extent, on good communications.

But what do we mean by 'communications infrastructure' here? Up until the start of the twentieth century we would have been looking at roads, canals and railways. Even a few years ago you would only have extended the list to include airways and telephones. But the past few years have seen a dramatic change in both the reality and perception of what a communications infrastructure should be. The arrival of high-speed, high-capacity telecommunications systems has taken the distance out of data. It is now possible to transmit information that, only recently, had to be physically moved.

The way in which information is generated, stored, transmitted and processed is changing in a way that is revolutionizing how many people work. In the very near future, everyone will have the wherewithal to be a publisher, a composer, an analyst. They will have access to huge amounts of data and will be able to process it with consummate ease. And those who have the skill to distil this sea of data into useful information are likely to be rare and highly prized (Gore, 1995). The end of the twentieth century is set fair to be recognized as the dawn of the information age, as significant a change as the earlier industrial and agricultural revolutions.

History has done little to prepare us for this new age. In terms of social development, the oral tradition that requires vital facts to be memorized has only recently passed. The advent of printing allowed ideas to be recorded for reference and
shared with many others. Usually these ideas were recorded in the form of structured text – a story or argument supported by reason, explanation or illustration.
We now have the prospect of infinitely malleable, instantly changeable (and,
often, context-free) data. The new age will require new concepts to cope with this
wealth of data and, perhaps, paucity of information.

The technical components that drive the information age are either in place or
soon to be deployed. Optical fibre systems already form the backbone of the wide
area communications network (Davies *et al.*, 1993). Local area networks provide
powerful single-site networks. Increasingly, the two are being connected to
provide the total area networks that give high-capacity service, irrespective of
location (Atkins and Norris, 1995).

As the information highway concept develops, the 'copper bottlenecks' that once
constrained speedy communication over large distances will be removed. The
network-imposed speed limits between computers and their users will disappear.
And it is likely to be the professional users along with the enthusiastic amateurs
who are in the vanguard of this revolution. There is a route for the creativity, innovation and analytical power currently confined to local areas, to burgeon into the
global arena.

But first, you have to know how to capitalize on the opportunity. Just as the fron-
tiersmen of the 1800s had to explore the physical structure of the Wild West, so
the high-tech entrepreneurs will have to map out their homesteads in cyberspace.

So the question is – how do you deploy technology that is not constrained by
physical limitations? And when you have deployed it, how do you use it to good
effect and keep it in line with ever-changing needs?

These are not simple questions. Even so, we can gain some insight on them by
examining the world as it is now. To start with, most people are familiar with
many of the common computing network elements – personal computers, workstations, local area networks, modems and the like. The fulfilment of the information age, though, lies in what you use the combination of these elements to achieve
and this leads, inevitably, to distributed computing: the processing of readily available data. This is the key to using the information highways to good effect.

In truth, the term 'information highway' should be revised to 'data highway' to
reflect the current situation. The purpose (to process data into information) to support the means (connecting computers together) has yet to be fully explored. This
is what our book is all about and the two questions in the above paragraph are
what we intend to answer.

Let's start to consider the path that has taken us to the edge of the information age
with a short 'parable' that encapsulates the evolution from the local to the distributed:

Once upon a time there was a Team. The Team gathered together every day in one place. There they worshipped and made offerings to the Great Blue Idol. Only a chosen few High Priests could approach the Idol in its sanctuary. Yet the Team worked well together and listened in awe to the Idol's pronouncements.

Time passed and the Priesthood became seen as an onerous burden on the Team. So it was that members of the Team were allowed to submit their offerings to the Idol without the intervention of the Priesthood. Yet still the' Idol retained its hallowed place.

Then one day life changed – forever. The creators of the Idol had a Great Idea. They created many smaller, less powerful Idols. These Idols did not require an elite Priesthood or a special sanctuary. These Idols did the sole bidding of their owner. Soon, every member of the Team possessed and coveted their own Idol. But could the Team still work together?

Read on …

Much of what follows is captured in this (very) short story. To be useful, we need to unfold the story and attach it to the real world. This chapter starts on this path by describing the main forces – commercial and technological – which drive towards a 'distributed world'. In doing so we aim to show the benefits (and a few of the perils) which we may obtain from distributed computing. Indeed, part of the argument will be that commercial survival itself will, increasingly, come to depend on effective distribution. It will be the only way of providing both the reach and the flexibility that will be essential to compete.

We then go on to discuss some of the ways in which several long-cherished assumptions about computing have to be turned on their heads in a distributed world, for example that local operations become remote, that monolithic centralized control has to be broken down and dispersed and that a closed, safe environment turns into an open (and potentially hostile) one.

By the end of the chapter you should be familiar with the major themes and issues associated with distributed computing. You should also understand why computers have had to change. This sets the background for the following chapters which describe how these issues can be worked out in practice.

1.1 The dawn of the information age

The outer surface of the information age is already familiar to many of us – the Internet, the World Wide Web and the like are all examples of globally distributed information systems. Evolution has been driven, as in previous revolutions, by the emergence of powerful new technology. In this case, explosive growth in the power and availability of personal computers and the increasing use of local networks has given many the freedom to do a great variety of tasks without moving away from the computer on their desktop.

Further to this, our expectations of having the world 'at your fingertips' have been raised. (Some would say that, in practice, the world is more likely to be 'in your face' than 'at your fingertips'.) The global data communications market, growing at 30 per cent per annum, is providing the infrastructure that allows high-speed connections between most sites, worldwide. It is now fairly commonplace for large organizations to have their own 'enterprise networks' connecting all their main offices and outlets. Local area networks are, increasingly, being connected together to form larger working groups. In short, the once isolated computer is being connected via a network to act as one part of a global processor.

On top of this, ideas of 'teleworking', 'virtual teams' and, indeed, 'virtual corporations' have been shown to be viable through this combination of computing and telecommunications. An information society is forming – and fast. Or, at least, that seems to be the intention of both suppliers and users.

One of the effects of having access to information anywhere you need is that the physical dependencies of many people and businesses are being diluted. Instead of being clustered around a particular place, many activities will be logically clustered around processing and communication infrastructure.

There will, in the information age, be a logical migration similar to the physical migration of the industrial revolution. The high-capacity connections now available from the large network operators will allow the distance to be taken out of information. And thus the locations in which we conduct business may well be chosen on social or aesthetic grounds, unconstrained, in the main, by physical access limitations. At the same time, there will be a need to reconfigure, change and modify the computing systems that people use as never before.

In reality, this is not a settled issue – far from it. The fact that we have made a start in effectively distributing the information systems, so vital to modern business, does not mean that we know all of the answers. Nor do we really know what impact the changes will have on the behaviour of those who use distributed systems.

From a traditionalist's standpoint, there are questions, as yet unanswered, about security, reliability, intellectual property and the like. Even the enthusiast would ask how people work well together when they are distant – even in another time zone.

Part of the answer to these concerns lies in appreciating the inevitable consequences of distribution. There are some changes to conventional wisdom that come with the removal of physical restraints. And there are some consequences of distribution that have to be addressed, just like the knock-on effects of any other shift in the operational ground rules.

The realities of what can be done (and how easy – or otherwise – it is to do it) are the prime target of this book. We intend to expose some of the constraints and unknowns of decentralization, as well as the capabilities and promises.

1.2 Local knowledge, global presence

Over the past 25 years or so, a number of factors have changed the nature of business competition. The particular drivers have varied from one industry to the next but there are common themes. Among these are increased similarity in available infrastructure, distribution channels and business practice among countries.

Additionally, there have been falling political and tariff barriers, a growing number of regional economic pacts that ease international trade relations and an increasing impact of technology in integrating business sectors. It is becoming more and more difficult to differentiate a job in publishing from one in journalism or even one in telecommunications!

Recent political changes in the former Soviet Union and Eastern Europe, the changing dynamics in the Pacific Rim area and the evolution of the European Union have all further fuelled an environment for global business competition (Frenke, 1990).

These factors, along with a fluid capital market that allows large-scale flows of funds between countries, have led to a situation where it is information that is a vital resource. (The working definition of 'information' here is 'data that has been processed so as to add value'.) With an increasing number of organizations operating on a global basis, the universal availability of information is a prerequisite to competitiveness. The point is readily illustrated. Not many years ago, it was the planes themselves that were the major cost in the airline business. These days they are easier to replace than the associated flight booking systems. Likewise, millions of dollars are made or lost by shifting capital around the world in a quest for short-term interest. (This sort of electronic turnover is put by *The Economist* at around $4 trillion per week – about the same volume as the US national debt.) It is not the cash that travels, rather the information required to call on it.

Information used to be something that was gathered to support the business. Now it *is* the business in many instances. Shared over a wide area it is a key resource.

In this context, many companies – large and small – see that their future survival depends to a large degree on expanding their operations to the global scale. A good number of them are devoting considerable resources and capital to setting up satellites away from their traditional home territory. There are two main drivers from the business viewpoint:

- First, globalization is seen as the only real way to grow. It not only gets to a wider, more open market but also allows the impact of currency fluctuations, skill shortages and other national factors to be minimized.

- Second, proximity to customers – and hence building a greater understanding of their needs – is seen as key to achieving the sort of mass customization demanded by many. An ideal combination – the aim of many – is to retain local knowledge and back it up with global presence and capacity (Cooke *et al.*, 1993).

Just as organizations have scattered their people around the world, so they are now distributing work. And it is important to be clear in the nature of this arrangement. It is not subcontracting or licensing but the establishment of a cooperating part of the main organization – a satellite – that just happens to be separated from the rest by time or distance.

In principle, the capacity of such organizations to react quickly is great. They should have the flexibility to beat more rigid and hierarchical structures every time.

This advantage is not easy to realize, though, as anyone who has been involved with a multisite project will know. You have to build a considerable amount of knowhow to make the organizational value chain smooth, efficient and effective. Many disparate areas – logistics, order fulfilment, and so on – have to be designed to work together. This means the integration of a range of systems, both automated and manual.

So, global competition requires the efficient operation of a distributed set of resources that support operations. And this means the establishment of a flexible computing system that provides a cooperating set of applications and data. This is easy to say, tricky to deliver.

Even so, many have risen to the challenge. Globalization is evident in industries that were recently very much domestic concerns. For instance, software development can now be developed as a 'follow the sun' activity with several cooperating teams working together across time zones (Lu and Farrell, 1989). The once national telecommunication operators are now forming global alliances (for example MCI/BT, AT&T/DBP) and are offering customized, managed networks that span the world. It is also interesting to note that companies who already have a global presence, such as AT&T and BT, are not immune from all this. They need to structure their systems so that they can easily be reconfigured to meet new service needs. Pressure on the networks providers' to adopt distributed systems principles in order to achieve the flexibility they need is evident in many of the standards bodies (see Appendix A).

The capability and availability of reliable telecommunications is, to a large extent, the enabler for organizations to generate and share information effectively, irrespective of location. Broadband data communication technology, such as frame relay and asynchronous transmission mode (ATM), make it possible to transmit volumes of detailed, structured information across the world in seconds, with little or no corruption. The basis for the information industry is here with both public and private networks that can operate at speeds similar to those used across computer backplanes (Gilder, 1993).

Once a multiservice network is available to connect powerful computing resources, the way in which the whole system is organized becomes key. It is now widely predicted that coordination among a network of activities (for example design, marketing, production and so on) dispersed worldwide is becoming a prime source of competitive advantage – the business battleground of the second millennium (Porter, 1986).

As the information age matures it will generate increasing pressure to change the way we work, both as individuals and as organizations (Ohmae, 1990). For the information-intensive company there should, in theory, be greater choice of the fastest, cheapest and easiest way to deliver the goods by:

- being flexible in responding to competition by sharing information between regions,

- reducing costs through selection of the cheapest or best resource, irrespective of location.

The impact on the individual will be no less dramatic. There will be less attachment to specific locations as it becomes easier to establish virtual teams – groups of individuals who can communicate and share information as they work together unaffected by the tyranny of distance. The rise of the 'information worker' and the 'telecommuter' has been evident for some years now. This is a trend that looks likely to continue. The extent to which people cope with this radical change in working practice remains to be seen.

All of the above is no more than an extension of what we already know. There are, in addition, new industries that will be enabled by a new capability. There will be products and practices that we do not yet recognize – just like the pastime of cruising that became popular in the 1950s as car ownership expanded, and the video shops that arrived in the 1980s when video players became popular. Both were a knock-on effect of new technology becoming widely available.

1.3 Anytime, anyplace, anywhere

So it looks as if advances in telecommunications will make information more readily available and easier to share. It will no longer be the preserve of a privileged few but will be obtainable by anyone with the equipment 'patience' and knowledge to reach it.

In this environment, it will become increasingly viable to have work carried out by 'virtual teams' – people who work together entirely through the network (Barnes, 1991). In an information-rich environment, it is these non-hierarchical groups of information workers who will come to predominate. A key factor in future business will be the bringing together of local and specialist knowledge and focusing it on a specific goal. The more traditional hierarchies – well-suited to the marshalling of large numbers of people – look set to wilt in the information age. Figure 1.1 illustrates this shift.

Some of the features that characterize the two organizational extremes are given in Table 1.1.

The main point is that the distributed scheme gets its flexibility by relying on individual action and initiative. For this to work, some form of operating framework needs to be put in place.

Once this is done, the combination of global reach and local knowledge (access to fixed resources, wherever) favour the distributed model over the hierarchical one. Expectations are that this approach will increasingly become a vital part of an organization's competitiveness (Naisbitt, 1994) and, with this, virtual teams will become a more central and important organizational feature. (This is characterized by Alvin Toffler as a move from bureaucracy to ad hocracy.) This leaves

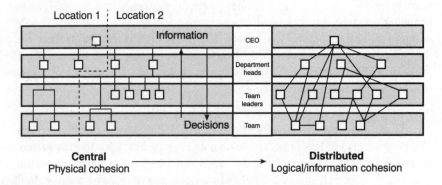

Figure 1.1 The move from hierarchical control to information networking.

Table 1.1 Characteristics of centralized and distributed organizations.

Central	Distributed
Rigid and procedural	Flexible and informal
Preallocated responsibilities	Collective responsibility
Top down decision	Decisions focused around key information holders
Hierarchical	Flat structure
Leadership vested in rank	Leadership dependent on situation
High cost of entry and exit	Low cost of entry and exit
Face to face predominates	Electronic communication predominates

the main challenge in this way of working – to establish common purpose in a physically scattered organization – as a priority concern.

It should be fairly clear that virtual teams do not just happen – they have to be managed if they are to capitalize on their flexibility. And this can be very difficult with so many interesting and readily available diversions to distract one from the day job. The temptation to 'surf the network' in search of weird and intriguing 'off-world' attractions (because they are certainly out there) will be great. Even if the temptation to wander in information space is overcome, there is still a challenge in focusing the diverse and distributed resources on the job in hand. (It is interesting to note that some individuals display a personality change when they are online. Teams may exhibit similar departure from type.)

To exploit virtual teams in the broadest sense, it will be necessary to implement procedures to monitor, control and synchronize distributed team efforts. With the comfort factors of personal contact and/or shared experience taken away, the value this provides needs to be replaced (Quarterman, 1989) or maybe enhanced in some way.

Certainly, it is the authors' experience that virtual teams are made, not born, and that even the best enabling technology will only pay dividends if matched to the people who know how and want to use it (Gray *et al.*, 1993).

Once this is achieved, though, it will probably become commonplace for products to be built as logical items – pieces of electronic data – for assembly by a suitably positioned and equipped agent. The extent to which the technology for the 'software integrated circuit' is with us can readily be gauged from later chapters.

To capitalize on technology, though, there have to be well thought out ways of working. For instance, individuals must be able to ascertain precisely what pieces of work are complete, which are still in progress and which have yet to be tackled. Also, they usually benefit from some idea of what a distant co-worker is likely to deliver (and when). With geographical separation often removing the option of asking the relevant person (it may be the middle of their night when you want to know), some overhead to supplant traditional methods needs to be put in place.

Exactly what has to be added in terms of process depends on the type of work that is being done. But given an infrastructure to link a group of physically disparate people, applications that they can use to work as one team and sensible working procedures, whole new working scenarios emerge. For instance (IEEE Journal, 1992):

- Collective design – where a group of experts, gathered for their specific knowledge rather than their being close at hand, contribute to a piece of work. The record of their combined deliberation is held, in some format, on a remote machine but is available for all to access. Review, edit and formatting of the document is carried out during production and any ideas or suggestions are loaded onto a bulletin board so that all involved can see what is going on. Pictures, voice notes and associated video clips can be added, as appropriate, both on and offline.

- Offsite servicing – where the performance measures of a remote piece of equipment are collected for a remote operator to effect required changes. This sort of application is already in place in some specialist areas. For instance, the adjustment of turbines when they first go into service (and for ongoing maintenance and repair) can readily be carried out without the physical presence of an engineer. Files containing operating data (one way) and adjustments (the other way) do the job.

- Follow the sun development – where the development of, for instance, software is divided into time slices to suit the normal working hours around the globe. As people shut up shop for the day in Tokyo, their working files are available to the team in Bombay for further development and at the close of the Indian day, to Frankfurt for test. Next day in Tokyo, the team find extended, tested code. As well as following the sun, this type of operation can also be an effective way of getting the right mix of skills.

- Electronic distribution – where people can sit in their office or their armchair to buy goods and services, rather than having to go to the shops or scour the trade magazines. (The Internet already features a number of electronic shopping malls and online catalogues – see http://www.internet.net, for example.) The ability to present high-quality pseudogoods, onscreen and to allow the user to select what they want, perhaps customize it and then pay for it, seems set to fuel the development of many types of 'transaction trading'. And this is likely to extend into related areas such as electronic software distribution as a means of upgrading/customizing user software both quickly and with control.

Each of the above makes a different set of demands on the underlying systems that provide the capability. Some require speed of response, others more in the way of control over the work in progress. Quite apart from the variety of technical demands, actually making these scenarios a reality and capitalizing on their promise is likely to require significant change to the way that many organizations are structured. The central control picture, where all commands flow out from a central headquarters, is not appropriate here. A more likely candidate is one where the various parts of the organization behave (within some set of general constraints) as autonomous entities. To work as an effective whole, each entity must know its role, its contribution and how the whole organization works together. Hierarchy is likely to lessen in importance as the emerging distributed lattice of network connections carries information, authority and complete work.

When considering what sort of support this type of organization requires, we return to the parable at the start of the chapter. The system needed will not be a centrally operated and maintained resource but a set of cooperating processors.

Just as with distributed teams this, too, requires discipline to work effectively. Each part of the system needs to know how to transfer information, where other parts of the system are, how transactions should be completed, and so on. Of course, commonality of purpose does not happen by accident. Distributed systems have to be planned in advance and this is what we now start to do.

1.4 The brave new world

First, we take a look at the basic requirements for flexible and reliable distributed computing systems in their capacity as the support structure for virtual organizations, along with the general trends that drive their deployment.

Given that human organizations are not static but are subject to change, this must be accommodated by the computers used to support the organization. As a consequence, systems will have to be provided as a collection of interchangeable components rather than a monolithic single resource. This will become more and more the case.

As organizations seek to add increasingly complex functions to their systems, suppliers will find it increasingly difficult to manufacture, sell and support a full range of system components. It is reasonable to assume that suppliers will cater for specific needs and will, therefore, be obliged to cooperate with other suppliers (or their products) when they are called on to assemble a working system. So the supply side is likely to consist of specialists and integrators.

Large organizations engage in many diverse activities, each of which can be supported by a computer system. For example, a manufacturing company may have computerized payroll, order handling, design and sales support systems. To make the best use of these systems they need to be linked to provide an enterprise resource. This is fairly straightforward when all the systems are of the same type but the diversity of requirements usually demands a diversity of hardware and software support. Distributed systems provide a route to achieving the integration required by the user without restricting the freedom to choose the most appropriate technology for each system component.

In a nutshell, these are the reasons why the computing world has had to meet the telecommunications world. It is a convergence driven by need rather than choice. That need (as we have already said) is, in the simplest terms, the user wanting to have the facilities now commonly available on a LAN across all of their network.

So how will technology evolve to cope with an evolving business need? We start now to look at the type of systems that will allow flexible, distributed applications to be delivered to flexible, distributed organizations.

The keys to getting to this are:

- Greater understanding of the basic principles and techniques that lie behind distributed computing. These set the overall structure for design, planning and operation.

- Consensus on how to organize and control distributed resources. These are the rules of engagement for the implementor. They are required to configure the systems.

- Techniques for dealing with those issues (such as security) that assume great importance in a world where you cannot see your valuable property, let alone lock it up in a safe place.

There are a number of golden rules that need to be taken on board by anyone who works in, or builds, a distributed environment. It is a fundamental change of paradigm for many people and is worth introducing at an early stage. There are a whole range of basic changes of philosophy and among the most important assumptions which need to be carefully (re)examined on moving from a central to a distributed system are the transitions:

- From central control to local autonomy. A distributed system may be spread across a number of autonomous authorities, with no single authority exerting overall control. Some constraints have to be agreed between the co-operating elements of the system. This means that issues of consistency between domains (for example what names are used, where information is stored, and so on) needs to be considered as part of a deployment strategy.

- From private to virtual networks. You will no longer own a lot of the tele-communications equipment and network connections that you use. Public domain and outsourced facilities are likely to become more of an accepted part of an organization's overall resource. The focus will swing from what you own to what you use. Security, branding and intellectual property may well become more burning (and difficult) issues than they have been hitherto.

- From go/no-go to partial failure. In the event of some part of a distributed system failing, the remainder can often continue operating without it. Indeed, in a large system it is unlikely that all parts will ever be operational simultaneously, nor will they all be out of action. A central system is either working or broken.

- From homogeneity to heterogeneity. There can be no guarantee that the components of a distributed system use the same (or even similar) implementation technology. The set of diverse technologies (and associated suppliers) will change over time. Interconnection and interworking standards are crucial in this context.

These general trends are revisited in Chapter 4, where the detail and colour required for practical application is added. In a distributed world, the principles outlined above need to be reflected through into system planning, design, installation and operation. In effect, they provide the new rules of the game for operational support systems. As we go into more detail in subsequent chapters, the way in which they are applied should become clearer. For now the list serves to illustrate the fact that distribution brings with it the need to revise the way in which information and support systems are built and operated. And given the 'distribute or die' message that emanates from many of the leading business schools, it seems a pretty good area to learn about.

Finally, there are a couple of more general pointers that might help in understanding the likely shape and demands of the information age. The first picks up on the final bullet point in the above list – the move towards diversity of supply. This is an important issue and can be further illustrated by looking at the current state of play in the two core areas for distributed systems – telecommunications and computing.

Fordism, the type of structured manufacturing associated most closely with the mass production of motor cars, but subsequently adopted in many other industries, is not appropriate in an age where consumer need has diversified. So, to remain competitive, manufacturers must be more flexible than hitherto. The opening of many of the world's telecommunications markets has led to the wide availability of customized global networks (frequently known as enterprise networks) that provide all of the connectivity an organization needs. In the already customer-oriented computing business, the pressure for open systems (which allow users to 'mix and match' processing boxes, databases, and so on) continues to grow. In short, both the relevant supply sectors are moving to support distributed systems. Whether they converge or collide remains to be seen.

A second issue is the balance and range of disciplines that organizations will have to apply, if they are to adapt to an environment where speed of reaction and flexibility are paramount. Figure 1.2 shows the main areas that the responsive, or

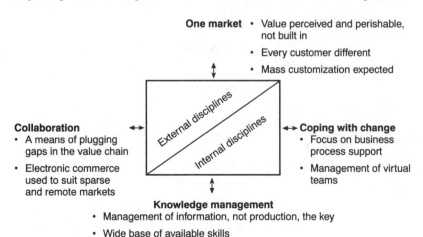

Figure 1.2 The disciplines for effective distributed organizations.

agile, organization will have to master. The concept of the agile company was introduced as far back as 1964 (Thomas Burns' *Industry in a New Age*). The idea has been more recently popularized in publications such as *Fast Company*.

Taking each of the areas shown in the figure in turn:

- Collaboration will become increasingly important as information and knowledge products rely on inputs from many sources. With delivery to the customer as a focus, the stitching together of the required elements in the overall value chain will be paramount.

- The market for many products will become increasingly fragmented. Each customer will appear to be the only customer as mass customization becomes more prevalent. The general move from one mass market to a mass market of one needs to be tackled.

- Coping with change will be more important with less tightly coupled structures. As timescales get shorter, the chance to optimize procedures will diminish. Mechanisms for spotting problems and reacting to them are needed.

- In an information-rich environment, the management of knowhow is vital. This requires a change of emphasis from the established production way of doing things. Value cannot be built in – it is perceived and also perishable.

There is little prescription that can be given here. Accumulated experience in this area does not really allow guidelines to be formed as yet. There are some general points that can be made – that internal efficiency will be less important, that links to customers will matter more and that service differentiation, management and branding will be real pressure points.

The impact of organizational and business pressures on information network provision should be clear. The level of responsiveness and inherent complexity of requirements will leave their design as a balancing act between a range of interests, some of which are shown in Figure 1.3.

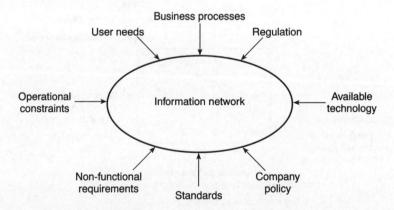

Figure 1.3 The influences that shape information network needs.

The final point in this chapter is that the sheer range of pressures, influences and unknowns that impinge on what an information infrastructure needs to provide means that a well thought out plan of action is essential. A lot of time and effort have been expended over the years working out what should be in that plan. The technology of distributed computing has gone a long way to anticipating the demands of the information age. But it takes a while to explain them, and that is what the rest of this book is about.

1.5 About this book

One notable effect of the industrial revolution was that it provoked a move from village to town life. There is likely to be a parallel move with the current information revolution, albeit logical rather than physical. Marshall McLuhan's 'information villages' from the 1950s look likely to evolve into high-tech towns by the year 2000.

To extend the analogy, the small information corner shop (already alive and well on the World Wide Web) will persist but will be joined by information banks, retailers and factories (the early adopting corporations of the information age).

There will also be a range of new facilities, ranging from the information pub, where entertainment and refreshment, even salacious gossip, can be sought (much like some of the less technical user groups on the Internet) to the community doctor for the sick of the information city.

Along with this will doubtless come a whole new range of problems that have to be addressed. Just as inner cities breed crime, so there will be a whole new breed of criminal – the information superhighwaymen. Security is a key feature of distributed systems. We will consider what needs to be done here.

The information age is still in its infancy. There are certainly thriving information villages but the towns have yet to appear. But appear they will, and sooner than many people think.

This chapter has set the scene, or at least raised some of the main drivers and influences on an increasingly distributed world. The next chapter takes stock of the way in which technology has evolved to enable distribution. It reviews the past 30 years or so and traces the route to the present day. Although based in technical progress, the chapter also reflects the parallel social and organizational changes that need to be understood for the present situation to be seen in context, and for the likely routes from this point forward to be understood. Chapter 3 explains a little more of the technology, this time from a user's point of view. At this point we are looking at technology as the 'magic' that lets you do what you want (or scuppers you completely).

For all of the hype surrounding the information superhighways, we are still dealing with a complex area of technology. Facts, knowhow and good judgement are all required to ride the highways successfully. Chapters 4 and 5 dive inside the magic to reveal the concepts, ideas and techniques that make it all work. Chapter 4 tells it the way it should be. Chapter 5 is more concerned with what you can really do – warts and all. The next three chapters are concerned with the effective use of all of these ideas.

Technology isn't the be all and end all. It still has to be applied with understanding. Chapter 6 explains the new technology in the context of the real world – one in which there are already many existing systems, people and practices. Deploying systems in a green field situation is relatively easy – this chapter is intended to help you through the complications that are introduced by (inevitable) history; your existing legacy systems.

Chapters 7 and 8, respectively, deal with common concerns or issues and some of the strategies and techniques for dealing with them. It is said that good judgement comes from experience and experience comes from bad judgement. These two chapters are based very much around the concerted experience of many years' worth of distributed systems development. We finish by taking a peek into the future – some of the great unknowns, and a few of the safe bets for the new millennium.

1.6 Summary

The advent of the information superhighway is bringing the 'global village' ever closer. More and more organizations are looking to decentralize their operations. And, as part of this, they are obliged to distribute the systems that support their business. In the words of Herbert Simon, 'The question is not whether we shall decentralise but how far we shall decentralise'.

This chapter has explained some of the main factors that are driving distribution, along with some of the attendant challenges. The main message is that those who harness the data abundant in the information age will be winners. Before then, however, the principles of distributed working need to be fully appreciated. The last part of this chapter introduced the most important shifts in thinking that you need in moving from a centralized to a distributed world.

CHAPTER 2

Where are we now?

'Our plan is to lead the public with new products rather than ask them what kind of products they want. The public does not know what is possible, but we do. So instead of doing a lot of market research, we refine our thinking on a product and its use and try to create a market for it by educating and communicating with the public' – Akio Morita, Sony Corporation

As recently as the 1970s there were no personal computers, graphical user environments or local area networks. Most households did not have a camcorder (in fact, the word was not even coined until after the product appeared) or a cordless telephone, and tape recorders were still using open reels. Automobiles, washing machines and central heating systems contained no intelligence and the compact disk was no more than a gleam in someone's eye. Yet, people had built a telephone network that allowed billions of people on the planet to speak to one another and astronauts had landed on the moon.

Over the past 30 years or so, our capabilities in producing electronic machines and applications has (to a reasonable approximation) doubled every year. Today, many people in western Europe and the United States have a personal computer connected to a network, a car with electronic cruise control and a software-controlled washing machine.

The ingress of technology into everyday life is readily illustrated. The intelligence embedded in the engine management system of the family saloon is greater than that installed in the first lunar lander. In fact, there are now telephones, wrist watches and even shavers that contain many thousands of lines of software and have a considerable repertoire of functions.

Behind all of this innovation lies the computer. The earliest of these would be all but unrecognizable to many people. By today's standards, they were huge, power-hungry machines with many moving unreliable components (prone to misoperation due, for instance, to intruding insects; hence the term 'computer bug') and few saving graces. Yet within the space of 30 years, they have come to affect the lives of all of us and form the core of most business operations. How did this happen? And, more to the point, what can we learn from our recent history?

This chapter sets out to explain some of the main steps in an impressive progression. It starts by describing a little of how we got where we are today or, more specifically, how computing has evolved over the past 30 years or so from an arcane specialism into a popular and ubiquitous issue for both the individual and business.

Seven ages of computing are described here. Each one of these provided a significant advance on its predecessor and sparked the wider use of computers. The developments that have (and look set to continue to) set the pace of change are explained, in particular, the relentless progression to distributed and networked systems. In the light of past progress, we consider some of the key challenges for the future.

2.1 The seven ages of computing

It is not that long since each computer was an isolated piece of equipment – useful but lonely. Advances in network technology and communication software have changed all that. We are now headed towards the information superhighway and total area networks, where the physical distance between computers will cease to be a major issue. In this brave new world, the effectiveness of computers as an enterprise resource will be limited not by their connectivity but by their ability to cooperate.

So what can we learn from the past in the quest to meet this challenge of cooperative working?

Looking back through history, it is easy to see that virtually all of the major developments in communication have had profound, and sometimes unexpected, impacts on society. The introduction of the printing press, the telephone, the television all exemplify this. In each case, something localized – ideas, speech, pictures – could suddenly be shared with a huge new audience, worldwide.

The impact of these innovations was rarely predicted and, even when it was, rarely accurately. (There is nothing new in this – before the computer came along Niels Bohr said that 'Prediction is difficult, especially of the future'.) For instance, Edison felt that music recording was a minor application for his gramophone – its prime purpose would be to record speeches. This may seem a strange stance in hindsight but at the time there was no music industry to appreciate or assess the potential of the new technology. Thinking was confined to the current situation with little consideration of the likely new order created by a new capability.

What value is there in looking back, then? Perhaps Henry Ford's assertion that 'history is bunk' holds true! Well, there are some useful things that we can glean from past events. For instance, there are general patterns that technologies tend to go through:

- replacement, when a new technology supplants an established one and sometimes introduces new ways of doing things;

- intensification, when the replacement becomes cheap, so it becomes popular and is widely used;

- dependence, when the technology becomes so embedded in society that it is taken for granted. It is common at this stage for the technology to spawn new social and operational structures.

And once you know where you are in the cycle of evolution, you stand some chance of seeing which way things are headed. So, having said that, let us look at the way in which computers have taken hold over the past three decades. Here is a brief resumé of the route to the present day – the seven ages of computing!

2.1.1 The custom computer age

By the early 1960s, the computer had emerged from the laboratory and was beginning to be accepted as a useful addition to business life. It was capable of carrying out laborious and repetitive tasks quickly and accurately. Many large organizations had a computer tucked away somewhere for processing volumes of data or performing complex calculations.

That is about as far as it went, though. The computer was kept in a controlled environment, well away from the mainstream of operations. There were no users, as such. The machine was tended by a team of specialists who were responsible for applying this new and, generally, ill-understood piece of technology.

The computer itself was a large, slow and fragile machine, especially when compared with the most modest of modern home computers. Its processing power was limited by the immaturity of the semiconductor technology on which it was based. The main memory was a physical magnetic core – low capacity and slow to access. Reliability was a problem and breakdowns were a regular feature. Finally, the input and output media were tape or punched card. Once programmed, jobs were submitted using one of these with the results usually taking a day or so to come back. In the early days this entailed low-level instructions closely tied to the

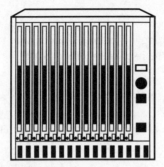

- No users as such
- Air-conditioned room
- Core memory
- Card or tape input/output

Figure 2.1 The isolated machine.

structure of the computer (machine code). This could do the job but contrasts with later programming languages, more oriented to the task than the machine.

A typical setup during the custom computer age is shown in Figure 2.1. The insularity of the diagram speaks volumes.

In action, the computer was limited in terms of the functions it could offer. However, it was fairly straightforward to instruct – early programming languages were simple, if somewhat cumbersome. The programmer was expected to cope with a range of challenges, from manipulating the computer hardware so that the logic of the program could execute, to putting dropped sets of punched cards back into the correct order!

In general, during this age, computer systems forced the organizations that they supported towards a central location to get specific jobs done. The organizations themselves tended to be stable and hierarchical and readily added computer services into their structure and procedures. This resulted in fixed computer centres for carrying out functions such as customer invoicing, payroll and billing. The technology partially replaced a labour-intensive task.

In summary, this was a time when users were subservient to a machine tended by experts. The computer served to calculate. It was an isolated, special-purpose machine that would take batches of work and return specified results.

2.1.2 The computer bureaux age

By the mid 1970s the computer had emerged from the backroom to some extent. During this time, computer bureaux selling time on their machine to a number of users flourished. In terms of usage, computers were beginning to be used as general purpose processing machines. Users could interact directly with the computer, albeit at a distance, and the turnaround time for jobs was of the order of hours, even minutes, rather than days.

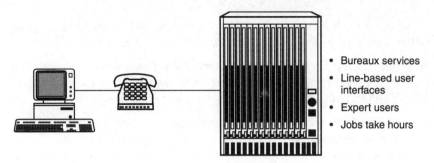

- Bureaux services
- Line-based user interfaces
- Expert users
- Jobs take hours

Figure 2.2 The accessible machine.

Computing was still very much the preserve of specialists during the bureaux age. Those operating the bureaux were concerned with the maintenance and operation of the computer itself. The users, on the other hand, were focused on programming – instructing the machine to achieve a result. With the details of a computer's structure becoming less intrusive, more general and more readable means of organizing and marshalling their power were established. Programming languages evolved during this stage to be structured and higher level, similar to modern-day offerings. Figure 2.2 depicts the situation during this era.

User access to the bureaux was generally via a modem (a device for converting the digital signals from a computer to and from analog signals that can be sent over a phone line) and telephone line. Connections tended to be slow, fixed and of moderate reliability. It was not unknown for a user's session to be corrupted in midstream so that they had to go back to the beginning. Also, more than one task generally required more than one computer session. The only variety of multi-tasking during this age relied on the user's persistence.

The user (that is programmer's) terminal connected to the modem was a primitive predecessor of the modern PC; monochrome, no pictures, no sound. Commands and edits were entered through a line-based (rather than full-screen) interface – an option driven by efficiency. With the user paying per processor cycle, the most direct input/output possible was preferred.

This age can be typified by a growing dependence on the computer, but also by a preservation of its restriction to specialist users. There were, however, the early signs of interaction between the user and the computer they were working on.

2.1.3 The minicomputer age

It did not take people very long to realize that it was better to have their own computers than to pay for time on someone else's. The advance of the mainframe computer as a commodity package was heralding the end of the bureaux era. The IBM 370 series (popular around this time) offered around ten times the processing power per dollar compared with the comparable IBM 7090 from ten years earlier. This trend would continue right through to the present day.

So, by the late 1970s, virtually all computer users had been brought together with the computing power they required. The typical picture was as shown in Figure 2.3, with direct terminal access to the company's mainframe systems.

This situation reflected the increasing importance of computers in business. It was, by now, necessary to have significant processing power on hand to carry out a range of control tasks and to handle ever increasing volumes of data and information. Because of this, turnaround times of hours and days became unacceptable. Access to the mainframe was direct, via one of the standard terminal types still in use today (for example VT100 or IBM 3270). The user could interact directly with the machine and line-based applications had given way to screen.

Further to all this, advances in technology, such as virtual memory and multitasking operating systems, were greatly extending the range of uses to which computers were being applied. Also, mainframes were beginning to be connected together so that their users could use resources on more than one machine. By now, computers were accepted as business tools for general use. Programming was still a specialism, though.

This early form of networking was popularized in a number of proprietary products, such as DECnet. This sort of facility meant that users could not only interact directly with the applications hosted on the mainframe to which they were connected but could also communicate with other users.

It was around this time that the first fruits of U.S. Department of Defense initiated experiments to increase the resilience of computer networks appeared. This work – started in the late 1960s – would take a further 10 years before achieving widespread adoption in the form of the now all-pervasive Internet.

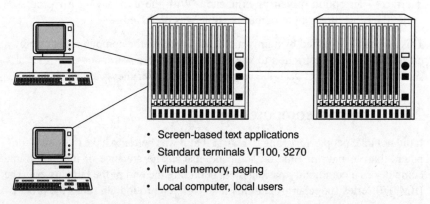

- Screen-based text applications
- Standard terminals VT100, 3270
- Virtual memory, paging
- Local computer, local users

Figure 2.3 The local machine.

This age can be typified by numbers of connected VAX computers providing the processing and communication infrastructure for many large organizations. The user was still dependent on the machine, though, and computing was still a specialist activity, albeit one that was beginning to involve people in a wide range of related disciplines. For instance, the design of telephone switches changed from a mechanical to a computing exercise around this time. The Ericsson AXE, AT&T No.5 ESS and BT System X switches were all stored, program-controlled devices – in contrast to the previous generation of physical cross-connect switches.

2.1.4 The early desktop computer age

The next era saw a significant shift of processing power away from the mainframe and on to the desktop. It was during the early 1980s that the first of the personal computers appeared (for example the Apple Lisa, the Commodore PET). With the popular adoption of the minicomputer (for example DEC's MicroVax and a host of UNIX-based processors) immediately beforehand, computing quickly moved from being reliant on a static core to being a local resource. The end user now had significant control as desktop and departmental processing power could be rapidly installed, as shown in Figure 2.4.

The tight-knit communities built up around (and reliant on) a group of large computers started to dissipate. The user could now choose to work locally (with limited power) or to connect to a more powerful, remote machine. The style of user interface – much closer to the familiar windowing environment – allowed some measure of user control over this.

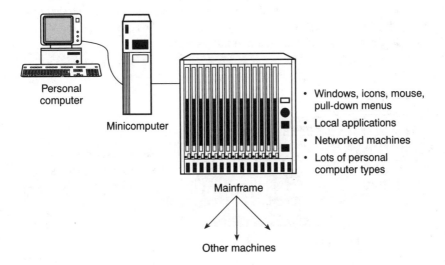

- Windows, icons, mouse, pull-down menus
- Local applications
- Networked machines
- Lots of personal computer types

Figure 2.4 The desktop machine.

One significant development during this time was the introduction of operating systems (most notably DOS) for the desktop machines. Local consistency in computing environments was thus broken and the irrevocable drift to distributed systems started.

This age marked the beginning of independence for the user. They now had some level of control and did not rely on a machine maintained by specialists.

2.1.5 The PC/LAN age

The trend started in the previous era picked up pace during the 1980s. During this time, the shape of most computer systems changed out of all recognition (see Figure 2.5), as did the extent to which they were popularly accepted.

There were several vital elements that contributed to this. The first was the adoption of a common standard for the desktop computer – the PC (based on the Intel 80X86 series of microprocessors, commonly known as the 386, 486, and so on). The PC was launched by IBM and was subsequently cloned by a large number of manufacturers. A huge amount of PC application software was produced very quickly thereafter. This, in turn, sparked mass computer literacy. Many people now knew how to build software. Even more knew how to use it, as computers were becoming more common in the home. Networking a set of computers into a working group, however, remained a challenge for the specialist.

Local area networks, such as Ethernet, provided the second vital element. These were managed networks that gave a user fast access to remote resources. They allowed resources (such as printers and file stores) to be shared by a number of users and sparked many of the ideas for constructing distributed systems. In the space of a few years the PC and LAN matured to allow local enterprise zones with file, print, program sharing and multi-user databases.

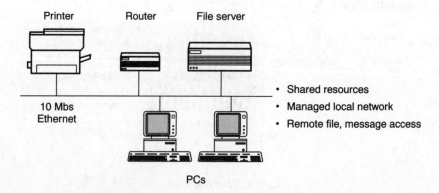

Figure 2.5 The local networked machine.

A lot of this progress was due to the advances in software for managing local networks (such as Banyan's Vines and NOS, Novell's Netware and IPX, Microsoft's LanManager). Typically, these provided a range of administration, troubleshooting and network management facilities that allowed the LAN to be set up and run to best suit user needs. In this era, information could readily be moved over longer distances by connecting into public data networks. User packages that implemented *de facto* standards such as Telnet and file transfer protocol (FTP) allowed files to be readily exchanged over long distances.

A third element in this time of rapid progress was the evolution of the database. The early 1980s saw the theory of relational data storage turned into usable product, first by Oracle and soon thereafter by Ingres (named after the French classical painter, Jean Ingres, because the original development machine for the product was likewise labelled), Sybase and others. Structured Query Language (SQL) provided a common interface to relational databases and this formed the basis for explosive growth in commercial availability.

In a very short time frame, computer users had enough power, data and applications to do a significant amount of useful work on their local machine, combined with the wherewithal to make use of remote machines. The distribution of work between local and remote resources gave practical substance to the idea of client and server software cooperating on a task. Programmers were no longer limited by memory or processing constraints, so efficiency and compactness were overtaken by functionality and usability as key concerns.

2.1.6 The superconnectivity age

Interworking across globally distributed systems characterizes the superconnectivity age (Quarterman and Smoot, 1993). The layout of the average computing facility had changed little from the previous age, as shown in Figure 2.6, but there are a few external signs of a new order taking hold.

The real change was only evident when you looked at a user's screen. Pages of information provided by and accessed by a global resource were now available (see Figure 2.7). By the early 1990s, the experimental work on distribution that had been started years ago came to full fruition. It was delivered in the form of suites of standard protocols for information transfer over the Internet. The popularity of the net soared as it became easy to use remote resources.

There were a few other subtle advances during this era. The reams of text on PC screens were being supplemented with pictures, sounds and moving images. The desktop computer was equipped with a compact disk (CD) drive, had a standard window interface and was capable of supporting multimedia. The speed of LANs had crept up from 10 Mbps to higher speeds (up to 100 Mbps) to keep pace with the increasing richness (and file size) of information transfers.

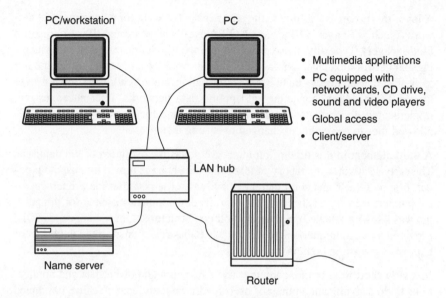

Figure 2.6 The networked machine.

Along with this increased capacity came advances in local network management facilities. The user could readily see and connect to a wide range of network resources. They could also support a number of operating systems on their desktop machine. Rather than having a DOS-based PC, many users had processing engines in front of them that were difficult to distinguish from early mainframes (in terms of capability, not size)!

The operating system for most PCs continued to be the standard MSDOS, developed some 10 years previously, usually with Windows loaded on top. The former was now showing its age (and its limitations – constraints such as a 16-bit architecture and 640 K base memory limit) were limiting innovation. By now, newer PC operating systems, capable of capitalizing on the new environments were being adopted. The likes of IBM's OS/2 and Microsoft's Windows 95 were making the PC a major processing element in its own right. The workstation on many desktops was already in this position.

And just as machines advanced during this period, so did applications and languages – object-oriented techniques in particular (a means of programming by defining discrete entities that cooperate to carry out a task) were advanced at this time and an increasing number of customized applications were being crafted through the use of (often graphical) software development packages. The information age was seeing the information user in a position to exert considerable control over their working environment.

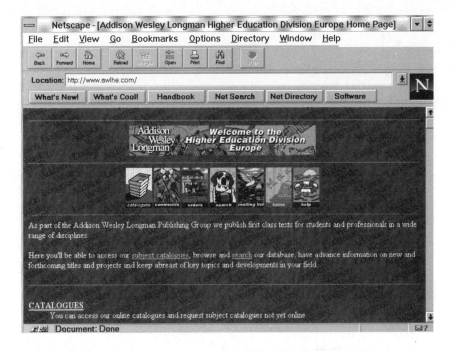

Figure 2.7 Access to information from the desktop – a page from the World Wide Web.

2.1.7 The information age

This age, which is still with us, is seeing the packaging and integration of the facilities from the previous age. Users are now being presented with a portable, flexible and easy to use computing environment, some of which is illustrated in Figure 2.8.

The user's machine these days can be small enough to fit into a briefcase or even a pocket. It comes equipped with software packages to send and receive fax messages, establish telephone calls and manage its own LAN connections. In effect, it combines the functions of many of the traditional pieces of office equipment and (with the addition of a few peripherals) is capable of replacing them.

From the user point of view, the computer is a multipurpose piece of equipment. It can be used wherever it is required and provides an easy to use window on a vast array of resources. The widely predicted growth of speech-based interfaces (instead of keyboards) is likely to broaden this perception. For instance, the Voyager system (developed at MIT) provides an interactive speech-driven street guide.

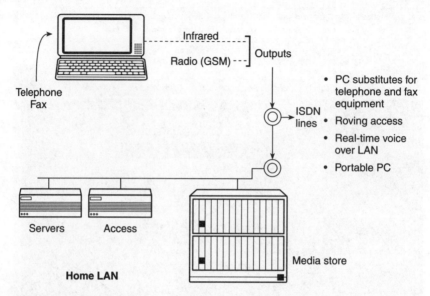

Figure 2.8 The roving machine.

The way in which machines are connected to networks is also more flexible than hitherto. The fixed cable and plug link has been supplemented with both short range (infrared) and longer range (radio) roving links. Standards in both areas allow usable data transmission paths to be established to both LAN and digital carrier services (such as ISDN). The Global Standard for Mobiles and Infrared Data Association bodies set standards for digital connection for, respectively, radio media and infrared. Both offer transmission rates of the order of 100 Kbps. This reinforces the multipurpose nature of the user's machine; it has the capacity to circumvent the traditionally separate telephone. Applications such as Maven and IP Phone permit people to talk over their data link; fax transmission packages and scanners are commonplace.

The advance in connectivity technology has been matched by the way in which application and information are integrated. The likes of World Wide Web, OpenDoc and object linking and embedding – all revisited in the next chapter – allow the user to find and use information from a huge range of sources.

LAN evolution also continued in this age, allowing a greater range and speed of information flow across the network. Established protocols, such as CSMA/CD, designed primarily to ensure fair access to a LAN bus, are being superseded. The LAN of the superconnectivity age is designed to be much more like a fast, local switch. For instance, the 100-VG LAN operates at 100 Mbps and gives priority to real-time data packets that arrive at the LAN hub. This approach makes it possible to send delay-sensitive data (such as voice and video) over the LAN, rather than relying on a separate network. And this means that interactive and real-time services can be made available over (multiservice) networks – currently local, soon to be global.

Network technology is doing a lot to make all of this possible. The speed of network connections allows remote machines to be treated as if they are backplane connected. Initially this was a luxury only available on a LAN over a few hundred metres, or a few buildings. The high speed, broadband network technologies and services like frame relay and ATM extend this range from a local hop to... wherever the network ends! The essential point is that a fast multiservice network, with plenty of local processing power and standards for information transfer (such as MPEG) make it viable to carry (real-time) multimedia across a wide area (Clarke and Norris, 1994). This may seem some way off for the person in the street but history shows that we continually underestimate the impact of technological progress from more than five years out.

We could go on from here to guess at what the future might hold. Perhaps computers will soon be intelligent enough to marshal all of the resources they need without explicit instruction. Perhaps they will evolve into information agents that provide personal assistance to their users. This may be interesting to think about but it is just fantasy – in reality, few are even at the leading edge. The real world still contains a considerable legacy of ages past and the pictures drawn so far are abstracted from true complexity.

For the purposes of this book, the aim has been to draw a picture of current capabilities and how they evolved. And, in doing this, it is clear that there have been some consistent shifts of emphasis through all of the above – from batch and central working to more distributed and interactive.

In fact, all of the points made in Chapter 1 have been reflected in the history of computing to date. The general themes throughout the seven ages have been faster processing, greater volumes of data and easier to use systems.

And there is little doubt that computers will continue to increase in power. It will become easier to exchange information, applications will become more and more powerful and computer-supported cooperative working (CSCW) will become more widespread – the norm rather than the exception (Reich, 1991).

So, we have gained the benefits of power and personal choice. However, we now have to harness these capabilities and face the challenges of complexity, diversity and isolated 'islands' of information.

Our brief historical outline gives some perspective on the current situation, at least in terms of how technology has enabled more sophisticated operations. Along with advances in technology, we have seen ever increasing expectations on the part of users. But what are the key factors that combine with new technology and rising user expectations to drive the future?

The answer to this question really follows on from taking stock of where we are. We have passed through the three evolutionary phases of replacement, intensification and dependence for computer usage. And computer dependence has spawned new structures – specifically ways of doing business that are centred on information rather than hierarchy or geography (Ohmae, 1990).

The next cycle to look at is distributed computing, that is, the convergence of computing and communications technology. This is probably closest to the first stage of evolution – that of replacement. Many organizations are striving to get away from special purpose, tailored systems and move towards a flexible deployment of their computing resources. The commonly used banner for this is enterprise computing (Simon, 1993), a concept introduced in the next section and explained in subsequent chapters.

For now, though, a resumé of where we are. One of the reasons for looking back in this section has been to show that technological advance makes it possible to do new things, to operate in new ways. And people have always been keen to exploit new ideas. In particular, if entrepreneurs see a way of stealing a march on the opposition, they will grab it. And sometimes they win, sometimes they lose. Either way, they explore new territory and show others a route to a pot of gold (or a white elephant). The next section should, therefore, be taken as the necessary background to inform that exploration. Some of the points may need to be moderated against the reader's background, current position and local environment. But one general trend likely to affect everyone is that of continuing change. This is likely to be endemic in the information age and it is safer to treat it as a planned-for exercise than a continuing adventure.

2.2 Enterprise computing

We have already examined the way in which the working environment is changing as technology allows more to be done (Morton, 1991). The extent to which computers and networks can be tailored to suit the particular needs of an organization have given rise to the concept of 'enterprise computing'.

In a nutshell, this is a computing infrastructure that allows everyone in an organization to share information. Like many other terms in computing, it comes overloaded with many alternatives and variants but it is the simple definition that we will stick to. Of course, there are many implications within the idea of enterprise computing, not least of which is the fact that the enterprise itself is fluid and geographically distributed, so requires comparable flexibility from its computing resources.

So the 'simple' aim of sharing information becomes one of getting computing systems (usually of different type, vintage and location) to exchange meaningful information in a usable time frame (Datamation, 1991a). The favourite buzz-phrase used by salespeople for this is 'seamless integration of applications, data and user interfaces among heterogeneous systems of all sizes'. And this is not easy, especially when computer systems (for all the advances in processing power per dollar) are still an expensive and critical business resource. These factors make it easy to see why people baulk at the thought of paying for the privilege of disruption, pending a promised Nirvana, when a tactical 'fix' might shore up the immediate problem or satisfy a particular need.

So why should anyone really consider the strategic option embodied in an enterprise approach? Let's look at a few of the drivers that are, increasingly, forcing the pace:

- Current limitations. There are a whole host of problems being experienced by computer-dependent companies. The amount of data being held and processed is getting out of hand owing to inconsistent entries, multiple creation of items, collation of information from many sources, and so on. The information that people need to do their jobs is often spread over a number of sources and retrieval from those sources is neither quick nor easy. There is a clear need for greater consistency and integration from the user's point of view.

- Expectation. It appears to many people that technology can do anything. The likes of client/server architectures, open systems, remote procedure calls, object-oriented design techniques and total area networks have raised expectations. There is a growing belief that enterprise networks can be constructed using these magic panaceas.

- Competition. Following on from the above point is the worry in many people's minds that their competitors will implement successful enterprise systems before they do. This is sometimes called the 'teenage sex syndrome'. Everyone wants it, everyone believes that everyone else has it and the few who are doing it have yet to get it right. And when competitiveness is driven by information, with the fastest and best winning, there is pressure to take heed of significant developments at the leading edge of the information business.

- Whole-life costs. It is becoming increasingly clear that point or tactical solutions to information-intensive problems often proven counterproductive. They may solve things in the short term but they have a worrying tendency to cause problems of their own downstream. The drive towards open systems in the 1980s exemplifies this concern – they promised greater choice for users and fewer integration problems. That concern has not evaporated and has now extended from the purchase of computing platforms into the wider area of information networking.

To date, the practicalities of real enterprises seems to have prevented significant realization of these drivers (Datamation, 1991*b*). It has proved to be a lot easier to espouse the virtues of enterprise computing than it is to say how they should be provided. In the words of Posch 'Enterprise-wide systems have not yet begun to be widely implemented and have not emerged as a clearly focused subject of interest, because no one knows how to manage them' (Posch, 1991).

In essence, this statement is still true. There is no concerted plan for the construction of commercial-strength enterprise systems. This should not come as a surprise given the variation in organizational needs across various types of business. Some of the responsibility for effective enterprise systems lies (and will always lie) with the end users. Clarity of requirements and purpose cannot be prescribed.

The technical basis for constructing cooperating distributed systems has come a long way since Posch made his observation (Coulouris *et al.*, 1994; Sloman, 1994), however there are some important advances in our understanding of how you go about building distributed systems, and this is the subject matter of the later chapters. Before this systematic treatment of a complex problem, we need to understand why the ideas have evolved as they have, and this entails looking at some of the general approaches that have been made so far.

One of the early attempts to satisfy the needs of a dynamic, information-intensive organization came from the suppliers of computing equipment. They each developed a similar (but different) plan for delivery. The result was that a considerable number of commercial 'enterprise architectures' have been developed over the past 10 years – IBM's SAA (1987), Digital's NAS (1988) followed by Hewlett-Packard's NWC and AT&T's AOE to name but a few (Systems Integration, 1990). Ideally, these should provide a set of components for system construction along with a route map to guide the builder. The absence of some (or all) of these elements has, in some instances, given rise to the term 'market-ectures'! In general, these all aimed at providing a flexible (and usually proprietary) blueprint for organizing a company's processing, data and communications. The very fact that it was the vendors who developed these enterprise architectures hints that they focus on optimizing the deployment of that vendor's equipment in providing the required facilities.

In practice, reliance on a single vendor, especially one who has thought out how to support enterprise computing, appeals to many people. It provides a ready-made, turnkey solution for the user, does not impinge on their core business and delivers products that are built to cooperate. The fact that one enterprise may have problems working with another remains, however.

This is where 'open systems' come into play. This is related to the concept of enterprise computing in that the idea is for suppliers to build to the same overall plan thus making interworking straightforward. Open systems have taken a rather different approach to that of the enterprise architectures. They started with a focus on interoperability and portability, first defining communication protocols, then operating systems' interfaces and then the component parts of distributed systems.

In reality, the development of open systems has been fairly slow and tortuous – a sign of the complexity and magnitude of the task (and to some extent, the willingness of all players to abandon their proprietary stronghold for more vulnerable common ground).

A point worth making here is that enterprise computing and open systems are very different, at least in the motivation behind them. They overlap, yes, but the former is all about supporting a particular set of user requirements and may be proprietary, whereas the latter focuses on interoperability and not on any specific application or user requirement. The two approaches, which can be described, respectively, as top down and bottom up, have now met at the level of system integration.

There are now standards and some common agreements on the building of distributed systems. These areas of agreement – the 'good things' to do in distributed computing – are explained and illustrated later. To close this chapter, we will consider the challenges in distribution and cooperation. These are the practical issues that need to be resolved before the ideas and technology that we have now can be relied on to provide tangible benefit.

2.3 Seven labours

It is already fairly clear that organizations are becoming increasingly fluid in order to continue competing in the 'nanosecond nineties' and beyond. (The optimist's version of this is 'agile', the pessimist's is 'chaotic' – actually, both apply.) With ever-shortening timescales, growing customer expectations and a global economy, the traditional centralized control and management hierarchies are no longer enough (Handy, 1990; Drucker, 1993).

More and more of an organization's decisions are being made at the point of contact (Morton, 1991) and so the relevant information must also be available there too. Technology started the meltdown of established structures. In turn, the new structures – virtual organizations and teleworking teams – are driving advances in technology.

The future of the global economy depends on the ability to transfer and process vast amounts of information across geographical borders, markets and organizations (Reich, 1991). The 'knowledge business' (Hague, 1991) is set to grow and this poses some significant challenges, rather like the labours presented to Hercules. In this case there are seven, not twelve. Even so, they are no pushover.

The latent capability of computer technology is quite frightening. There is very little that cannot be done with the vast array of powerful tools on or near the marketplace. Most power tools, however, have a tendency to wreak awful destruction if abused. This section focuses on the potential pitfalls of the distributed world. There are no solutions proposed at this juncture, these come later. For now the aim is to raise the main issues, which become much easier to plan for and avoid once you know where they are!

2.3.1 Information management

Information consistency is vital. It is a key resource and there is a huge amount of it out there! By way of illustration, the U.S. Library of Congress has between 22 and 25 million books. (No one is quite sure of the real number – this figure is an estimation based upon miles of shelf occupancy!) With the sum total of recorded human knowledge doubling every 3–4 years, it is clear that paper-based technology will soon run out of space. So computers and databases will just have to cope.

In essence, the challenge of ensuring good information is to make sure that it has some essential features:

● integrity (it is correct);

● topicality (it is up to date);

● completeness (it covers all relevant aspects);

and finally it should add value by extending the user's knowledge in some way. It may be new or it may shed new light.

Anyone who has used the World Wide Web cannot fail to be impressed by the sheer volume of information that is available (nor by the temptation to surf aimlessly around the sites). Control over information, its location, relevance, accuracy, timeliness and availability at point of use, is vital. And it will become a much bigger job with higher capacity networks that extend the user's catchment area and tools that speed the generation of networked data.

The heart of this problem lies in the fact that the rules and metaphors of information representation simply do not exist. With modern technology allowing all authors to be publishers, the temptation to generate electronic verbiage aimlessly will have to be controlled. The fact that a network server is as easy to set up as a client illustrates the ease with which anybody can contribute whatever they wish. Consumer review becomes a major obligation.

2.3.2 Service management

With large investments in infrastructure and the central role it plays, people will expect direct support for their business process. The network should help them to do their job not get in their way. The configuration of new and complex technology to match this expectation is a major challenge.

Simple connectivity does not mean cooperation. To provide service (as perceived by the user) requires a level of intimacy and embedded intelligence between system elements. With networks, software and applications all getting more complex and diverse, ways of configuring (and reconfiguring) systems to align with business process needs will have to be attended to.

2.3.3 Network management

The Internet is so widespread that it has many options for fallback. Yet people still lose service because of equipment outages. End-to-end network management will be an increasingly important concern for any organization that relies on its computing resource. The implication of this in the modern context is that there are many diverse, scattered elements that need to be kept in step, monitored and kept operational. Availability constraints and physical spread mean that this cannot be achieved without automation. And this can only be achieved with another set of computers!

So, network management becomes an overlay of the distributed systems already in place. Standard interfaces and protocols for managing remote equipment, along with commercial, purpose-built management systems make the task easier. The ever increasing demands on end-to-end availability across the globe mean that this challenge cannot be safely ignored (Stallings, 1993).

2.3.4 Security

With information *the* business currency of the next millennium, its protection is paramount. But the spectre of the information superhighwayman looms whenever and wherever there is appealing booty on offer.

Information is power and, more and more, it is also money (this is illustrated by the operation of 'First Virtual Holdings', a network-based bank that opened its (electronic) doors in 1994), but the ease with which electronic information can be copied, erased, manipulated and modified makes that power subject to abuse. The dangers of a widely distributed information system can readily be appreciated by looking at what can happen on the Internet. Here, it is relatively easy for the non-expert to be attacked – there are instances of forged e-mail, private data being taken without consent and illicit access and damage to protected files. The way in which network addresses are translated into names makes it relatively easy for someone to pretend to be someone else. A message from Queen@Windsor could readily be sent from a PC in Oklahoma.

Firewalls and encryption go some way to protecting information but the trusting nature of widely used network programs make total safety virtually impossible (the fragility of security in a networked and distributed environment is discussed in detail via spurious USENET newsgroups alt.security and comp.security.misc). People are likely to want to preserve their recently won ubiquity and ease of access and many of the access restriction schemes have been cracked.

One of the more demanding of the Herculean tasks was to tackle Kerberos, the three-headed dog. Kerberos has changed form into its modern guise as a security control method. It promises to provide part of the answer here and is revisited in Chapter 5.

2.3.5 Complexity

With computer and communication technology both stretched to enable the distribution of resources across the information superhighway (Gore, 1995), it is impossible to drive progress from a purely technical viewpoint. Sheer complexity precludes this.

A superior understanding of integration, complexity control and information planning will have to be established. Early notions of the challenge of computers were based around the harnessing of a superbrain. The actual challenge is less well defined. It consists of controlling a mass of different interests and sources of information, all generating new ideas, innovations and opportunities at a staggering rate.

2.3.6 Usability

This is the other side of security. The temptation in barring unwelcome access to information is to make it difficult for everyone. Access control methods are needed that allow the right people to use systems without being unduly frustrated by multiple logon requests. Of course, there are many other aspects to usability but that would be a book in it's own right.

2.3.7 Flexibility

Change is inevitable and networked computer systems are expensive. They need to evolve to meet changing requirements. They are not throw away items that can be swapped every year or so. Changes of business condition, acquisitions and mergers will always change the shape of the processes and functions that computer systems need to support. Given this, they cannot be brittle artefacts specialized for a specific or set requirement. Other angles on this are to say that systems need to be scaleable, so that they can grow over time, or integratable because organizations are dynamic.

An overall plan, architecture, or route map needs to be adopted in the face of this need. This gives some consistency of approach in systems development and gives hope that the new can be integrated with what is already in place.

This is not an easy task and, perhaps, equates to one of those faced by Hercules – to clean out the Augean stables. A difficult job that attracts few bouquets and is very visible if skimped.

How you deal with these issues is the subject of Chapters 6, 7 and 8. For now, our concern has been to set the context in which distributed systems have evolved and to explain the nature of the challenges in that evolution (and, perhaps, a few of the consequences of not meeting them).

There are, of course, other factors that impinge on the design and deployment of distributed systems. For instance, both cost and regulation will drive the shape of their business case; differentiation and branding when physical presence is removed may be an issue; and the protection of intellectual property may affect the way in which systems are used.

These are concerns that vary from one instance to the next, however. Our concern will be to address design issues that affect any distributed system and to provide guidelines that reflect best practice.

2.4 Summary

Computers have become very versatile. The have evolved from specialized, isolated and slow machines into the ubiquitous enabler for everyone. Nowadays, they can be used for a huge variety of applications – wordprocessing, information storage and retrieval, calculation, data manipulation and communication. What is more, all of these facilities can now be provided on the same system and that system can be distributed across a worldwide network. In the space of 30 short years, the computer has become an indispensable part of our lives. It enables many of the accepted services, pleasures and capabilities of everyday life.

The information distribution and processing power of the computer means that business could not function without them. There is little doubt that computers have reached dependence level. They used to be a business – now, in many cases, they are the business!

This chapter has illustrated the evolution of computers, showing how they first replaced manual processes, then moved to one per desk as prices fell and finally became the main working interface. Many people are now dependent on electronic mail, distributed files and networked information to operate, and that level of dependence is quite easy to see in the ubiquity of global applications such as airline reservation systems and automatic teller machines.

In short, the computing systems have ceased to be local resources with a fixed point of access. A global information community is forming across the previously rigid boundaries of different disciplines and a 'network culture' is beginning to emerge. Systems need to cope with this and the observation made in 1988 in *Fortune* magazine, that 'Software that will enable people to collaborate across barriers of time and space is one of the hottest frontiers of computing research' should now concern us all.

CHAPTER 3

The user's view

'Discovery consists of seeing what everybody has seen and thinking what nobody has thought' – Nagyrapolt Szent-Gyorgyi

The heart and soul of any system lies in what it does for the user. Technical capability and business operations provide sound reasons for doing things in a certain way but it is the people in the system that ultimately determine how, indeed *if*, it is adopted. There are numerous instances of perfectly viable systems that had to be withdrawn from service because they were 'rejected' (often subtly) by their intended users. The BBC TV programme *Arena* devoted a whole episode to such failures in the health sector alone.

So far we have described the pressures and opportunities that are driving organizations to spread their wings. The way in which technical capability has evolved to support that general drift has also been covered. It has been established that there is both a need and a means of satisfying it. So, how will this translate in practice?

This chapter presents a view of distributed computing from a user's point of view. It concentrates on what a user can see and do 'from the desktop'. The aim is to address the questions 'how do I know distributed computing when I see it?' and 'why should I care anyway?' Both of these questions will be revisited at the end of the chapter.

To start with we describe a little of the current state of play – what distributed systems offer their users at present. We describe a few of the facilities that many users have come to expect, along with some of the evolving ideas that look like they will become widely adopted. Along with this we look at the impact of globally distributed systems like the Internet. Going on the basis that past behaviour is a good indicator of future practice, the way in which these facilities have been used and are evolving is discussed.

From this, we move on to look at some of the key happenings just behind the scenes – the tools and techniques that provide the user with the computing world that they want to have. It should come as no surprise that many of these are to do with distribution. Some of the topics explained in depth in later chapters are introduced here.

In particular, we look at some widely used services like electronic mail and network-wide file sharing along with more embedded technologies such as networked and distributed databases, multimedia, object linking and embedding (OLE) and 'groupware'.

To close, we consider the implications of these new enablers. At all times the emphasis is on putting each area of technology in its appropriate context from a user's point of view.

3.1 A window on the world

We have come a long way since computers presented the user with a stack of cards, a paper tape or even a fixed screenful of information. The user relationship to computer systems that required separate links to be set up for each discrete transaction is also long past. The expectation these days is to be presented with the screen equivalent of a desktop where you can see and attend to a number of jobs in parallel.

Given the situation, users want to be able to make good use of what he or she sees in front of them. The joy of having everything you need in a series of windows on your PC soon evaporates if you cannot readily manipulate the information on hand as you see fit. So information must not only be easy to get hold of, it must also be easy to use once you have it. And this means effective cooperation with whichever machines provide the data or processing that is required to do a particular task, irrespective of their physical location.

Expectations are well illustrated by looking at the personal communications offered via the Internet. This provides a good model of what users will expect any distributed system to offer, so will be described here in some detail.

3.1.1 The Internet

This is a network of computer networks that share a common way of communicating. It has grown dramatically over the past 25 years or so, and now links together as many as 40 million people across the world. Estimates vary widely, but there is no doubt that the Internet community is a large one. What is of interest here is the way in which this situation has come about – what it is that has provoked such growth.

The Internet was a research project sponsored by the US military. The idea was to develop some way of removing reliance on a central computer in the event of a bomb or suchlike. So how did it come to be something that is used by a global community of users? Let us start by considering what people use the Internet for and how the technology that was developed supports this.

On a day-to-day basis, most people on the net use the facility to send and receive mail messages, to exchange files and to access data on different computers. This has been enabled by the widespread adoption of families of protocols, for example the Internet protocols including TCP, Telnet, FTP and a host of others. These allow most users to communicate with most remote services, irrespective of local equipment type. This is the very technology developed to reduce reliance on a central computer. So the solution to a specific problem found wider application, and the Internet was born.

Over the years, the Internet has done much to bring down national and organizational barriers to enable information working. And the way of working that it has sparked cannot be ignored – it is already as embedded into communications culture as are the telephone and the fax machine. It could not be as readily removed, a point reinforced by the dramatic growth in the number of users, the amount of business transacted and the number of services now offered.

The Internet works by passing data using standard communications protocols, which can be used on many types of computer and which work over almost any network, both local and wide area. Internet protocols are *de facto* standards and preloaded on most computers. The Internet offers a simple naming and addressing scheme, whereby resources (and this covers services and people as well as information) on the network can be readily located.

So why is the Internet so popular? There are a number of reasons, the main ones being that

- no one 'owns' it – it relies on mutual trust and voluntary efforts, so there are few mandatory controls and restraints;

- it is genuinely global and gives access to a huge set of users at low cost and with relative ease;

- it engenders a level of social and cultural openness – there is a willingness for people to help each other;

- it provides a vast amount of information and a lot of useful applications, many freely available and in the public domain.

We can expand this last point by looking at some of the more useful applications that are available and are commonly used on the Internet.

3.1.2 Electronic mail

This is a widely used and long-established application of the Internet. It is now commonplace for businesses, television programmes and government bodies (as well as individuals) to give out their electronic mail (e-mail) address as a matter of course.

From the user's point of view, this facility works through packages (in the form of software clients) available on almost any system (PCs, UNIX workstations and Apple Macintoshes) that allow them to connect to mail servers within the Internet. Well-known examples of software packages are MS-Mail, xmh, Eudora and NewWave.

The mail servers within the Internet provide the backbone of the mail system. Some servers are provided as commercial messaging services, probably the best known being Compuserve and America Online. They all store and forward mail between themselves using common protocols and addressing formats. For the exchange of electronic messages, the Internet uses the simple mail transfer protocol (SMTP).

Although different in terms of look and feel, all of the e-mail packages allow messages to be sent to any other Internet user. The common form of addressing is

name@location.organization.type.country

For instance, M.Norris@axion.bt.co.uk is a user name followed by a location identifier, followed by a company name, followed by identifiers that place the person in a company (as opposed to .edu or .ac, for academia or .gov, for government) and in the UK. (There is no country extension for the U.S. – they were first, rather like the UK with postage stamps.) There are variants on this but the formats are similar and readily decipherable.

There are many applications of electronic mail – from the simple exchange of messages to more complex interchanges of information. This is reflected in the layers of sophistication of both the Internet technology and its mail capabilities.

The former can be illustrated by the way in which information sent through the mail system can be 'tagged' so that the recipient knows how to deal with a received file. This is effected through a development in the base technology called MIME (multipurpose Internet mail extensions).

Just as the base technology (sometimes, quite reasonably, referred to as 'under-wear' – its absence or low quality can cause signs of discomfort on the surface) has reduced the degree of internal system knowledge required of the user, so new facilities have eased operations. Special mail servers, known as list servers, pro-vide the user with an intelligent e-mail distribution service that can forward mail to a group of people of a known list. By sending mail to a list server's address (for-mat as above), with the word 'help' in the body of the text, the server will return a help file that tells you how the list server works. You can then choose to sub-scribe to that list and, when you send a message to the list server, it will forward the message to all members of the list (yourself included). The list server also inserts a unique message number in the 'subject' field so that you can follow a dis-cussion, refer to earlier issues, keep tabs on what happened and when, and so on.

MIME and list servers are but two of many examples of the way in which a dis-tributed system evolves from being technology centred towards being user centred.

3.1.3 Bulletin boards and discussion groups

Moving on from the essentially interpersonal e-mail facilities on the Internet, there are also a range of 'broadcast' services – bulletin boards and discussion groups. Bulletin board systems (BBSs) provide a central repository where public messages can be posted for all to read at their leisure, much like an office notice-board. BBSs pre-date widespread Internet use and are often accessed by dialling up directly over a modem link. Access can be restricted to a closed set of users and even with a single BBS there may be restricted noticeboards.

Discussion groups are best exemplified by the USENET news system. This appears rather like a giant world-wide BBS. However, there is no single central repository. News articles are held and accessed from a local system and local users can post or reply to articles. These locally generated articles are then copied out to and new articles are received from neighbouring systems at regular inter-vals. So articles ripple out to news sites across the world over a matter of hours or days. USENET also pre-dates the Internet and in the early days all news was carried over point-to-point dial-up links. Now the Internet itself carries the bulk of news traffic.

USENET groups are identified by names such as uk.telecom, rec.tv.dr-who and so on. There are categories of groups (such as those beginning with rec which are all concerned with recreational activities) and some articles carry considerable amounts of useful information. For instance, many of the FAQs (Frequently

Asked Questions) posted to groups provide concise facts, figures and contacts relevant to the group – a rich source of (usually) high-quality information.

Overall there are about 10 000 groups. Most of these are accessible to everyone. A proportion are private and are used for closed user group discussion (for example within a company, project, and so on). A good group to start with is news.announce.newusers.

3.1.4 File transfer

Applications that allow the sort of file transfer required to get hold of a FAQ are typically bundled with TCP/IP packages. So most PCs, and so on, have an FTP client program that enables file transfer from remote machines. Simple FTP clients can connect to FTP hosts, view directories of files and download them, if they choose.

There is usually some form of access control for FTP access – you have to provide a user name and password, just as if you were logging on to any computer. Some FTP servers allow anonymous login. This entails giving the user name 'anonymous' and supplying your Internet e-mail address as the password. This is useful in allowing free access to stored information.

The above examples give some idea of the uses that people have found for the Internet. Many organizations use some of the available services to ease and enrich their work. An increasing number have come to rely on the Internet to carry out part of their business (for example using the file transfer facility as an integral part of remote testing). To quote from *The Economist*: 'In the high-tech world, if you're not on the net, you're not in the know.'

This is a trend that looks like continuing and new applications that draw on having a global community seem to arrive with increasing regularity. In particular, several recent enhancements have made Internet-based information search and retrieval facilities considerably more powerful (this is covered in the next section).

The rapid adoption of the Internet has been sparked, to a large degree, by altruism. A low cost of entry combined with the availability of the high quality of public domain tools contributed from across the user base has kick-started a worldwide community.

This, in turn, has prompted changes in the way that many people now use computer systems. The volumes of data associated with the expanded user base has meant that user access has had to evolve in order to cope. A new form of user front end (again provided to users in the form of a 'client' software package) is now being widely used to access a host of new services. This facility, known as World Wide Web, eases the navigation of a vast and growing information space. The World Wide Web was originally developed as an information-sharing facility at CERN, the European high energy physics laboratory. So physics research is relevant to the average person! We will describe it in some detail, as it is very much the user-friendly window on global electronic communications.

3.2 A World Wide Web

Since the Internet already provides a means for any computer to communicate
with any other, the World Wide Web is a globally distributed application. It can
be regarded as a development of earlier page-based information services (such as
the BBC's Ceefax service), although with a number of differences:

- The pages of information may contain pictures, sound and links that allow
  the user to navigate between pages of text simply by clicking on key words.
  So the World Wide Web is a multimedia application.

- It is not constrained by length of page. In practice a 'page' of information can
  be any length, although it is customary to present a 'home page' to introduce
  a server and to structure subsequent information for ease of reading.

- It is readily expandable both in terms of users and the facilities that it provides.
  The separation of World Wide Web into 'client' and 'server' components
  means that it is very straightforward to add extra clients and servers to the
  system (see http://www.leeds.ac.uk./ucs/www/handbook/handbook.htm/
  for details of exactly how this is done).

- Client and server can negotiate the document types that they will use.
  Typically a server offers pages based on a standard page description language but can also provide proprietary formats such as MS-Word.

A typical page of information from a World Wide Web server was shown in the
previous chapter (Figure 2.7). This illustrates the mix of pictures, text, and so on,
and, more significantly, shows how users are presented with a view of the available information (rather than just having to know where to go to find what they
want). The significance of the underlined text will be explained shortly!

The client software that allows a user access from virtually any type of terminal
(PC, Macintosh, UNIX workstation and most others) is available from a number
of sources, although the major growth of the World Wide Web has arisen through
the distribution of the Netscape and Mosaic browsers. It is interesting to reflect
that Mosaic started life as a humble student project, yet has come to have significant impact on the use of the Internet by virtue of its intuitive appeal to users of
a widely distributed system. For most users, World Wide Web, Netscape and
other popular browsers are practically synonymous.

Pages of information retrieved from a server are displayed in a window, much
like that displayed by a wordprocessor. Certain words on the page are distinguished either by displaying them in a different colour or by underlining them (as
in Figure 2.7). Each such item is a hypertext link, and clicking on it results in the
bringing up of a new page of information in the user's window. Effectively, each
page can include links that allow the user to navigate straight to an associated
page.

When the user clicks on a link, the client application decodes the reference and retrieves an appropriate page from the server – this page could be anywhere and need not have any other association with the machine on which the first page is kept.

As far as the user is concerned, it is their client software that decodes the reference and selects the next page. The user does not have to get involved in finding resources. Resource addresses come in the form of uniform resource locators (URLs). For example http://www.internet.net takes you to the interactive shopping resources on the network. Often, the user does not have to know the URL – it is usually associated with a link in the text. So, in much the same way that the postal service evolved to mask routing decisions from the user of the service, the World Wide Web system provides its users with transparent access to information. The focus is on information, rather than on where it resides and the routes that are needed to locate it.

3.3 New horizons

As noted in the previous section, pages of information delivered via World Wide Web may include pictures, sound or video. Apart from touch, taste and smell, the user would appear to have access to the full gamut of communication experiences. What more could they want?

In reality, there are readily identifiable new horizons to be explored. The two main areas here are access and interaction. Taking these in turn:

- Access. In operation, anything more than simple text can take some time to retrieve over all but the most advanced networks. There are special, high-speed networks such as SuperJanet (Joint academic network) in the UK and Mbone (Multimedia backbone) but, in the main, these are for research rather than general use. In view of this, clients such as Netscape may be configured to load only the text and display markers in place of other items. The user is then able, selectively, to click on the markers if they want to download pictures, and so on. So, the speed of access currently tends to impose some sort of limit. And this means that users have to exert control over their usage in order to ease demands on their network (and get acceptable response times). The likely move here is towards faster, more integrated networks (Atkins and Norris, 1995), which will both remove existing limitations and (most likely) spark further developments.

- Interaction. The quality and quantity of information available from the World Wide Web is surely impressive, but it is still just a source of predigested information. Users can readily find items of interest, take a local copy of some information and respond to the provider. So there is a constraint on the amount of processing that a user can do at present. Just as the capacity of current networks limits the speed/volume of information that a user can get to, so this constraint limits the extent to which they can process that information.

The maxim of faster, better and cheaper is clearly not exhausted in this area and the user is likely to see significant further developments. Rather than trying to guess how and when these advances will come, we now dwell on some of the likely implications.

Both the World Wide Web and the Internet are open services with many well-respected contributors leading to a large part of their success. For illustration, servers can be accessed at Xerox PARC, NTT, IEEE, the United Nations, Open Software Foundation, AT&T, BT, NASA, the White House… and most of the major universities. They are available to anyone who can organize their own network access and they rely to a large extent on the integrity and quality of the information providers for successful operation. Servers are spread all over the world and there is no form of centralized control. This goes back to the original design philosophy of having resilience against a point of failure. It makes the Internet inherently unstoppable. Each server is set up and run independently of all others, the only constraint being that it conforms to the shared standards. The connections within the Internet vary widely, with the vast majority using modems and dial-up access over public telephone lines. This variability of infrastructure extends to the connections between servers (usually the larger computers on the Internet). A few have high-capacity links, the majority are less well heeled.

Even so, the breadth of Internet facilities continues to grow. Originally, it provided little more than basic intercomputer communication. This is no longer the case. In addition to having information on the World Wide Web, the Internet carries both video and voice communications over the same links. Applications such as Maven (for voice) and CU-SeeMe (for video) extend the range of the Internet. The quality may not be all that the user would like (at least, not for early applications) but the grip of electronic communication is becoming tighter. The diversity of application will doubtless increase with the likes of virtual reality (via VRML) and component applications (via Java).

For all the usefulness and excitement, the value of having an open and largely uncontrolled network can be viewed another way. The way in which the Internet is set up means that there is no guarantee of quality or of security. The systems, and the information they provide, depend on peer trust and (distributed) goodwill and expertise. This arrangement makes them ideal for some purposes, less so for others.

Adoption to date has been fuelled by the breadth of information providers, the variety of applications and the availability of significant desktop processing power. There are few bars on information provision. There is no 'Bit Police' as such. See Negroponte (1995) for an in-depth analysis of this and other aspects of media control. Furthermore, it is now almost as easy to provide a service on the Internet (that is, to set up a server) as it is to use it. This, combined with the sophistication of authoring tools, allows just about every author to be their own publisher. There is good precedent here. Desktop publishing tools provided powerful capability which was often abused when the associated professional discipline of their application was not present. The reader needs to question both the validity and the source of information from such a distributed and open network. Free cheese, as they say in Russia, only comes in mousetraps.

3.4 Under the covers

To provide something as intuitive and appealing as the World Wide Web requires a lot of thought and action behind the scenes. This section takes a peek under the covers at some of the things that are happening to allow users to navigate, search and use a mass of information.

The World Wide Web model gives a good basis for what the user wants – access to resources from all over, yes, but at the information level not the network level. So what else is going on that will enrich this promised cyberland? It is possible to see what sort of world truly distributed systems will put us in. Here are some of the key technical developments and underlying concepts that promise to provide users with everything they might want.

3.4.1 Networks

A network to connect one resource to another is a basic prerequisite for any communication system. Over the years many different networks have been used to link cooperating computers, from analog lines built for voice traffic through to digital links dedicated specially for data traffic. Just as there are several types of network, so there are different capacities. Long-distance links tend to be of limited throughput (perhaps a few tens of thousands of bits per second), whereas local area networks have tended to offer considerably more bandwidth (typically tens of millions of bits per second). Also, each network type has been designed with a particular type of traffic in mind.

The sheer variety of transport mechanisms capable of getting bits from one machine to another has led to the user seeing a very diverse platform. In the past, this has demanded some understanding of the underlying communications network from the user but has posed no fundamental problem. With the advent of widely used multimedia information, the association of different types of data with different carrier types becomes an issue.

Emerging network technologies such as asynchronous transfer mode (ATM) provide a single mechanism suited to the whole range of information that the user expects to carry. It provides a multiservice network capable of transporting voice (which is tolerant of transmission errors but is delay sensitive) as effectively as it transports data (which is sensitive to transmission error but not delay).

So there is every prospect that distributed systems can be built on a general-purpose network rather than having to be crafted to fit onto a set of individually focused platforms. There is, of course, more to it than that! The design and technology of multiservice networks is a huge subject in its own right (Atkins *et al,* 1996) – the very heart of the much vaunted information superhighway. This term – popularized in the early 1990s – has been satirized as the information super-hypeway. Failure to materialize as quickly as hoped is due, in no small part, to the sheer complexity of the task.

We will not dwell on this here, however. We are more concerned with connecting information than with joining boxes together. You certainly need a fast, uniform connection but the very fact that there is a prospect that the latter can be done is enough for now. Investing in the necessary equipment is a choice for the organization or individual!

3.4.2 Data

Good information relies on getting, keeping and making available reliable data and this means the efficient design and use of databases. The database has come to form the core of just about every information-intensive system. It is usually represented in design diagrams as a single box or icon. In reality it may be a number of physical resources, all of different pedigree, scattered over a wide area. From the user viewpoint, however, data is data and should be available to them in a consistent format, irrespective of where it is held or how it is retrieved. To achieve this goal, we need to understand a little of the relevant technology.

At the simplest level, a database is no more than a persistent collection of data, a place where you can store information for later reference or use. In practical terms fast, high-capacity databases have come to be an indispensable part of most computer-based systems. They provide the essential currency that is exchanged, manipulated and processed.

In a computer system, databases can store information in a number of different ways, ranging from the very simple (for example entries in a text file) to the more sophisticated (for example an object-oriented datastore). This spectrum of implementation options reflects the fact that the way in which information is stored is usually dictated by the way it is to be used. So, the challenge of designing and building a complex database structure may be made all worthwhile by the ease with which it operates.

There are a number of types of database:

- Hierarchical. This was the model adopted in the earliest of the commercial databases (before 1980). In this instance, the records held in the database contain both information and pointers to other record types. So, for instance, a database of customers and their addresses would be stored as a record of names along with a pointer to a record containing the associated addresses. This type of database has been largely superseded by the relational type, primarily because the latter is better suited for queries that have to navigate the stored data. For bulk data retrieval, however, this type is still useful.

- Relational. This is the most common type of database at present. It works on the premise that information can be kept in the form of a series of linked tables. A table may be a set of addresses with associated names and telephone numbers. For example, each row of the table would refer to a different person, each column to a different piece of information. The database works by having keys defined on the columns so that the user can readily pick up an entry in the table from the key of their choice. This may sound simple, but practical complexity is evident when you consider that a single database of this type can store several hundred gigabytes. The *de facto* standard used to access relational databases is the structured query language (SQL). This language can be used directly for one-off queries or can be embedded in application code when more systematic access is required.

- Object-oriented. This is a relatively new addition, at least in terms of having commercially viable products. As the name suggests, this type of database stores objects. Each object consists of a set of attributes and a set of permissible actions; an altogether much more complex entry type than either of the above. The importance of object orientation in achieving effective distribution is dealt with later in this book (see Chapter 4). For now, the point is that the general trend in storing information is becoming increasingly user-oriented as technology has allowed the database to become more of an information store.

The above reflects the general trend in database technology over the past 30 years or so. The emergence of object-oriented databases has been in line with the migration to distributed systems (which, in turn, has been driven by the user's desire to distribute his or her operations and operate at a global level).

The single aim that links all of the above is to present the user with a single view of the data they require. This is easier when it is all stored on one machine – less so when the variety and location of physical stores is wider (a point illustrated in Figure 3.1).

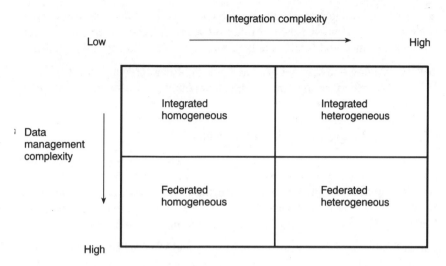

Figure 3.1 The cost of having distributed information.

The main point here is that the preservation of a single logical database (which is what the user actually wants to see in most instances) is more difficult when the systems are distributed. Not only is data management (keeping it consistent, up to date, at known status) more complex but also the integration of the required constituents is more difficult.

Having said that, the technology and knowhow is available. It is the application of what exists that will determine whether users get what they want. So from the designer's point of view the architecture of information beckons – we are not there yet but we do have the components to build with. To go with this, there are applications to match.

3.4.3 Applications

A general picture built up in this chapter is of a user getting information from a range of sources and then using it for his or her own purpose. There are facilities that allow this by enabling compound documents to be produced that contain active links to their parent application. Microsoft's OLE (object linking and embedding) and Taligent's OpenDoc are two well-known examples. These allow users to incorporate different types of data without having to concern themselves with the application that originally created or manages that data. The techniques that have been developed for this provide a living reflection of information that has been created and that lives elsewhere – in another file, on another machine, on a remote site, perhaps. There are two essential concepts here:

- Linking – establishing a live connection between data and the parent application (for example pasting a link from a drawing package into a text document so that modifications to the source are reflected in all linked copies).

- Embedding – taking an object and placing it in a foreign application where it looks after itself by virtue of having a link back to its parent application. The 'object packager' utility available on most PCs exemplifies the idea; it allows the user to create an object (which consists of a body plus associated icon) and then paste it into another application.

Object linking and embedding is essentially a client/server way of doing things. The client/server concept is explained fully in later chapters. For now, the essential idea is that the client asks for a service, the server provides it. (It is worth noting that this definition of client and server holds for the duration of an interaction. The terms do not apply generally to a particular machine or process.)

An OLE client application can accept, display and store linked objects. A server can edit or manipulate the object in response to a request from a client application. The essential point is that this way of working is user centred rather than application centred. Everything revolves around what users want to achieve with the information in front of them – they do not have to manage a set of applications to achieve a result. The system is set up to manage this.

Finally, we have some underlying concepts that allow some of the technology to be delivered and are required to make good use of it.

3.4.4 Objects

An object can be anything from a single cell in a spreadsheet through to a complex set of related items. The principles of working with objects are covered in detail later (see Chapter 4) but for now, the salient point is that they provide an intuitive means of defining complex and diverse systems in a uniform way. It is obvious that OLE is based on the concept of objects, less so that other aspects of distributed systems are too.

3.4.5 Work organization

Technology adoption changes patterns of work and in turn, patterns of work make demands of technology. The essential point that needs to be appreciated, however, is that people change at a much slower rate than technology and so put a limit on the rate of change that one can realistically expect. There is considerable evidence that when technology is forced on people it tends to be fought and, quite often, rejected (Norris and Rigby, 1992). As John Locke said many years before computers appeared: 'New opinions are always suspected and usually opposed, without any other reason but because they are already common.'

But when people do change their behaviour, it can have a significant impact – one part of a system can allow something to be done and the rampant adoption of that new facility can radically unbalance the rest of the system.

The ease with which information can be posted onto the World Wide Web is a case in point. Authoring tools for creating high quality Web pages complete with pictures are readily available (a huge number of these are available on existing net sites). A credible and attractive set of pages can be made available to an unsuspecting public in a matter of minutes.

As stated earlier, the technology of the World Wide Web makes every author also a publisher and this has profound impact on the amount (and, most likely, quality) of information that is available. A modest book, like this one, takes years of research, entails months of writing, undergoes numerous reviews and requires the efforts of many to produce. A similar amount of text can be placed before a global audience overnight with few constraints.

So, open and free environments have attendant problems which need to be taken into account in the way they are used. How people do things on a closed, private (readily limited and controlled) system may not necessarily transfer into one where the job is the same, but the technology leads people to change the way in which it is done.

Working through electronic media, especially when unregulated, demands new approaches (Kostner and Books, 1994). The appropriate practices have yet to be developed, fully tried and tested for this. One thing that is clear, however, is that people behave differently on the Internet than they do in more customary social circumstances (Sproull and Kiesler, 1991) and are likely to do so with any system that takes the distance out of information. Groupware, a term coined to describe the way people work in virtual teams (Johansen, 1988) is young and evolving.

One thing that is clear is that we are at the stage where a lot of information is under the control of the user, not the provider. Subject to access rights (which on the World Wide Web are virtually without bound), users can get hold of what they want, link it together in any way they wish and present it as suits their tastes.

The level of mutual trust on the Internet has given rise to a user view that transcends previous company, national and discipline boundaries – it is easy (and therefore commonplace) to examine peripheral issues. The richness of the distributed computer network makes information working more exploratory, less prescriptive or directed.

3.4.6 To be resolved

It should be fairly clear that there are a number of operational issues that have yet to be resolved – work organization in a distributed environment being but one. Given this situation, there is a very real need to re-examine a number of the practices that are currently taken for granted. High up on this list are the security, privacy, legal and copyright issues. Currently, most of these are governed by rules that rely on physical phenomena (national boundaries, ownership, and so on) which are difficult to transfer into the virtual world.

By way of illustration, it is interesting to consider what rules should govern a file from a Canadian database that is accessed by a Briton for processing and storage on a French computer for the use of a Japanese client. This example would come to life if the contents of that file contravened French law and might result in a libel or defamation case in the UK.

Not only does such open electronic exchange stretch existing law, but also the new forms of exchange (multimedia) have no precedence, so it is not clear where the law to cover this should start from! Until this (and other) questions are answered, there may be blocks on the progress of distributed systems, or at least some heavy influences on their deployment.

But it is not our intention to suggest how such issues might be dealt with – merely to point out that they are part of the overall picture of distributed systems; something that the user should be aware of and have some guidance or strategy for dealing with.

3.5 Graunch and go

A long-term ideal of the computing industry would be to simply plug equipment in and start using the full range of facilities – plug and play. The word 'graunch' is used here as, in practice, a considerable amount of user effort is often required before you get to go!

For all the advances in computing and communications, we are still some way from having a ready-made box of components from which to build the systems we might like. The prospect of treating computer systems as commodity items that simply need to be plugged in and used is still somewhat distant. There are some areas where things are getting close to the ideal (for instance, interfaces such as WinAPI, protocols like TCP/IP, both ubiquitous). There are other areas where the ideal is altogether more distant.

It would be naïve to expect the simple compatibility of a Whitworth nut and bolt. Distributed computing systems are far too complex and multifaceted for this. The challenge should be apparent from straightforward things such as domestic power outlets. These vary across Europe in physical layout (two or three pins, round and square), in delivered frequency (50/60 Hz) and in power level (from 110 to 220 V).

There is a general evolution of most products, however, from crafted to standard. For instance, at one time all guns were handcrafted items. Each one was produced on a one-off basis by a skilled and experienced gunsmith, who subsequently became the sole source of replacement parts. The shortage of such skills in the U.S. led to the first of the mass-produced guns – the famous Peacemaker of the old West. This was made possible by a system of manufacture that used machines that were set up and operated to standard settings.

At a stroke, the skill shortage was eased (experts were still needed but their productivity was greatly improved) and reliance on a single source was removed. It is not that all guns became the same, rather that variety had been reduced and there was some measure of standardization at the component level.

This move towards variety reduction and interchangeability of parts has been repeated time and again since this example. And the general flow of development is the same – lessons of history can be learned. It should be clear by now that the dawn of 'plug and play' in the world of computing is some way off. This term generally refers to the ability to connect together compatible hardware and software so that the system that results is immediately ready for its intended purpose. The focus, for now, is on variety reduction, with the skilled craftsmen on hand to set the machines up and the informed technician to operate them (in practice, this role often falls to the user!).

As with gun manufacture, the elimination of variety is precluded by complexity and discouraged by the commercial imperative that suppliers should differentiate their product.

But there is now a clear overall shape to a distributed system – some overall structure, common across many installations. It would be wrong to suggest that there is, as yet, standardization of computer systems but there are areas within which informed choices can be made.

3.6 The shape of distributed systems

And so to the first question posed at the start of this chapter – how do you know a distributed system when you see or use one? Well, they certainly do not have any sort of physical shape. In fact, they should appear to the user to be no more than a fairly comprehensive set of resources just like any other system, only with more variety in the services and information on offer.

But behind all of this, there is a logical shape beginning to emerge. And here are some suggested criteria against which a system could be measured:

- Wide area access. This is enabled by the evolving transport networks that provide an adequate platform for carrying the variety of services to be delivered to the end user. The issues here are all about capacity and availability of links and are usually covered under the banner of network design (Atkins *et al.*, 1996). The need is for an enterprise network that adequately supports enterprise computing. Given the expectation that distributed systems will be built to deliver many types of information, the transport will have to be multiservice. From the user's 'plug and play' viewpoint this is rather like having enough power available once the system is plugged in.

- Basic services. These are the mechanisms that are put in place to allow user applications to be built. The concept of client/server is probably the best known of these, but there are many interchangeable parts now defined. The importance of interworking and information exchange standards/guidelines has not escaped the attention of either the supply industry or of the relevant government bodies (Gore, 1995; Bangemann, 1994). This is the subject of the next four chapters and equates to selecting the right box with the right type of plug.

- User focus. In action, there should be little to distinguish a distributed system from one that is localized on a single site. That is the point after all. So the focus of application development will be on presenting the user with a view of the services and information they want to work with, without demanding knowledge of the way in which it is delivered. The aim will be to give the impression to the user that all the services on offer are seamless. It should be possible to manipulate information on the desktop, irrespective of source.

- Business focus. Stepping back from the above point, there is the ultimate aim of speeding the user's business activities. The system should provide a faster or better way of working, as discussed in Chapter 1. This is largely a matter of planning and (a much overworked term) business process re-engineering. Exactly what is needed and how it is best achieved varies from one enterprise to the next and so the question is one of taste – choosing the relevant power tools for the job in hand (Norris, 1995).

And finally, to make it all happen as it should, systems will have to be built in a way that allows them to combine global reach with local feel. The answer to the second question posed at the start of this chapter – 'why should I care about distributed systems' – should be taking shape in your mind by now. The answer is likely to depend on circumstance. Some will care because they want to know what can be done. Others will be concerned with how they achieve it. A few may even care simply because it is interesting. All should know that distribution is a fundamental shift that cannot be ignored.

The way in which the available technology and knowhow is deployed to good effect and used to benefit from the potential will be a key differentiator, and that is where we focus attention from here on.

3.7 Summary

This chapter has considered distributed systems from the user point of view. It has looked at the way that systems, distributed or otherwise, are presented and then moved on to consider the various options for storing the currency of the computer system, that is, the data. The glue that joins these two together, the network, has been described and, for completeness, the patterns of use and their impact on what is acceptable has been examined.

These all fit into a model of distributed systems described in the next section. The one element that has been omitted so far is the procedural element that allows the user to access the data they want over the network. This is the 'application' area and is what the designer, builder, commissioner of a distributed system needs to know about.

And so, after much going around the edges of distributed systems to the guts of what is entailed in making them happen. By now we should

- be convinced that they are a fact of life
- have an idea of what the user wants and expects
- know where technology is and how it got here
- be aware of challenges of distribution.

All we need to know now is what are the concepts, standards, guidelines, dos and don'ts of constructing them. In other words, a systematic explanation of how to design for distribution. And so to the next chapters.

Electronic references

There is a vast amount of online information that is relevant to this chapter – too much to catalogue in any detail. The following references are good starting points. In the absence of a citation in the main text for each of them, a few words of explanation are attached.

http://pclt.cis.yale.edu/pclt/default.html

A very comprehensive and authoritative guide to connecting to the network. It starts by explaining basics – TCP/IP and the theory of networking – then moves on to catalogue the various pieces of hardware and software that help you to get the most from your connection. A similar offering suited to the Macintosh is located at http://web.nexor.co.uk/public/mac/archive/welcome.html.

ftp://win.tue.nl/pub/security/admin-guide-to-cracking.Z from win.tue.nl

This gives a practical guide to network security and explains how an organization can check its security by breaking into its own facilities.

http://info.cern.ch/hypertext/Datasources/WWW/Geographical.html

Here is a source of a huge amount of information on network providers in different countries – basically, a list of all of the registered World Wide Web servers (but a very large list)!

http://www.leeds.ac.uk/ucs/WWW/handbook/handbook.html

This is a detailed guide to the World Wide Web. It explains all of the practicalities, such as what the various browsers do and where you get them, how you set up a Web server and how to go about putting information online.

http://gnn.com/gnn/gnn.html

One of the network navigators. This page is easy to follow and gives ready access to a whole host of information sources.

And finally, for 'definitive' text on the Internet, the following documents can be retrieved from is.internic.net (for example ftp is.internic.net).

RFC-1208   Glossary of networking terms

RFC-1207   FYI: Answers to commonly asked 'experienced Internet user' questions

RFC-1206   FYI: Answers to commonly asked 'new Internet user' questions

RFC-1178   Choosing a name for your computer

RFC-1150   FYI on FYI: Introduction to the FYI notes.

The files are stored at an anonymous ftp site, so can be accessed by replying anonymous at the login prompt.

CHAPTER 4

The big ideas

'A stand can be made against invasion by an army; no stand can be made against invasion by an idea' – Victor Hugo, *Histoire d'un Crime*

Distributed computing ought to be easy. After all, it is only a case of tying together computers with networks. We are getting pretty good at the business of building fast, cheap, well-understood, commodity computers. We have been creating successful communications networks for decades. We know how to make computers talk to each other over these networks – so where's the problem?

Unfortunately, it is not as simple as that. Distributed systems tend to take our long-cherished assumptions about how computer systems function and turn them upside down. For example, most computer systems only really do one thing at a time. This is most obvious in the familiar personal computer running DOS. This manifestly only runs one program at a time. Microsoft Windows does a very limited form of multitasking – but here an application generally only runs when another one will let it. Even true multitasking systems such as UNIX, VMS, OS/2 and Windows NT only provide an illusion of doing more than one thing at a time by 'time-slicing' between competing processes.

Multiprocessor computers do execute more than one program simultaneously. However, most applications only exploit a single processor and so see the same one-step-at-a-time sequential path through their code. Things are very different in a distributed system. Here, parallel execution of applications is the norm. And this is only one of the reversals of behaviour that need to be handled. Some others are shown in Table 4.1.

Table 4.1 Reversed assumptions.

Centralized system		Distributed system
Local	In a distributed system some things will not be local, by definition. Some parts of an application may, literally, be running on the other side of the world	Remote
Sequential execution	With more than one system in use, applications will truly be running in parallel	Parallel execution
Synchronous	Most local interactions are serial and synchronous. Distributed systems introduce a much greater degree of asynchronicity and unpredictability	Asynchronous
Centralized control	Distributed systems may encompass several autonomous subsystems. No central control may be desirable or possible	Decentralized control
Total success or failure	Distributed systems can continue to operate if some parts fail or are unavailable. In a large distributed system it is unlikely that all parts will ever be fully available	Partial success or failure
Fixed location	Components of a distributed system are not bound to a fixed location. They may be relocated from time to time – even while in use	Changing location
Static configuration	Aspects of system configuration other than component location may also change 'on the fly'. For example, duplicates of components may be introduced to share processing tasks	Dynamic configuration
Homogeneity	There are no guarantees that all of the components of a distributed system employ the same technology, or that those technologies will not change over time	Heterogeneity
Unification	As systems grow or need to involve independent parties an imposed single structure becomes unworkable. Collaboration, cooperation and coexistence are essential	Federation
Private	Many things that were private become exposed to public view in a distributed system. This includes communications and structure	Public
Shared state	In a single, centralized system the current state of the system can be shared and known by all components, for example through shared memory. In the distributed world such shared state can no longer be assumed	Local state
Single design	A large, dynamic distributed system rarely springs to life fully formed. Such systems are more the product of organic growth. Components need to be designed to be used and reused in such an environment	Cooperating components

Each of these reversals brings a degree of increased complexity along with a set of attendant difficulties. None of these problems is entirely unfamiliar to programmers. However, many of them have been the provinces of specialists within particular application niches. Parallelism is the domain of the mathematical 'number-cruncher', asynchronous event handling the strength of the 'real-time' programmer and so on.

We may be forgiven for thinking that it will require a new breed of designers and programmers to be able to cope with and exploit this brave new world of distribution. It is for this reason that a great deal of effort has been expended in trying to make the distributed world look as much like the cosy, familiar 'single system' world as possible.

This chapter introduces some of the main ideas which have been applied to trying to tame the unruly distributed world. We start with one of the seldom stated but often sought goals of distributed systems: transparency.

4.1 Transparency – smoke and mirrors?

Transparency is all about hiding unnecessary levels of complexity from users and developers. We talk about 'transparency' because it is the process of making the unnecessary details invisible. If we talk in terms of hiding complexity then it could equally well be considered to be 'opacity'. It all depends on your point of view. You do not need to know the details of how an internal combustion engine functions in order to drive a car. In the same way, most users of distributed computing technology do not, and should not have to, care about how the 'distributed magic' happens to make things work. Any distributed system may provide and use a number of different types of transparency. A few of these are shown in Table 4.2.

Some of these transparencies may seem esoteric or impractical, but any user of a modern computer system has probably experienced each of these to some degree. A form of location transparency is seen where remote machines are accessed by name rather than address; access transparency is well illustrated by network file systems and so on. It is, in fact, a key feature of the concept that different degrees of transparency are appropriate or desirable in different circumstances. Distribution transparency is not supposed to be an absolute, all-or-nothing concept.

Table 4.2 Distribution transparencies.

Transparency	Meaning
Location	Components of the system are identified and located by name rather than physical network address
Access	The mechanisms (networks, protocols) by which components of the system are accessed and interact are hidden
Failure	Partial or complete failure is hidden, perhaps by automatically retrying failed operations or restarting 'dead' components
Replication	Some components of a system may be replicated but appear as a single unit to the rest of the system
Migration	In some systems components may migrate between different physical locations while in operation, unknown to their users

To return to the metaphor of the car, there are cases where people need or want to get under the bonnet and tinker with the engine. So it is with distribution transparencies. Sometimes it is not possible to hide complexity without a heavy cost, for example in performance or code size. It may also mean sacrificing flexibility and function. In some circumstances a user may be willing to handle more of the gory details in order to achieve particular ends.

Equally, just as with cars, someone has to be able to get in and fix things when they are broken. Complete location transparency is fine in theory, but how would you find and fix the location service if you could not access it by absolute address? For all these reasons, transparency needs to be selective.

4.2 Messaging – the electronic lifeblood

Having said that a major goal in building distributed systems is to hide complexity from users and developers, it does not always seem like that in practice.

At its heart, all distributed computing comes down to an exchange of messages between cooperating processes. The basic underlying structure is rather like that of a huge, bureaucratic organization which is limited to doing all of its business by exchanging a constant blizzard of interdepartmental memos. This may be a slightly unnerving illustration but fortunately computers, unlike humans, are sufficiently obedient and unthinking to make such a scheme work!

The memo analogy is also useful to illustrate a further point. There are three basic ways of sending messages around a system. In paper-based terms these would be personal messages, copying to a distribution list and 'blanket' bulk mailings. In computing terms these are generally known as peer-to-peer communications, multicasting and broadcasting.

You could argue – and some people do – that the best way of hiding the differences between distributed and standalone systems is to make the single system behave more like its distributed relation. In this case it is less the presence of distribution that becomes transparent as its absence. Complete environments have been built explicitly around a message-passing model. All communication, local or remote, takes place through an exchange of messages.

There are two principal advantages to the message-passing view of the world. The first is simplicity. Every interaction is handled in a completely consistent manner and there are no special cases for local or remote operations. Only a few operations are needed to manipulate messages. The most basic are some form of *send* and *receive* or *put* and *get* functions.

These basic facilities are usually augmented by a naming scheme to select the destination of messages, some form of queueing mechanism to provide buffering, and methods for selectively retrieving messages based on their type. This simple set of primitive operations provides great flexibility, which is the second advantage of the approach. It is possible to construct arbitrarily complex interaction schemes from this small set of tools. This gives an application developer the greatest possible control over the system.

These advantages of simplicity and flexibility can also be the greatest weaknesses of the technique. For many purposes message-passing schemes are just too basic and low level. Programmers want to deal in terms more familiar to their usual experience of computing. Similarly, flexibility is a two-edged sword. A limited repertoire of commonly used interaction schemes will be sufficient to handle most eventualities. Developers do not want to have to reimplement new schemes and protocols each time they build a system. Finally, debugging such systems can be surprisingly difficult when messages have to be traced and the current states of interactions tracked.

The next chapter describes the most commonly used 'off the shelf' schemes available within the industry and the technologies that support them. Most build on and hide the message-passing basics at their core. They integrate with the single-system environment to a greater or lesser extent. Before moving on to consider these technologies, however, there are a number of other concepts which we need to cover.

4.3 Clients, servers, peers, agents – what's in a name?

The term 'client/server' is one of the current shibboleths of the computing industry. Systems are sold on the basis of being 'a client/server solution' or 'the answer
to your client/server needs'. Often the usage of the terms is confused. Does a
client/server system mean a set of PCs clustered around a larger central box? Can
dumb terminals connected to a mainframe be classed as clients? Can a server system itself be a client? How does this fit with 'manager–agent' or 'peer-to-peer'
interactions?

In this minefield of terminological inexactitude (a euphemism originally attributed to Winston Churchill and in the same tradition as 'being economical with the
truth') we need to be clear what all these terms mean and how they relate to each
other. There are, unfortunately, no universally accepted meanings but we will try
to give a set of definitions that should help you to understand the varying ways in
which the words may be used.

The first thing to realize is that many of the terms describe not so much concrete
entities as the roles that different components of a distributed system adopt within interactions. It is quite possible for a single component to act in different roles
at different times. Often particular components perform the same sort of interactions and adopt the same role every time. So it is that a component that usually
acts as client, for example, often gets referred to as 'the client' as a kind of
shorthand even if that does not fully describe what is really going on.

4.3.1 Clients and servers

We will start the process of mapping out the web of distributed computing terms
with *client* and *server*. Within any given distributed computing interaction, one
party will initiate the interaction and the other will respond. The one making the
request adopts a client role and the one responding that of a server. These definitions are a reasonable starting point, but they do not really paint the whole picture. This is because the terms 'client' and 'server' have a rich set of overtones
associated with them. To understand these, a slightly more practical perspective
may be useful.

Another way of viewing the term 'server' is as a component of a distributed system which provides a reusable set of services to the rest of that system. The whole
point of distributed computing is to have different parts of an application running
in different locations. The decision as to 'which bits run where' is seldom performed automatically and never on a machine instruction-by-instruction basis.

Never may be a slight overstatement. There are some specialist environments, such as data flow architecture processors, under which such things could be done but 'never' is good enough for all practical purposes!

The most basic principles of modular design lead to an application being broken up into reasonably coherent chunks each of which provides a set of related services. In a non-distributed system, these chunks might well end up as libraries of reusable code. In a distributed system, they will probably end up as independently executing servers. The relation between the server as 'supplier of services to the system' and clients then becomes fairly obvious – a client is a consumer of those services.

There is, of course, still more to the concepts of client and server than we have described so far. A server is often seen as a passive entity, waiting to answer requests made of it. A client is, by contrast, often seen as the active party, making requests of servers. It is also usually, but not necessarily, the case that an interaction between client and server is synchronous – a client makes a request and then waits for a response. Another important aspect of a client/server relationship is the interface between them. The topic of interfaces is the subject of a later section (see Section 4.5). At this stage it is sufficient to say that the interface is the contract between a client and server describing how they will communicate.

It is easy to see how the common concept of a 'file server' on a LAN fits with what we have described here. When people talk about a file server they generally mean a machine that holds a central store of files which it makes available over a network to be shared by a number of other machines. Each PC or workstation has the illusion that remote files are part of the local file system. This is, of course, a distributed computing application containing client and server components. This is also a good example of how the term 'server' gets stretched and overloaded. It is often used to mean either the software or the machine on which it is running. This is not usually a problem until you start talking about the server (program) running on the server (machine) ...

4.3.2 Beyond 'client/server'

The basic client and server concepts are fine as far as they go. However, once you start to explore real problems which distributed computing needs to solve, a number of questions arise. Some of the most important of these are:

- what stops a server from also being a client?
- what stops a client from also being a server?
- what happens when a client and server need to know what they have said to each other in previous interactions?
- how can a server interrupt a client to tell it something it might need to know or vice versa?

The answer to the first of these questions is very simple – nothing at all prevents a server from itself being a client of other servers. During the course of providing its services a server may need to make requests of other system components to do its job. This is entirely in line with what you might expect from a distributed system. A client's initial request to a server could result in a cascade of further requests to other servers behind the scenes.

You might reasonably expect that the answer to the second question – what stops a client from also being a server? – would be equally straightforward. Unfortunately, it is not. To understand why this is the case we need to return to the idea of a server as being basically a passive 'responder' and a client as an active 'requester'. Normally a server will sit around waiting for incoming requests from clients. In servicing those requests it can easily initiate further interactions itself as a client. But how can a normally active client simultaneously sit and wait for incoming requests as a server does?

Ultimately, one of the cleanest and most powerful answers to this problem is the use of multithreading and concurrency. This provides for multiple simultaneous threads of execution within a client (or server). In this case the client is able to do two things at once – one thread can wait for incoming server requests while another performs the functions of a normal, active client. This topic is covered in more depth in a later section (see Section 4.6). However, there are other techniques that can be applied in certain circumstances.

One of the ways of handling the client-as-a-server problem is by the use of a 'conversational' style of interaction. A conversational interaction is, as the name suggests, a dialogue between parties in which each speaks alternately. The thread of the interaction winds back and forth between the two partners. Thus a client may issue a request to a server which in turn responds with a request for more information from the client. In providing the requested information the client has effectively become a server.

You could argue that the client does not truly become a server in this interaction because it can only act in this way in a specific context. In truth, it does not really matter. This is a technique which can be applied to solving a particular set of problems. It may be useful to think of it turning a client into a server in some circumstances but if that does not apply to the problem at hand then do not force the issue!

In practice, the more common use of conversational interactions is in sharing a knowledge of the current state of a set of related interactions between a client and a server. This leads on to the answer to the third question: what happens when a client and server need to know what they have said to each other in previous interactions?

In Table 4.1 one of the reversed assumptions was the move from globally shared data to localized state information. In a single system it is easy to maintain a globally accessible view of the current state of the system in memory. A client and server separated by a network on physically separate machines do not usually have a common data store. Further, a server listening for requests from the world at large could receive requests from any number of clients in any order. In order to be able to respond correctly to these requests each interaction must take one of two forms. In the first 'stateless' case, each client request must supply sufficient information for the server to be able to respond without any additional information. In the second 'stateful' case, a server must maintain a local context for each client and a client request will specify the context which the server should use when responding.

The stateful and stateless approaches can be illustrated by considering a server which provides access to data held in a number of files. In the stateless case, a client request might say 'return 56 bytes from file READ.ME starting at byte 597'. The stateful alternative might say 'return the next 56 bytes' – but this requires that READ.ME has been opened in a previous request and some form of context has been established.

There are advantages and disadvantages to either approach. A stateless server is often more simple to design and implement but can then suffer from problems of maintaining consistency. For example, without knowledge on the server that the file READ.ME is in use, another client could be allowed to remove the file, causing the request for more data to fail. Section 8.2.3 covers these topics in some more detail.

The final problem is one that occurs very frequently in system and network management applications. A component that is usually a passive server occasionally wants to become more active, often when it needs to 'shout for help'. Management systems usually use a somewhat different terminology than the usual client/server pairing. The terms most often used are 'manager' and 'agent'. In broad terms these are synonymous with 'client' and 'server' but there are some complications.

An agent is a special type of server which provides a standard view of a set of system or network resources. A manager is the client that makes requests of an agent either to report on or alter the state of those resources. So an agent for a printer might be able to report whether the printer is currently online, for example. It might also respond to requests to take it offline or to swap to using a different paper tray.

The complications arise when the agent detects that some event has occurred. Say, the printer has nearly run out of paper. It is possible that the printer would return an error to a user saying 'out of paper' in the middle of a print job. However, it would be better if the person responsible for keeping the printer topped up with paper could be notified before this occurred. This is where the concept of 'notifications' comes in.

A notification is an unsolicited message sent out by a server to inform interested parties that some event has occurred. There are various ways in which this can be implemented so that it does not imply a network-wide broadcast but in principle it is really a message 'to anyone out there who happens to be interested'.

4.3.3 A summary

All of the interaction styles that we have discussed so far are illustrated pictorially in Figure 4.1. In each of the diagrams A and B are two communicating processes. The arrows show the flow of interactions between them (moving from top to bottom over time).

4.4 Partitioning – it will all end in tiers …

Having covered some of the basic interaction styles between two components of a distributed system a larger question arises: how do you partition function, between two, or more, of those components. This is where we run across the 'tiered' models of client/server computing. The most common of these are the single, two- and three-tier models. This section explains some of the different interpretations of these terms and their implications.

Probably the easiest place to start is, perhaps surprisingly, with the so-called 'three-tier' model. This starts from the premise that there are basically three types of logic within any application, be it distributed or not. These three categories are presentation logic, application logic and data management logic.

4.4.1 Presentation logic

Presentation logic is concerned primarily with the display of information and interacting with an end user. Presentation often employs a significant amount of processing, particularly with the availability of ever-increasing power on the desktop.

When the only means of presenting information was on an 80 character by 24 line display the potential for creative presentation was severely limited. Presentation logic in this environment is often relatively trivial with menus and forms being the norm.

Today, many users want to interact with applications by 'point and shoot' methods. Busy executives expect to see sales figures presented as glitzy graphs or eye-catching animations. The advent of multimedia facilities will enrich the presentation possibilities yet further – the virtual reality spreadsheet could be just around the corner! But however impressive it looks, it is all presentation logic.

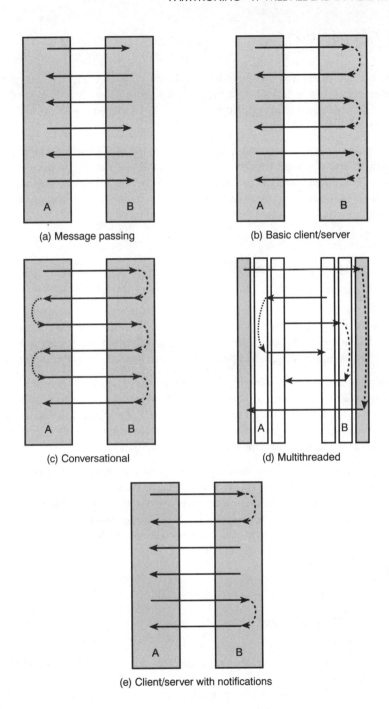

(a) Message passing

(b) Basic client/server

(c) Conversational

(d) Multithreaded

(e) Client/server with notifications

Figure 4.1 Interaction styles.

4.4.2 Application logic

With so much such effort being put into producing slick and seductive user interfaces it is sometimes difficult to remember that presentation is only part of the story. The real 'guts' of an application are generally independent of the look and feel presented to a user.

Consider, for example, a typical spreadsheet application. The underlying logic is concerned with applying various functions to tables of data to produce sets of results. Most spreadsheets allow those results to be displayed and presented in various ways – tables, graphs, pie charts, and so on. In all cases the supporting application logic is the same.

4.4.3 Data management logic

If application logic is all about manipulating data in different and interesting ways, there is usually a much more fundamental task to do with storing and managing the basic data itself. Sometimes this is as simple as just being able to read and write data to long-term file storage. In other cases this can be a much more complex task.

Let us return again to the example of a spreadsheet application. Many such applications have the capability to draw data from tables in a separate database. A spreadsheet might well be used to retrieve a set of sales figures, for example. It could process them in different ways – perhaps calculating monthly averages by sales region – and then store the results back in the database.

In a multi-user environment, however, many other people could be performing similar or different operations on the same data. The data management logic within the database has to ensure the overall integrity of the data in the face of potentially conflicting requests, perhaps by using locking mechanisms. Another example of data management logic might be the need to ensure that items of data were of the correct format or facilities to 'filter out' data which a particular user was not authorized to see.

4.4.4 Putting it together

The reason the model is described as tiered is that usually presentation logic 'sits on top' of application logic, which in turn draws on data management logic. Presentation is the closest part of an application to a real user and the 'raw' data often seems furthest away. Having identified the three tiers there are obviously several ways in which the function of those tiers can be split between a client and a server. This is shown in Figure 4.2.

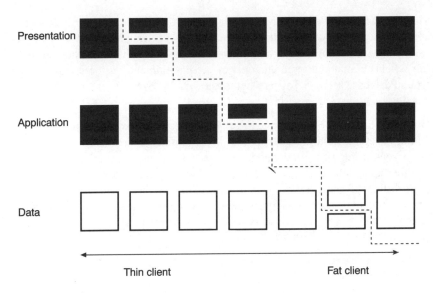

Figure 4.2 The client/server break.

Figure 4.2 illustrates where the break between client and server can be inserted. The portion above the dashed line is logic in the client and below the line is in the server. The 'thickness' of the client increases as more and more logic gets placed in the client and less in the server.

The thinnest client, shown at the extreme left, has no logic at all. This best represents the classic 'dumb' terminal attached to a central machine. All the logic resides in the central machine and it is stretching the definition to its limit to call this a 'client/server' system at all. This is followed by 'split presentation' as might be represented by an X Window system terminal. The client becomes progressively more fat until the other extreme is reached where the entire application resides in the client – the typical standalone PC.

Each of these ways of cutting the cake has its own advantages and disadvantages. A thicker client requires more local processing power but less network traffic and less sharing of potentially common code and data. A thin client can be 'lean and mean' but might generate more network traffic and a greater load on a server. Some of these trade-offs are the subject of Chapter 8.

4.4.5 Three tiers, three boxes?

Of course, the next logical progression is to ask the question: why just stop at one cut between client and server? You may have noticed that each of these splits described above turns the three-tier model into a two-tiered implementation.

Many of the current client/server technologies in the market support this sort of approach. The most common products, such as those using Microsoft's ODBC or from database vendors like Sybase or Oracle, make the split at the data tier. Here 'fat' clients containing large amounts of presentation and business logic cluster around database servers. This is what is known as a 'two-tier' or sometimes 'first generation' client/server system.

However, one of the main advantages in recognizing the three kinds of logic within an application is that you can start defining boundaries between them. Once you do this you can define interfaces to components which can be reused by other applications. If you lock large amounts of logic into a client it is much more difficult to reuse it for other purposes. This topic is expanded in Section 4.5. For this and other reasons many people favour splitting the three tiers of an application between more than just a single client/server pairing. However, this is where a subtle confusion starts to creep in.

Many people have observed that the old-fashioned mainframe system is very good at some things – in particular managing very large volumes of data. Similarly, personal computers are generally well equipped to perform demanding presentation tasks. Finally, there has often been an investment in quite high-powered but 'commodity' local application or file servers, perhaps running some flavour of UNIX. Following this line of thought often leads to the following equations, particularly in organizations who already have a large investment in existing infrastructure:

$$presentation\ logic\ =\ personal\ computer$$

$$application\ logic\ =\ local\ server$$

$$data\ management\ logic\ =\ central\ 'mainframe'$$

In many ways this is not a bad first approximation for a wide range of applications. However, it should not be taken as a hard-and-fast rule that 'one tier equals one box'. It is certainly a good design principle to try to separate the different processing roles as much as possible. So, for example, software on a desktop machine might primarily be a client concerned with presentation while a server process may implement a particular set of application logic.

This 'one-to-one mapping' principle is by no means an inviolable rule. There are sometimes good reasons for the borders between roles to be a little diffuse. This is particularly the case where performance considerations are paramount. For example, it may be better to place some elements of application logic alongside presentation code in order to avoid excessive client/server interactions. However, the cost of this 'blurring' is that function may not easily be reusable and duplication of effort can result.

In practice, different splits of logic will end up in different physical tiers for different applications. The whole picture might look more like that in Figure 4.3. Here presentation is mainly in the end-user workstations, application logic is mainly in the mid-range systems and data management logic is primarily back in the mainframe. However, for some purposes the split could be very different.

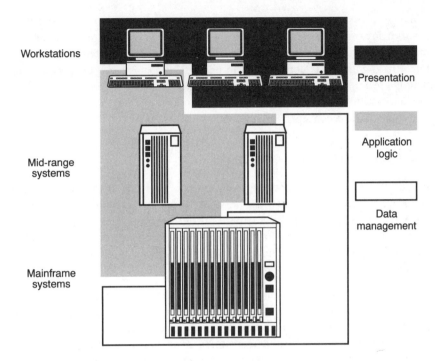

Workstations

Presentation

Mid-range
systems

Application
logic

Data
management

Mainframe
systems

Figure 4.3 Three tiers in practice.

4.5 Objects – a rose by any other name

The English language has the largest vocabulary of any in the world – some 500 000 words. However, people usually employ only a very small subset of this immense resource. Often we cram a wide range of interpretations into the space of a single word or phrase. Sometimes the old, familiar connotations of a word help to shed light on and give clarity to a new meaning. Sometimes the result is just plain confusion. Nowhere is this more obvious in the field of computing than with the term 'object'.

The ideas of 'object orientation' are becoming more and more widespread and accepted within the computing industry. In truth these ideas are not new – much of the initial work was done 20 years ago. It seems to be the case that it takes about 15 years or so for ideas to work their way from research into acceptance in the 'mainstream'. This has been the case for structured design methods, local area networks and many other tools and techniques. The work at Xerox's Palo Alto Research Center (PARC) on the Smalltalk environment (Goldberg, 1984) is seen by many people as some of the most influential.

Although perhaps coming from a different starting point, distributed computing shares many of the characteristics and concepts held to be fundamental to object-oriented design. Non-programmers may find some of the following discussions rather hard-going. It is not essential to understand all of these concepts to cope with the rest of this book, with the possible exception of Section 5.4, but a little familiarity with the jargon may help. If it is any consolation, many programmers find some of these concepts difficult too!

4.5.1 So what is an object?

An object is a 'chunk' of closely related processing and data. It has a well-defined boundary or interface. The interface provides a set of methods for interacting with the object. You can ask an object to perform a processing operation supported by its interface and that operation may return a result or change the internal data of the object in some way. You cannot, however, directly examine or alter the internal state or implementation of the object.

In many ways this description of an object is very similar to the concept of a server we have discussed above. However, the object fraternity would rush to point out that there is more to object orientation than just interfaces and operations. Although there is no universal agreement, there are generally three or four characteristics which are held to be essential for any system to be counted as object-oriented. These are encapsulation, inheritance, polymorphism and dynamism. If you like your terminology with fewer syllables per word, you might like to think of these as hiding, breeding, pretending and finding.

4.5.2 Encapsulation – hiding

Encapsulation is all about hiding an object's internal implementation from outside inspection or meddling. To support encapsulation you need two facilities: a means to define the object's interface to the outside world, and some form of protocol or mechanism for using the interface.

An object's interface says 'this is what I guarantee to do, but how I do it is my concern'. At least one author on the topic of object-oriented design (Meyer, 1988) describes an interface as a contract – the object promises to provide the specified services and a user promises to abide by the defined interface. The mechanism for using the interface might vary. It could be a form of procedure call, sending a message or something else entirely.

There are two primary benefits to encapsulation. The first is one of simplifying the job of users of an object by hiding things that they do not need to know. The second, and more important benefit, is that it is much easier to maintain a degree of consistency and control by prohibiting external users from interfering with processing or data to which they should have no access.

To draw an analogy, encapsulation does for software what integrated circuits do for electronics. An IC is a bundle of circuitry which has a well-defined interface (the pins) and which supports a published set of operations. There are often a number of ways in which the circuit could be designed and implemented but provided that it responds correctly when presented with the right inputs a user will neither know nor care. It is also impossible for a user to examine or modify the internal workings of the circuit.

Distribution is the sincerest form of encapsulation. From the description above it should be obvious that a 'server' is practically indistinguishable from an encapsulated 'object'. If the server or object with which you wish to interact is physically separated from you by a network it is impossible to violate encapsulation by perhaps 'peeping under the covers'. The only means you have of interacting with a remote object is by a specified protocol through a defined interface.

4.5.3 Inheritance – breeding

Inheritance in object orientation comes in two closely related but subtly different forms. The first form is 'inheritance of definition'. One of the strengths of object orientation is the ability to say something like 'object B is of the same type as object A but with the following modifications'. If you are at all familiar with object-oriented terminology you will probably recognize this as 'object B's class is derived from object A's class'. However it is phrased the basic idea is this – an object's interface can be defined in terms of behaviour inherited from other classes of object plus some modifications, additions or deletions of its own.

A common, but still valuable, analogy is with the classification of animal and plant species. For example, a domestic cat can be described as a member of the kingdom *Animalia*, phylum *Chordata*, subphylum *Vertebrata*, class *Mammalia*, subclass *Eutheria*, order *Carnivora*, family *Felidae*, genus *Felis* and species *domesticus*.

This is a shorthand way of expressing a large amount of information – even if it does not immediately look like it! In plain English it means that a cat is an animal (*Animalia*), with a spinal chord (*Chordata*) and a bony skeleton (*Vertebrata*). It is further distinguished in that it is warm-blooded and suckles its young – a mammal (*Mammalia*). Even more specifically it is a placental mammal (*Eutheria*) as opposed to a marsupial and is also a meat-eater (*Carnivora*). Of all of the types of carnivore it is a member of the cat family (*Felidae*) along with, for example, lions and cheetahs. It differs from these in some respects, however, and so is categorized as *Felis* while they are grouped together as *Panthera*. Finally domestic cats (*Felis domesticus*) differ, if only slightly, from wildcats (*Felis silvestris*).

Each level of description extends that preceding it. The description of a domestic cat inherits all of the characteristics of the categories above it without them having to be respecified. So it is with inheritance in object orientation.

People complain about the number of jargon terms introduced by computing, but object orientation makes do with just one basic unit of grouping, the class. One class inherits from another 'above' it in the hierarchy. This is commonly known as its superclass. A descendant class is known as a subclass. The relationship between classes is usually described either as inheritance – a subclass inherits from its superclass, or derivation – a subclass is derived from its superclass.

The advantages of inheritance of definition are twofold. First, there is obvious economy in expressing an interface in terms of a set of already defined portions with a small amount of extra, specific detail. The second advantage is in the lessened potential for introducing errors. It is easier and safer to specify a small set of changes to an already defined and probably working interface than to respecify the whole thing from scratch.

The second form of inheritance flows naturally from the first. It can be described as 'inheritance of implementation'. Suppose as a programmer you have an implementation of an object of class A and then define a B class as inheriting all of A's behaviour but just adding one extra facility. It would be very useful if you only had to write the code for the new function and then the B class reused all of the remaining A class code automatically. This is precisely what happens in object-oriented programming environments.

So, do these inheritance features form part of a distributed processing environment? The best answer is probably 'if you want them to'. In many standalone object-oriented development environments the two facets of inheritance are inextricably entwined. Within these systems inheritance in definitions leads to inheritance in implementation – and they do not necessarily work correctly if you try to implement things otherwise. In a distributed environment it may be useful to specify interfaces by using inheritance. However, once an object is at the other end of a piece of wire there is no way to tell if its implementation uses inheritance or not. Encapsulation applies here as much as anywhere else!

4.5.4 Polymorphism – pretending

The third 'classic' object-oriented characteristic is polymorphism. Literally this means 'many forms' and it refers to the ability of an object of one class to be treated as if it were of another class. In object-oriented programming this facility is usually only available to classes related by inheritance. So, objects of class B derived from class A may be able to substitute for objects of class A if they preserve the interface of class A as a subset of their own. It is not usually the case, however, that another class, say C, which has precisely the same interface as class A can be used in its place. This is because the mechanism used to implement polymorphism is usually dependent on the shared code base that comes through inheritance of implementation.

However, things are a little different in the distributed world. If the object at the other end of the wire claims to support a particular interface and implements all of the necessary protocols it is impossible to tell if it is a 'real' object of that type or not. It really is a case of 'a rose by any other name would smell as sweet'. So in this environment 'polymorphism' is probably more usefully thought of as 'compatibility'. In OSI network management they coined the term 'allomorphism' (literally, 'other forms') to describe this. Compatibility seems like a perfectly adequate English alternative.

4.5.5 Dynamism – finding

The last member of the object quartet is not universally accepted as essential but is a common characteristic of many object-oriented environments. It is hard to pin down a precise definition but dynamism comes in broadly two forms: dynamic typing and dynamic binding.

Dynamic typing is largely a matter of flexibility in a programming language to defer finding an object's precise type until runtime. In a statically typed language the type of every object must be fully defined to a compiler before it will allow a program to be built. Dynamic typing allows some things to remain ambiguous until the program is actually run.

This ability is related to, but different from, polymorphism where objects of different types may be used interchangeably but the types are still known.

Dynamic binding is the facility that allows the creation and instantiation of objects to be deferred until they are needed at runtime. This means that modified versions of objects may be found and loaded without having to rebuild the entire system.

While dynamic typing has little to do with distribution, dynamic binding is a fundamental and essential component of the distributed world. We will cover the topic in much more detail in Chapter 5, in particular Sections 5.1.4 and 5.4.

4.5.6 Types of interface

Of the properties of encapsulation, inheritance and polymorphism the most important in the distributed world is probably encapsulation. Much of the process of building a distributed application is centred on defining and using interfaces. There are many forms that these interfaces can take. Much of the next chapter is devoted to looking at the available technologies that support different kinds of interface. However, it is worth a brief look at some possible approaches before we delve into the finer detail.

The example in Section 4.3.2 of the interface for managing a printer is a good illustration. Let us start by considering the simple problem of determining and controlling whether the printer is online.

One possible interface method might be to make the characteristics of the printer appear as attributes of a remotely accessed database. The interface definition could be in terms of entries in a database table and the access method and protocol could be standard database mechanisms such as SQL. So, there would perhaps be a column in a table containing a true or false value depending on whether the printer was on or offline. Reading the value from the table provides a view of the status. Changing the value would cause the printer status to be changed accordingly.

You may be thinking at this point, particularly if you have a grounding in object orientation, that such an approach does not really provide encapsulation. After all, you have apparently direct access to an item of data which belongs to and should be controlled by an encapsulated 'printer object'. Would not a 'better' interface be one which provides explicit calls to enable or disable the printer? Perhaps, but things are rather more subtle than they may appear at first sight.

There are at least two levels of encapsulation going on even in the database-style interface. The first is hidden subtly by phrases like 'changing the value would cause the printer status to be changed'. In practice, there are a number of ways in which this might happen. It is true that in an 'intelligent' printer there may be a direct mapping from a change in the database to software changing the real printer status. However, another perfectly valid implementation would be for the management software to send a message via a radiopager to a human operator saying 'press the offline button!' All this is encapsulated behind the simple 'change the status value' interface.

The second level of encapsulation is that there does not have to be any form of 'real' disk-oriented database at all. Provided the print management software can respond to access requests exactly as if there was a real remote database it could store and retrieve the printer status however it wanted – in RAM, by detecting the state of the 'online' button or by another request paged to the hassled operator to type the answer in.

4.5.7 Stability in a changing world

One of the reversed assumptions mentioned at the beginning of this chapter was the move from static to dynamic configuration. In any system made up of a large number of components it can be very difficult to determine and control the current inventory and status of those components. In a distributed system the problem is even greater. If you need a practical demonstration of this sort of issue, walk into any office containing more than one personal computer. You will be hard-pressed to find two machines with truly identical hardware and software configurations – even if 'everyone uses the same systems around here'.

Such apparent unruliness and fluidity in configuration is seen by some people as nothing short of sloppiness. Great stress is placed, rightly, in many organizations on maintaining and enforcing good configuration management procedures. But there are times when totally rigid control is more destructive than helpful. As Emerson put it: 'a foolish consistency is the hobgoblin of small minds.' In any large system different components need to change and develop at different rates. Forcing all changes only to be introduced *en masse* on a fixed release cycle can result in accumulated delays and a sudden influx of instability as a whole set of new bugs simultaneously jockey for position. Software configuration management is a huge topic in its own right and beyond the scope of this book. There are a variety of approaches to release management within the industry and none of them are perfect.

In a distributed system different components may be owned, developed and managed by different people. It is essential to have the ability to allow these components to be changed at different rates while still preserving the overall function of the system. As a further potential problem, intricate and ill-defined linkages between components can lead to subtle 'knock-on' effects as one component is changed. Fortunately the solution lies once more with interfaces.

Figure 4.4 shows a single system made up of several components. The components can be grouped into several closely related areas, indicated by the shading. Each of these components is linked to one or more of the others, as indicated by the solid lines. If those components are closely coupled to one another then a change in one component may have to be reflected in a number of others. An example of close coupling might be through the use of a data structure in a shared memory area. If one component needs to add an extra element to the data structure for its own use, all other components sharing it will have to be modified even if they have no use for the new element.

The next picture, Figure 4.5, shows the same system divided up into three smaller subsystems. Each closely related group of components has been kept together but now defined interfaces have been placed between the subsystems. In a distributed environment there is now the opportunity for these subsystems to be run in separate locations. There is also a degree of flexibility introduced which allows each subsystem to evolve at different rates, provided the interfaces are maintained. A possible later state of the system is shown in Figure 4.6.

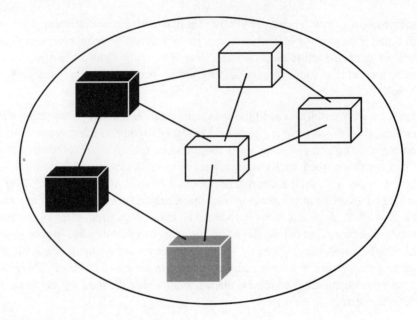

Figure 4.4 Single, closely coupled system.

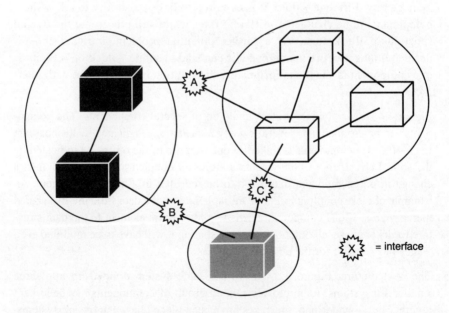

Figure 4.5 Split application with interfaces.

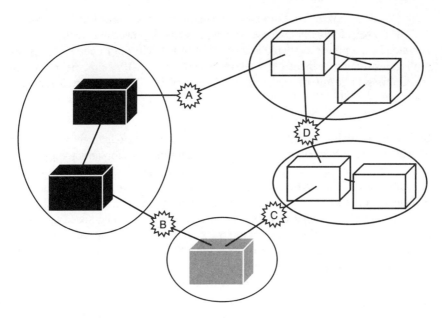

Figure 4.6 The system evolves.

You may be questioning by now what is so special about the design of distributed systems. Is not this after all just good modular or object-oriented design? As so often happens, the same basic good ideas crop up time and again in different guises. This is no exception – distributed processing merely reinforces lessons already learnt in other contexts. It adds some extra constraints and flexibility but in many ways you may find that you know more than you expect already.

4.6 Parallelism – many hands make light work

For many enterprises distributed computing is seen as the way of unlocking the data imprisoned in isolated systems. This in itself is a sufficiently large gain to make the process worthwhile. However, another view is that distributed computing also allows a potentially huge amount of raw computing power to be harnessed and applied to problems.

4.6.1 Multiprocessing – divide and conquer

Think for a moment how much computing power a typical small- to medium-sized company has at its disposal. Imagine the company main office – there may be 20 PCs and a couple of file server boxes connected by a local area network.

Each PC is a 75MHz Pentium-based machine and the file servers are maybe 120MHz boxes. Individually these are not particularly powerful machines but the combined total power available is over 1000 MIPS. MIPS, of course, stands for million instructions per second – but more commonly MIP is now held to mean meaningless indicator of performance! The absolute values are irrelevant, the point is that if all of the power can be orchestrated and applied to a single problem the results could be spectacular.

So if there is such a wealth of cheap computing power at our fingertips why do we not see the supercomputer manufacturers shutting up shop and going home? There are several reasons for this, the most fundamental of which arises from Amdahl's law. This can be stated as 'the minimum runtime of an application is inversely proportional to the degree of parallelism inherent within the application'. To understand what this means consider how you would speed up a program by applying multiple processors to it. If the application consists of two completely independent threads of execution through the code, which do not access the same data or depend on each other's results, it could be split into two parts and each thread run simultaneously on a separate processor. You could then get a total speed-up in the elapsed runtime of 50 per cent.

So imagine now an application of which 90 per cent can be divided up in arbitrarily small chunks and executed on a huge array of processors. What is the maximum speed-up that you could possibly obtain? Perhaps surprisingly, the best you could ever achieve is a factor of 10 increase. The reason should be obvious after a little thought. If 90 per cent of the application can be split up that still leaves 10 per cent which only has a single thread of execution through it. So you will always be left with that bottleneck as a limitation on total runtime.

The most fundamental reason why we do not see the office LAN as a supercomputer is this – most typical computing applications are single-threaded. In many cases there is not much inherent parallelism to exploit. In other cases the applications have not been designed that way. There are a number of reasons for this – many computing languages do not have the necessary constructs to express parallelism, environments do not easily support it, there is not the call for it or it is just too hard for some people to get their minds round. There are some environments, such as the occam language (INMOS Ltd, 1987), which embrace parallelism as a fundamental part of their vocabulary, but these are not always considered to be 'mainstream'.

However, there are some notable examples where distributed parallel computing has been applied. A very high-profile and glamorous one is in the field of computer graphics. This is highly computer-intensive and the techniques typically used such as 'ray-tracing' are very amenable to a divide-and-conquer strategy. The film *Jurassic Park,* for example, employed a network of Silicon Graphics workstations to generate the spectacularly realistic dinosaur animations and even then each frame took an hour's processing to produce. A slightly more dubious demonstration is the capability of the widely available UNIX security tool

'Crack' (Muffett, 1992) to use a network of machines to show up poorly chosen passwords by repeated trials of passwords generated from a dictionary.

Just to illustrate that distributed parallel processing is not just applicable to the esoteric and exotic applications we can offer one more mundane business-based example. The switches within the telephone network generate huge amounts of data, literally terabytes. Much of this data is of very little use in its raw form but it has to be correlated and condensed before it acquires much meaning. To a large extent such data can be divided up into unrelated chunks which can be processed in parallel before later consolidation. The authors know of at least one such system which employs a network of loosely coupled but cooperating workstations to perform just such a process.

4.6.2 Synchronicity and asynchronicity – do not disturb

Although there is potential in exploiting parallelism and multiple threads of control to gain greater processing power there is another aspect which is particularly interesting for distributed computing. Section 4.3.2 has already touched on the idea of using multithreaded clients and server to overcome some of the limitations implied by a rigid client/server model. One of the main uses of multithreading can be in 'ironing out' the asynchronicity which arises in the distributed world.

If you are communicating with another system you may be able to engage in a structured dialogue so that you know what is supposed to happen next or you may have to face the fact that something is going to arrive sometime but you do not know when. In a single-threaded environment the usual way of handling this is to have a form of 'event loop' – the application constantly checks for incoming events and handles them as they come in.

Sometimes this is a very natural way of doing things, for example in building a graphical user interface where the application is driven by responding to the unpredictable actions of a user at the terminal. However, this model can have its problems. If one of the actions resulting from an incoming event needs to perform a long-duration operation, such as communicate with another system, it will block the whole application. This can be avoided by performing an operation which initiates the function and makes a note to come back later to pick up the result. However, this can rapidly lead to increased complexity and a break in the natural flow of the application logic.

The diagram shown in Figure 4.1 illustrated a number of interaction styles of which one, (d), employs multiple threads of execution. In this environment everything within a thread appears simple and synchronous. If the thread needs to perform a blocking operation it can – execution carries on in another unblocked thread. These threads themselves could run on different processors or be scheduled and time-sliced on the same processor.

A common use of threading is within the implementation of a server. A main 'listener' thread waits for incoming requests. When it receives one it starts up a separate thread to process the request while it goes back to listening. In this way the server does not choke up if the requests require long-lived operations. If you are familiar with the UNIX inetd daemon this is similar to the process it performs except that the 'thread' is in reality a new UNIX process.

Of course, multithreading is not magic. The cost of employing multiple threads is having to deal with contention for data access and synchronization between threads. This is where concepts like mutual exclusion locks or 'mutexes' and semaphores come in. Yet again, these ideas are not new and will be familiar if you know anything about operating system design. This book is not the place to cover these matters, but there are a number of others which address these topics in as much detail as you would wish, for example Silberschatz and Galvin (1994).

4.7 Federation – peaceful co-existence

One of the fundamental reversals described in Table 4.1 is the move from a 'unified' to a 'federated' view of the world. This, and the related idea of a shift from centralized to decentralized control, makes some people rather uneasy. Is not one of the benefits of distributed computing held up by its proponents that you can bring disparate systems together into a single, unified system? Then the term 'federation' also raises hackles with others as implying the devolution of either too much or too little responsibility!

So is federation really essential? What does it really mean anyway? Is not a grand, unified scheme inherently better? To answer these questions it is instructive to look at the world's largest and most successful distributed system – the international telephone network.

Federation is about carving up a system into 'domains' and assigning responsibility for owning, implementing and managing those domains. It is a recognition that some problems are just too big or involve too many independent parties to impose a single structure. Federation is also about agreeing how those domains will present themselves to the rest of the world and how they will cooperate. Both of these aspects are obvious within the telephone system. Each country owns and operates its own system. The number allocation schemes and network infrastructure vary widely from country to country. However, there are some basic agreements that let the various network operators cooperate.

The most obvious agreement seen from the user's viewpoint is the format of telephone numbers – that they should consist entirely of digits. If they did not then it would not be possible to dial them from other members of the federation. (In fact, this does happen. There are a few payphones left in Australia which have characters in their 'numbers' which can only be dialled via an operator. Less extreme, but no less frustrating for others is the growth in the use of mnemonic numbers particularly in the U.S. which are printed in terms of the letters found on U.S. telephone keypads. Fortunately, most of these 'numbers' are for 800 or 900-type services which can't be accessed from overseas anyway. But that's another problem...) There are also agreements on the country code prefixes which identify who owns the rest of the digit string. In fact the specification of format pretty much stops there. There is generally some way of accessing the 'global namespace' but even that differs from country to country – 011 in the U.S., 00 in much of Europe and so on. Underlying the numbering schemes there are various internationally agreed standards that let the basic telephone networks converse but these are largely invisible to a telephone user.

The degree of autonomy within a federated domain can be very great. For example, most UK dialling codes gained an extra digit in April 1995. While this does have an impact on non-UK telephone companies it is largely in the human-oriented side – publications, procedures and so on. As far as the federation mechanisms are concerned it is largely a question of: 'I recognize this part of the system as belonging to you – I have done my bit, here is the information you need so go away and finish the job.'

4.8 Who cares about distributed *processing* anyway?

The stress of this chapter has been very much on distributed computing and processing. But what about data? For many enterprises today corporate data is seen as their most valuable asset. Even on the Internet, the explosive growth is apparent not in distributed processing applications but in the use of distributed information services such as the World Wide Web. Does not this mean that distributed data is more important than distributed processing?

The first answer to this is that distributed data does not just happen. Providing distributed data is a distributed processing application. The concepts described so far are as fundamental to the process of distributing data as to any processing of that data. File servers, WWW servers and distributed databases all employ client/server models, provide encapsulation, rely on federation and so on.

The second answer raises a philosophical question about how you wish to construct your applications. It may be that the only commodity which you can or wish to share with others is data. Within an office you may give other people access to some of your files on a file server but you are unlikely to allow them to use up processing power on your desktop machine to run a distributed spread-sheet application.

What, however, would you do if you were the vendor of an online encyclopaedia on the Internet? Would you rather provide people with access to the entire data-base for them to suck off and rework chunks at will – or would you rather pro-vide a sophisticated look-up service which allowed users to find the information they wanted but allowed you largely to preserve your intellectual property base and perhaps to charge more for the value-added service? We will return to some of these issues in Chapter 9.

The fundamental benefit of, and problem with, allowing unfettered data access is one of flexibility. Database vendors are providing sophisticated tools which allow you to easily construct client/server applications which sit around their databas-es. These applications can be easy to develop because you have access to a wide range of data. However, the owner of the data loses a measure of control over how that data is accessed. The solution is to move towards a more service-based interface providing access to the services which the data owner wishes to provide and control. But this, of course, comes at a cost of flexibility. There is no hard-and-fast answer but you should try to be aware of what choices and trade-offs you make.

4.9 Summary

This chapter has introduced the key ideas underlying distributed computing. Starting from the reversed assumptions that characterize the distributed world it has described the fundamental ideas used to handle these. One of the major underlying themes is that of 'transparency'.

The chapter has set the context for some commonly used terms in distributed computing. It has also shown how some other concepts from the single-system computing environment, such as object orientation, acquire new significance in the distributed world.

Many technologies are an attempt to hide the complex distributed nature of sys-tems. They try to provide developers with a more familiar 'single-system' view of the world. The next chapter describes some of the real technologies that imple-ment and build upon these basic ideas.

CHAPTER 5

Big ideas in practice

'Many ideas grow better when transplanted into another mind than in the one where they sprang up' – Oliver Wendell Holmes Jnr

If the previous chapter described some of the main ideas underlying distributed processing, this chapter is about putting some flesh on those bones. Fundamental concepts need to be understood, but there is often a large gap between good ideas and practical solutions. The gap can only be bridged by some fairly detailed explanation.

The ideas of Chapter 4 have been given life by a number of different technologies. As is so often the case, the technologies have been developed by different people, to solve various problems under a wide range of conditions. It should be no surprise that there is no 'one true solution' to all distributed computing problems.

We will start by looking at remote procedure calls. The reason for choosing this technology is not that it is inherently better than any other but it is a widely used and fairly general purpose tool. In describing it we will have to introduce and explain a wide range of concepts which are equally applicable to other mechanisms. For this reason the section on remote procedure call is much longer than the others. (Please do not assume from the imbalance that the authors believe that remote procedure call is the best or most important solution to all distributed computing problems. On the other hand, we do believe that it is important to understand it!) We advise you to read it even if your main interest is in the technologies described in later sections.

This chapter is the most technically demanding in the book. It should still, we hope, be comprehensible to readers with a reasonable familiarity with common computing concepts. Because we want to give a view of the broad spectrum of relevant technologies this can only be an introduction to each of them. The references cited throughout the chapter will, we hope, provide pointers to further more detailed sources of information.

5.1 Remote procedure call – the distributed cover-all

For many programmers distributed computing can be seen as an unwelcome addition to their workload. After all, it can mean having to deal with a whole raft of dirty issues – network protocols, machine byte-order dependencies, unreliability, asynchronicity and so on. It falls on the application developer to have to handle all of this but very little of it seems to add much value to the application in hand. If you were writing a system to monitor, model and control the processes in a chemical plant then it is a difficult enough problem to begin with – you probably do not really want to have to worry about such details as connection-oriented versus connectionless protocols!

One of the most useful general purpose tools at the disposal of distributed application developers is the remote procedure call system. As its name suggests, a remote procedure call – most commonly just referred to as an RPC – makes a remote operation appear just like a local procedure call.

The reason that this is attractive is that the procedure call – a feature available in just about every programming language in common use – is the natural way to express a temporary transfer of control to 'somewhere else'. It just so happens that in the case of an RPC the 'somewhere else' may be another machine. In terms of the transparencies introduced in Chapter 4, RPC is largely about providing access transparency – a remote access looks precisely the same as a local one.

A good RPC system hides all of the issues of data conversion and network protocols and may also provide other facilities such as recovery from communications failures, location transparency and integrated security. The procedure call illusion is generally maintained on both sides of the remote operation. An RPC client calls what appears to be a local procedure and an RPC server usually implements a matching function which 'magically' gets invoked to perform the requested operation. The server procedure returns a result in the normal way which in turn appears as the result of the client's procedure call.

The ideas behind remote procedure calls first appeared in print in the mid-1970s. However, the first practical experiences of building a general purpose RPC system were described in a classic paper by Birrell and Nelson (1984). This paper, which still makes excellent and instructive reading, describes development done at Xerox in the early 1980s as part of the 'Cedar' project. This extensive and thorough work has provided the underlying ideas for practically all RPC systems built since. It is interesting to note that Birrell and Nelson anticipated nearly every aspect of a complete RPC system design including integrated naming, location and security services. It has only been in the past few years that commercial offerings, such as OSF DCE, have reached the same level of functionality.

So how is the illusion of a remote procedure call obtained? There are generally three main components to an RPC system: interface definition, stub generation and runtime support.

5.1.1 Interface definitions

We covered the importance of interface definitions in fairly abstract terms in Chapter 4. However, for an RPC system the interface definition is the cornerstone of the development process.

Most RPC systems define and use some form of interface definition language. (The language is often – unimaginatively – just called 'IDL'. This can lead to great confusion in some circumstances over which IDL is being used). The purpose of an IDL is two-fold. Firstly, it describes precisely what services are provided by servers supporting the interface. Secondly, it provides the source for generating the 'stub code' which provides the glue between the client and server in an RPC interaction. We will return to the role of the stub code later.

Interface definition languages vary from system to system although many of them share a common heritage and are syntactically very similar. An example interface definition using the IDL provided by the Open Software Foundation's Distributed Computing Environment (OSF DCE) is shown in Figure 5.1.

The example shows a simple interface to a fictitious share-dealing service. It provides two operations. The first retrieves a history of the last 10 share price movements for a specified company. The second function makes a request to trade a number of shares in a given company at a specified price. The actual price obtained is also returned via one of the function parameters.

Although the precise syntax may differ from system to system, the example illustrates a number of features common to many systems. The main components of an IDL definition are generally:

- an interface name for, mainly, human consumption;
- some form of 'globally' unique identifier for system use;
- definitions of the interface procedures and their parameters;
- definitions of data types which will be manipulated.

The example in Figure 5.1 shows all of these facilities.

```
[
uuid(0062CD62-0D10-1BFA-874B-0260AC2F121E),
version(1.2)          ←——————————— Unique identifier
]                                   and version

interface ShareDeal←
{                         ←——————————— Interface name
    import "dce/utctypes.idl";

    /* Data type definitions */

    const small SHARE_HISTSIZE = 10;

    typedef struct
    {
        float sell_now;
        float buy_now;
        struct
        {                 ←——————————— Complex data-type
            float mid_price;           definition
            utc_t time;
        }
        history[SHARE_HISTSIZE];
    }
    ShareInfo_t;

    typedef long ShareStatus_t;
    typedef enum {SHARE_OP_BUY, SHARE_OP_SELL} ShareOp_t;

    /* Remote Procedure Definitions */

    ShareStatus_t         ←——————————— Interface procedure
    share_get_info(                    definition
        [in, string] char *company_name,
        [out]        ShareInfo_t *info,
    );

    ShareStatus_t         ┌——————————— Special parameter
    share_trade(          │             attributes
        [in]         ↙    ShareOp_t buy_or_sell,
        [in, string] char *company_name,
        [in]         long number,
        [in, out]    float *price
    );
}
```

Figure 5.1 Interface definition (DCE IDL).

Some of these features are probably fairly obvious. You would naturally expect a remote procedure call system to provide a means for specifying what remote procedures are available. Some of the other aspects are more subtle and deal with known problems arising from distribution.

The first problem arises in reliably identifying the interface. If you are going to try to invoke a remote service you would like to have some confidence that you and the remote system will agree on which service you mean. A simple approach is to give the interface a name, such as ShareDeal in the example.

Unfortunately, in any large network where services could be provided by many independent sources, it rapidly becomes very difficult to guarantee that good, mnemonic names will be unique. If you wish to trade with several stockbrokers each may provide a different interface to their service but all could claim the interface name ShareDeal. Such contention needs to be handled.

There are several possible solutions to this. The first is the 'registration authority' approach. A central body might be set up to own and administer the naming scheme. It could hand out new, guaranteed, unique names on request. The obvious disadvantage of this is that it requires all parties to cooperate with and submit to such an authority. This might prove undesirable or impractical, particularly if there are a large number of transient or essentially private interfaces.

There are, however, circumstances where this scheme works. An example is in OSI network management where interfaces are registered under the auspices of the International Standards Organization (ISO). In practice, ISO carves up the name space into a hierarchy and delegates responsibility for parts of the tree to other organizations. Also, it is really object identifiers (OIDs) rather than textual names which are uniquely assigned. However, each interface does effectively end up with a unique named position within the hierarchy. Similarly, blocks of Internet addresses are assigned centrally by the InterNIC. In other, non-computing fields such schemes are in common use for assigning globally recognized identifiers like international standard book numbers (ISBNs) and universal product codes (as shown on bar-code labels).

Another approach to solving the identification problem is to allow human-readable names to conflict but to assign an additional (numeric) identifier to the interface to be used by the RPC system itself to resolve conflicts. The string of hexadecimal digits shown in the example is the DCE solution to this. DCE employs so-called 'universally unique identifiers' or UUIDs which are generated in such a way that it is very, very unlikely that any two UUIDs will ever conflict. (It is extremely unlikely if you forgive the hyperbole of the term 'universal' – on a global scale you're pretty safe!)

There is, however, a further twist to the identification problem. In the 'good old days' you constructed a program by linking your object code with system-provided libraries. This process pulled in the library code and made it part of your final program. The system libraries might subsequently be upgraded or removed but your program would generally continue to run without any dependence on, or knowledge of, such changes.

Then came shared and dynamically linked libraries. Here the library code is not linked permanently with your program but rather is pulled in as needed at runtime. This was hailed as a Good Thing (See *1066 and All That* originally sub-titled 'A Memorable History of England, Comprising all the parts you can remember, including 103 Good Things, 5 Bad Kings and 2 Genuine Dates'. It is otherwise completely irrelevant to the subject matter of this book but well worth a read if you need a light-hearted break from distributed computing technology! (Sellar and Yeatman, 1993). The reason this was a good thing was because it allows program code and memory requirements to shrink. It also allows old programs to benefit from bug fixes or optimizations in new versions of the library. Unfortunately, if incompatible changes are introduced into the library it can also cause existing programs to crash.

A common solution to the shared library problem is to assign a version number to the library. The number can indicate upwards-compatible revisions or 'sorry, your program will break' incompatible changes. Runtime dynamic linking can select an appropriate version if one is available.

In RPC systems the problem is similar but even more acute. If you own a stand-alone system you can at least choose whether you will upgrade system libraries. In a distributed environment you may have no control whatever over the system at the other end of the wire. A versioning scheme is also a common solution in RPC systems. The DCE example shows a version number (1.2) which contains a major and a minor version component. The major and minor versions in this case are 1 and 2 respectively. The rule is that clients which require a variant of this interface with the same major version and a lower or equal minor version can interoperate with this server.

The scheme under which the minor version is incremented when backwards-compatible changes are made and the major version incremented for incompatible changes is based upon the interface designer's honesty and altruism. DCE itself does not enforce it. A backwards-compatible change might be to add a new function to the interface – old clients would not know about it and would not care. Removing a function would be an incompatible change. Netwise RPC is another system which uses a similar mechanism.

The great advantage of versioning interfaces is that you gain a good degree of flexibility in subsequently changing distributed applications. Old clients can continue to operate smoothly to a server using a new, backwards-compatible version of an interface. The clients can be upgraded as necessary in a controlled manner rather than in a 'big bang' approach.

Interface identifiers and versioning are very useful tools and represent pretty much the current state of the art in RPC systems. However, perhaps an even more attractive solution in the longer term is a 'trading' mechanism. This topic is covered further in Section 5.5.1.

Assuming that you have managed to identify your interface successfully you come to the real meat of the interface definition – the set of operations to perform. In the example, the procedures are defined in a syntax which closely resembles the C programming language. A procedure may return a result (of type ShareStatus_t in the example) and take a number of parameters. Although the RPC procedure definition looks very like a 'normal' procedure definition there are some subtle differences. The most important of these is the addition of some information informing the RPC system how the parameters will be used.

In a local procedure call parameters may be used to provide input to the routine or to provide storage in which results may be received. In particular, parameters may point to shared data storage from which the procedure might fetch input data or into which it might place results. However, in an RPC there is no common storage and all data has to be transmitted over the network. So the RPC system has to be told whether a parameter is providing data from a client to a server or vice versa. This is the purpose of the parameter attributes.

The attributes [in], [out] and [in,out] in the example describe whether a parameter is an input value, an output value or both an input and output value respectively. There may be other sorts of attributes which provide further hints to the RPC system such as the [string] attribute which says that the parameter is a C-style null-terminated character string.

The final aspect of the interface definition is the set of data types which can be manipulated by the procedures. Some basic RPC systems have a fixed repertoire of the commonest data types. In this case an RPC operation is limited to dealing with perhaps a variety of integer and floating point numbers, character strings and so on. This may be sufficient for many purposes. More sophisticated systems allow you to construct and use arbitrarily complex compound types including linked lists and arrays of structures. DCE is such a system and the example shows several examples of this.

5.1.2 Stubs

Interface definitions are useful in their own right as a piece of documentation on a set of remote services. However, the real magic in RPC systems comes in the generation and use of so-called 'stub' code.

RPC stubs are the pieces of code on either side of a distributed application which provide the illusion of a remote operation happening as a local procedure call. There are two distinct sorts of stub code: one on the client side and the other on the server. The client stub provides a set of locally callable procedures whose signatures match those in the interface definition. When a remote procedure call is made the client stub communicates with the server stub which arranges for the real implementations of those procedures (supplied by the application developer) to be invoked on the server.

Stub code is generated from interface definitions by a tool usually known as a stub or IDL compiler. An RPC client program is created by linking the main body of the application code with the client stub and RPC runtime support libraries. The stub code is treated just like any other module. A server program is created in a similar manner using the server stub code.

In the example given in Figure 5.1, the client stub provides share_get_info() and share_trade() functions to be linked into the client program. However, rather than performing the logic of these operations the functions encode each of their input parameters – those with the [in] attribute – into an appropriate form for transmission across the network. The stubs transmit the data across the network to the server where they are decoded and supplied to the corresponding 'real' procedures as parameters.

When the remote procedure completes the server stub captures the results – the function return value and parameters with the [out] attribute – encodes them and transmits them back across the network to the client. Finally the client stub decodes the data received from the server and the stub function returns exactly as any other local procedure. Figure 5.2 shows this diagrammatically.

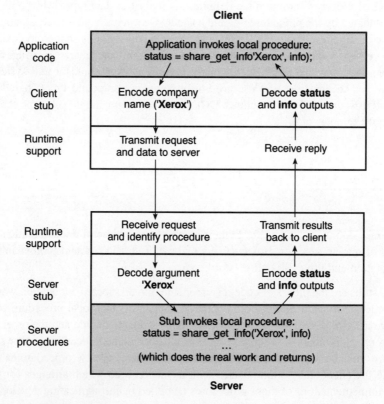

Figure 5.2 Stubs in action.

Marshalling

The general name for the process of encoding RPC data for transmission is marshalling and the reverse process, converting transmitted data into local data structures, is called unmarshalling.

There are a number of ways in use to represent 'data on the wire'. These systems differ in detail but share some common features. Primitive data types such as integers or character strings can usually be handled directly. Complex data structures have to be flattened out and broken down into their components. This is often known as 'serializing'. (The terms *marshalling, serializing, flattening, encoding* and even *pickling* are all in common use to describe essentially the same function of converting a data structure into a flat stream of bits for storage or transmission.) The receiving stub code contains the mechanisms to reassemble this stream of data into a copy of the original.

Depending on the complexity of the data structures, the marshalling code may also have to manage other issues such as the dynamic allocation and freeing of memory. This can be a very complex process. However, it is one of the strengths of the mechanism that a good RPC system can handle even the transmission of linked lists, trees and other very complex data structures between client and server without the programmer having to write anything more than the interface definition.

The marshalling processes would end with the disassembly–reassembly mechanism if all machines shared a common data representation. Unfortunately there are wide variations in hardware architecture and so some means of handling the translation between, for example, ASCII and EBCDIC character sets or 'little endian' and 'big endian' byte orders has to be found.

One approach to solving this translation problem is to have every system converse using a single *lingua franca* – each system converts its data to a common format before transmission. This mechanism is used in Sun's External Data Representation (XDR) format (Sun Microsystems, Inc.). This approach is simple, requires a single set of encode–decode routines and in many cases XDR maps directly onto the native representation used by a large number of machines.

Another way of tackling the problem is to adopt a 'receiver makes it right' philosophy. Data is transmitted in native format along with sufficient information for the receiver to be able to perform whatever translation is necessary. This mechanism is used by the DCE Network Data Representation (NDR) (X/Open CAE Specification C309, 1994). It has the advantage that if two communicating machines share a common data representation then no conversion is necessary. The disadvantage is that the number of encoding and decoding routines which must be supported is much greater. (In theory, the number of routines is infinite as someone could always – perversely – invent a completely new processor architecture having, say, 55-bit words with five 11-bit bytes. In practice, NDR defines a limited set of data formats representing the overwhelming majority of architectures. A completely new processor would have to convert data to and from the 'nearest' format for transmission.)

Both XDR and NDR encode data largely in terms of primitive data items supported in most programming languages. They can directly represent integers, character strings, double precision floating point values and so on. There is another more generic format called Abstract Syntax Notation One basic encoding rules (ASN.1 BER, see (ISO/IEC, 1990a, 1995)). ASN.1 is a programming language-independent way of describing data structures. The BER describes a way of translating ASN.1 into a data stream which could be transmitted across a network. This format is used in many formal standards particularly those for network management. There is also a draft ISO standard for RPC (ISO/IEC) which uses ASN.1 BER but it is not widely implemented.

5.1.3 Runtime support

RPC stub code can be large and involved, particularly if complex data types are being handled. But producing the code to encode and decode data structure from the network data is obviously only part of the story. The next step is to manage the transmission of the data between the client and the server. This the stub code does in conjunction with the runtime support infrastructure.

Binding

The first and most fundamental task is to establish some form of communication path between client and server. This process is generally known as *binding*. In a single, non-distributed application a similar binding process often happens when program modules are linked together. It used to be the case that the only option was a form of linking, known as *static binding*, in which all calls between modules were resolved once in building an executable program. All of the modules and pieces of library code were bound together into a single, immutable program.

The distributed analog of static linking is to embed the network address of servers into clients. This is, of course, possible but the resulting application suffers immediately from a loss of flexibility – if the server needs to be moved to another machine then the client will fail to find it.

In modern systems static linking of programs is frequently replaced by dynamic linking. A dynamically linked program does not contain code from modules or libraries directly but rather has references to modules which are pulled in at runtime. The references often consist of a name, a version and a set of locations in which to look for matching modules. This gives flexibility for the dynamically loaded modules to be changed independently of the main program – they can be modified and moved around provided that the versions remain compatible and the location stays within the known search path.

The ability to bind to a server by name, version and search path is even more applicable in a distributed system. It gives a good degree of flexibility and provides location independence and transparency. There are some additional requirements and opportunities in the distributed case but in many ways dynamic linking and client/server binding are very similar. The similarities become even more striking when we look later at technologies such as Microsoft's COM (see Section 5.4.4) which underlies their object linking and embedding (OLE) mechanism.

One of the complications in a distributed binding is tying down the precise location of a server. Many communications protocols require two pieces of information to identify a channel uniquely. The first is some form of machine address, for example 132.146.106.16 is an Internet protocol address of a single machine. (Note to the insatiably curious – yes, that machine exists and it corresponds to the textual address newton.axion.bt.co.uk.) Again this address could be hard-coded but a far better approach is to be able to locate a server by some sort of name which can be translated at runtime to the appropriate address. This is usually done by using some sort of 'directory' service. This topic is covered further in Section 5.5.1.

However, having located the right machine there may be many servers running on that machine each of which is listening at a particular communications end point, or 'port' in Internet parlance. So how does a client know which server is listening on which end point?

One approach is to assign well-known end points to specific servers. This is precisely the approach adopted for common (non-RPC-based) Internet services such as telnet and ftp, which listen on ports 23 and 21 respectively. Unfortunately, this method is not very flexible or practical except for very commonly used services, particularly when you consider that there are only 65 535 ports available when using Internet protocols. The solution more commonly adopted is to have a special end point mapping service on each machine. When a new server starts up on a machine it obtains a random, spare end point and then informs the end point mapper. When a client wishes to communicate with the server it asks the mapper, which *does* listen at a well-known end point, for the appropriate end point for the target.

Figure 5.3 shows how the binding process is carried out in a typical RPC system. (Again, the particular details of the example are based on DCE but the principles are the same for many systems.) The client application needs to use the functions of a ShareDeal server. When the client needs to communicate with a server the RPC runtime code sends a request to a directory service requesting the location of a machine supporting an appropriate server. The directory service finds a matching entry for the server type and returns the protocol type and appropriate network address of its host machine. The runtime support then sends a request to the end point mapper on the target machine to complete the binding process by finding out to which end point the desired server is attached.

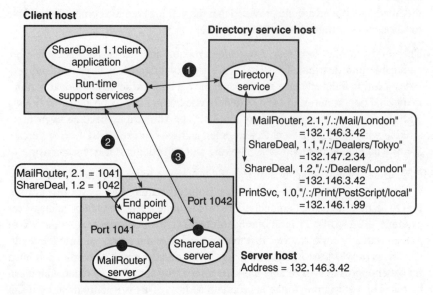

Figure 5.3 Binding to a server.

There are many ways in which the 'right' server can be selected. In the example the client code might specifically have asked for a particular server by name – in this case "/.:/Dealers/London". Another approach might be for the client to ask for a list of all compatible servers and choose one itself or even just let runtime code handle everything completely transparently. All of these schemes are possible and supported in different ways by different RPC systems. Unfortunately, most of these issues are beyond the scope of this book.

Communication

Whatever the means of binding, having found the right protocol, machine and end point a communication channel can be set up between the client and server and the real business of the RPC can finally start.

The basic communications function of the runtime is to take the data buffers created by the stub routines and pass them between client and server. However, in performing this task there are a number of issues the runtime code may have to handle. These include:

- breaking large data buffers up into smaller chunks for reasons of efficiency and to avoid choking clients or servers;

- detecting lost packets and managing time-outs and retransmission;

- handling client or server failure and performing necessary clean-up.

The usual default mode of operation for remote procedure calls is to guarantee 'at most once' semantics. This means that if the remote procedure gets invoked at all then it will only be executed once for any matching client invocation. The weakness of this is that if an RPC fails part way through there is, in general, no way for a client to know what state the server was in – did the remote procedure execute or not? For this reason RPC has been dubbed, perhaps somewhat unfairly, as a 'send and pray' mechanism. This weakness is addressed by mechanisms covered later in the chapter.

'At most once' is usually the form of execution that is wanted but there are often mechanisms to specify that a particular RPC should have different semantics and which may be more useful under some circumstances. The most common of the alternate RPC semantic forms are 'idempotent', 'maybe' and 'broadcast'.

Idempotent – literally 'same strength' – operations are those that always produce the same result when given the same arguments. A function which accepts an array of floating point values and returns the standard deviation could be declared as idempotent while a function that appends those same values to a file could not. Idempotent operations can be implemented more efficiently than 'at most once' operations.

A 'maybe' operation is a sort of one-way, no-guarantees call – a client invokes the operation but neither expects a result nor cares if the server fails to receive the call. This may be useful, for example, for notifying interested parties of non-critical status information.

A 'broadcast' operation usually employs a network broadcast facility to solicit replies from any servers that happen to be listening. It will take the first reply it receives and is mostly only used in boot-strapping operations.

Other features

To round off the functions of the RPC runtime we will briefly cover some other facilities it may provide.

Depending on how the binding process was originally performed it may be possible for the runtime support to rebind to another server in the event of a failure being detected. In any event the runtime is responsible for error detection and for signalling such errors to the calling application in an appropriate manner.

A very important feature of some RPC systems (notably DCE and, to a lesser extent Sun's secure RPC) is the ability to provide a variety of security mechanisms 'under the covers'. These facilities range from basic authentication of clients by servers, through two-way authentication, data integrity checks, to fully encrypted information transfers. These topics are covered further in Section 5.5.2.

5.1.4 So what use is RPC?

By now you should have a fairly good understanding of what a remote procedure call system is, how it is constructed and the complexity that it hides. You may be less certain, however, about how RPC is best used and what its strengths and weaknesses are.

The strengths of the RPC mechanism should be fairly obvious from the discussions above. To summarize, an RPC system:

- provides a good general purpose tool for a large number of distributed computing tasks;

- supports a familiar and simple programming model – the synchronous procedure call;

- hides a great deal of complexity including network protocols, data representation, server location and security exchanges.

Remote procedure call techniques have been used to build a very wide range of systems. For example, one of the reasons that Sun's RPC technology has become so widely available is that it was used to implement Sun's network file system (NFS – see Section 5.6.3). This is the *de facto* standard network file-sharing mechanism on most UNIX-like systems.

The weaknesses of RPC are perhaps less obvious. The most commonly cited ones include:

- a perception that RPCs are inefficient and carry a large overhead;

- the requirement that both client and server speak a common network transport protocol;

- the fact that a synchronous RPC model is not well suited to all distributed applications;

- the observation that 'at most once' semantics are not always a good enough guarantee;

- an implicit assumption that RPC servers are fairly 'heavyweight';

- the requirement to make a distinction between local and remote procedure call at build time.

Other technologies provide answers to some or all of these weaknesses and their different approaches will form the subject of the following sections. It is worth taking a little time at this point, however, to understand each of the objections.

Efficiency

The first objection to the cost of a remote procedure call is probably the one that carries least weight. It is certainly true that for any particular interaction or application you could always devise a more efficient protocol. However, any general purpose distributed computing mechanism will have to solve all of the same problems tackled by an RPC system.

Common protocols

The requirement that both client and server speak a common network protocol can be a more real issue.

Most RPC systems both hide network protocols and are designed to operate over a large number of them. Some of the longest established products in particular, such as NobleNet's EzRPC and Netwise's RPC Tool, provide support for a wide range of network protocols including Novell's IPX/SPX, Internet TCP and UDP and IBM's SNA protocols. However, each RPC interaction is essentially point-to-point within a network. It must be possible to establish a direct connection between client and server. In a very large, heterogeneous system it may not be desirable, or even possible, for every client to be able to use a wide range of protocols to access all possible servers.

The usual solution to the 'common protocol' problem is to employ some form of gateway. Often this means creating a form of 'proxy' server which provides the same interfaces to a client as the real server it is trying to reach. The proxy server fields requests using the client's protocol and passes them through to the final destination using the server's. This approach works, but can become unmanageable and unreliable on a large scale as each of the servers have to be built and maintained to reflect changes in the 'real' server interfaces.

Synchronicity

The synchronous nature of RPCs is probably the biggest issue with the technology and certainly the one that causes most 'religious fervour' from its detractors. RPCs will always take longer than local procedure calls. Where a large amount of data transfer is required the waiting time between invocation and return can be considerable. Particularly in an interactive application it is unacceptable for a program to apparently freeze while waiting for an RPC to return.

One approach to solving the 'freeze up' problem is simply to split an RPC into two separate calls – the first initiates a long-running action and returns immediately, the second can be called later to pick up the results. (There may be a state maintained between client and server or the first call may return some sort of token which can be redeemed later by the second call. It is a bit like the difference between having your shoes repaired while you wait and receiving a ticket when you drop them off which you present when you pick them up later.) This can work well for a large number of applications.

In Chapter 4 we described how the same sort of situation can be handled by the use of multiple threads of execution. However, while the multithreading model is powerful it is not always easy to apply in practice. The complexities which can arise from managing multithreaded access to data could outweigh the simplicity gained from the RPC model. In addition, system-supplied libraries or third-party products may not themselves be 'thread-safe'. Code that is not thread-safe may malfunction if called by different concurrently executing threads. Problems usually occur when a routine contains private storage and one thread overwrites what another has just written to it. This sort of problem can make it difficult to construct robust threaded applications.

Reliability

As we have already mentioned above, when an RPC fails it can leave the system in an unknown state. Of course, this problem applies in local procedure calls, but in a distributed system there are many more bizarre, interesting and unexpected ways in which things can fail! For many applications, for example those concerned primarily with information retrieval, this sort of failure is not a great problem. However, there are cases when it really does matter that the system is not left in an inconsistent state. You may not be too pleased if your bank tells you that the reason your account became overdrawn was because they were crediting your deposits using 'at most once' semantics!

There are a number of strategies for dealing with these issues. One sometimes applied in long-running numerically intensive applications is that of regular 'checkpointing'. This the process of taking a snapshot of the system from which its state could be recreated later if necessary. For many business applications 'transactional' semantics are required. These may be layered on top of the basic RPC mechanism. This is covered more fully in Section 5.3.

Heavyweight servers

You are unlikely seriously to consider using an RPC to perform the simple addition of two numbers, although you will probably find a myriad servers of this trivial type in existence, all built by people 'just getting the feel of the technology'. An RPC is a fairly complex operation and so you are likely to want a server to perform a substantially more valuable function in order to make the cost worthwhile. RPC servers often take a good amount of effort to build and are generally run as long-lived processes that do not just spring into existence for a brief period and then pass swiftly away again. This does not sit easily with all programming models, particularly with the notion of small, lightweight objects. We will return to this subject in Section 5.4.

Development choices

RPCs certainly provide a good degree of transparency, but there is a definite point in developing an application at which the choice between local and remote operations has to be made. At best the decision can be postponed until modules are linked together to form the final program. In practice the need to control the binding process and other matters tends to force the decision somewhat earlier into the development process. An RPC looks very similar to but not quite like an equivalent local call. To provide complete access transparency it would be best if the local versus remote decision could be postponed until runtime and the local and remote operation look truly identical. This too is covered is Section 5.4.

5.2 Messaging – back to basics

In looking at how an RPC system is built we have had to address a large number of issues. To obtain the illusion of an RPC requires a potentially large amount of code. There is a school of thought that maintains (with some justification) that a simpler set of tools can get the job done more easily in many circumstances. This is where messaging comes in.

The remote procedure call model transfers both data and the flow of control of an application across the network. Back in Chapter 4 we noted that the most basic operation that can be performed between two cooperating processes is for one to send a message to the other – the transfer of data alone.

Software developers are often both creative and optimistic. However, their creative urges are not always well contained. When building an application that has any element of distribution there often seems to be the urge to 'just whip up a little message-passing mechanism'. The basic idea is deceptively simple – all you need is a 'send' and a 'receive' function. Unfortunately, programmers' optimism over the scope of 'a little mechanism' becomes a problem as the simple idea begins to accrete more and more function – protocol independence, data translation, naming, queueing, priority delivery, replication and so on.

Developers have been building message-passing mechanisms for many years. For this reason there are a whole plethora of different types of system that march behind the message-passing banner. This section tries to give some outline of the main types. Of necessity the characterizations are fairly broad but, we hope, still useful.

5.2.1 Do-it-yourself messaging

There are probably more 'home-brew' message-passing systems in existence than any other distribution mechanism. Without much thought the authors can recall at least five applications they have worked with in as many years, each of which built its own message-passing mechanism. Some of these home brew systems included:

- a simple synchronous messaging mechanism for communicating a request and receiving a response between UNIX and MVS systems;

- a mechanism used to communicate between a few tightly coupled processes (implemented in the C language), passing messages consisting of the string representation of LISP-like lists;

- an interprocess 'event notification' messaging system used within a management system for an X.400 mail messaging system!

One of the authors also has to admit to implementing at least two other such mechanisms one of which, curiously, was built on top of DCE RPC! In his defence he would point out that these were purely for demonstration purposes and that neither has been, or was intended to be, used in production systems ...

We have good evidence to believe that this sort of situation is found in many other software development organizations. It is easy to think that such diversity is unnecessary. This may be the case and it is likely that a large amount of 'wheel reinvention' has happened throughout the software world.

Sometimes the do-it-yourself mechanism tailored to a particular task may provide the best solution to the problem. One of the other in-house systems alluded to above was developed in response to just such a situation. In this case the application itself was not really distributed and ran mostly on single-user workstations except for communicating with some specialized hardware. However, a number of these workstations were connected to a LAN and there was a requirement that a supervisor should be able to 'hook into' another user's workstation and watch their work in progress. The application was designed as a set of cooperating objects which interacted by sending messages to each other. The supervisor function was implemented by having the message-passing mechanism send all messages both to the local user's application and on to the supervisor's.

Most messaging mechanisms in existence are unlikely to see the light of day beyond the project for which they were crafted. However, there are some notable examples where more general purpose technologies have been developed and are available.

5.2.2 Message passing

Although message passing is not new, it is only within the past couple of years that commercial products providing what has become known as 'message-oriented middleware' (MOM for short) have started to emerge. Typical of these products are Covia Technologies' Communications Integrator, Peerlogic's PIPES Platform and Message Express from Momentum.

The fundamental aim of these products is to provide a very simple mechanism for asynchronous, high-performance communications between applications. The basic service offered is the ability to send a parcel of data to a known destination and, of course, to be able to receive incoming data. This data will be delivered as soon as possible by whatever means necessary including routing over multiple networks and protocols. This form of messaging supports peer-to-peer interactions and provides network and location transparency.

A typical messaging system is shown in Figure 5.4. Each node on the network has a 'message manager' (the 'MM' boxes in the figure). The function of the message manager is to present a simple, consistent interface to applications, represented by the shaded, lettered boxes. Each message manager can speak one or more network protocols. In the example MM 1 might be on a PC and can use the Novell IPX and SPX protocols. MM 2 could be on a UNIX machine and is able to communicate using Internet TCP, Novell IPX or IBM SNA protocols. Each message manager knows about its immediate neighbours, or at least those message managers with which it can communicate directly over a shared protocol.

When an application, for example A in the diagram, wishes to send a message to another, say Z, it merely passes the data to the message manager specifying Z as the destination. The message manager adds an address label to the user's data, wraps it up in an appropriate network protocol 'envelope' and sends it off. In the example the source and destination systems do not share a common protocol. However, if the message is sent to MM 2 using IPX this can then deliver the message to MM 3 using SNA.

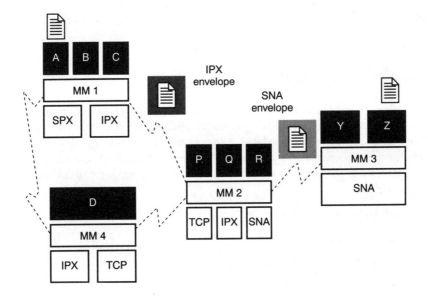

Figure 5.4 From A to Z with messages.

The full details of the network layout might be known to every message manager but in a large network the overhead of keeping all nodes' maps up to date would be very great. In practice it is more likely that things will be configured so that a manager knows either how to deliver a message directly if it can or to forward it to another manager which might be able to if it cannot. An intermediate message manager does not have to understand anything about the content of messages which it forwards. All it has to do is receive a message enclosed in a protocol envelope, take the message out, look at the address label, place it in another envelope and forward it on. (Of course, it might have to go via another network protocol hop, but the principle remains the same – extract the message, find its destination and send it on.)

The message system is also likely to provide a degree of location transparency by translating symbolic names for network end points (applications) into messaging network addresses.

It is this ability to deliver messages transparently over a web of different networks and protocols that means that these systems effectively build a single, homogeneous 'virtual' network out of the underlying real networks. They could, therefore, accurately be described as 'virtual network messaging' systems – however, the conventional term is the true, but rather broad, description of 'message-passing' system.

The basic programming interface to message-passing systems is generally a model of simplicity. There are the send and receive routines and there needs to be a means for an application to register itself with a message manager so that it can be a valid end point for messages. However, the term 'message passing' and this simple interface does not really do justice to the full range of facilities which these systems provide.

What is in a message?

In explaining what else messaging systems can offer we first must look in slightly more detail at what really is in a message. Above we described the message manager as adding an address label to the users' data. This is true, but is not the whole story. The manager adds a block of control data, some of which is supplied by the message sender and some automatically by the manager. Control data typically includes:

● the destination address

● the sender's address

● a system-generated identifier

● the message type

● a priority.

The reason for the destination address should be obvious. The sender's address is included both so that a receiving application knows where to send any reply and also so that the messaging system itself knows where to route notifications in the event of an error. Stamping each message with some form of unique identifier, perhaps a sequence count, allows messages to be correlated and duplicates eliminated.

There are generally three types of interactions which are supported by messaging systems. These are asynchronous 'one-way', synchronous 'query–reply' and forwarding. These are reflected in the message type.

One-way messages

Sending a message is essentially an asynchronous operation. Some messages are 'one-way' operations in that no response is expected. In this case once the data has been passed from an application to the message manager the application should be free to continue processing. The message manager will deliver the message as soon as it can but the sending application does not have to wait around until it has happened – although it does want a high degree of confidence that it will get through. For this reason this mode of operation is often called 'fire and forget'.

From the discussions so far it might appear that the message manager is providing little more than a layer of network protocol independence. However, there is rather more to it than that. The basic philosophy of message-passing systems can be summed up as follows:

● if the destination is reachable, get the message through as soon and reliably as possible;

● if the destination is not reachable then report the error back to the sender as soon as possible.

Of course, it is not always possible to deliver a message immediately. There may be a large number of messages being sent over a slow, shared communications link or the target application may be busy processing a previous message. For these and other reasons a large part of the job of the message manager is to perform buffering, temporary queueing, rerouting around failed links, message retransmission and other such tasks.

There are some other factors that can affect the basic delivery of a message. One of the facilities offered by a number of messaging products is that of message prioritization. As well as specifying a destination for a message it can be useful to specify a priority for it. This can be used by the message manager to ensure that high-priority messages are given precedence over lower priority messages and are delivered first. A classic example of this is in systems management – an application probably does want to know as soon as possible if the system is going to be taken down in 30 seconds' time!

Query–reply

We have talked so far about sending messages but have said very little about receiving them. The usual facilities which are provided by messaging systems are either block while waiting to receive a message or to perform a non-blocking 'polling' operation which returns immediately if no suitable message is available. It is also common to be able either to receive the next available message from any destination or to select the next message from a given destination.

The query–reply mode of operation adds a little extra to these basic functions. It is common for an application to send a message to which an immediate reply is expected. In practice this means performing a 'send' followed immediately by a blocking 'receive' – two asynchronous operations turn effectively into a synchronous one. If the sending messaging system is told that the message sent out is a 'query' and the destination system returns a 'reply' type message then the message manager can correlate the messages accordingly.

Additional features may also come into play in query–reply mode, for example the message manager may be able to notify the calling application if the reply is not received within a specified time limit.

Forwarding

We have already covered how messages may get relayed 'under the covers' across protocol boundaries. However, the same capability can be used explicitly by applications to good effect. If an application cannot handle a particular message, it can by forwarding it on to another which may be able to. This second application can 'cut out the middle-man' and reply directly back to the originator of the request without involving the intermediary.

5.2.3 Message queueing

In the 'message-passing' view of the world, if a destination application is not reachable within a fairly short time then there is a serious problem. For many applications this is precisely what you want – if the recipient is not there then there is no point in carrying on. This is typically the case in systems such as those concerned with online transaction processing (OLTP). For example, the Covia Communications Integrator mentioned above was originally developed to support the Galileo airline reservation system in the U.S. Most messages are from booking offices to central reservation systems. If these reservation systems are not contactable then, given that seat allocations usually need to be confirmed on the spot, the booking offices have a serious problem!

There are, however, situations when a rather different model is appropriate. To take a similar example, consider a showroom selling and planning fitted kitchens.

A customer may just have spent an hour discussing floor plans and selecting a dozen units for installation in six weeks' time. When the order is entered the remote order-taking system might be temporarily unreachable. In this case it is far more reasonable to save the order details locally and queue them for later transmission when the system becomes available again rather than just failing. This then is the domain of message queueing.

Message-queueing systems are in many ways similar to message-passing systems. The basic model of sending a parcel of data to an end point within a virtual network still applies. However, in this case the message system takes the data and places it on a local queue – possibly in memory but often backed up in persistent storage on disk. It then transfers the message from the local system to a similar queue on the remote system.

This 'store-and-forward' approach is similar to that used for electronic mail. However, there is a subtle difference. In a queueing system the message stays on the local queue until it can be delivered to the remote system. This is much the same as e-mail. But rather than ultimately being actively delivered to a final recipient it stays on the remote queue until an application explicitly removes it. (You could argue that the same happens with e-mail – a message stays in a mailbox until it is consumed (read) by its recipient. However, the basic message transport system delivers mailbox-to-mailbox.) There are some other differences too, as we will see in a moment.

Figure 5.5 shows how a message passes from application A to remote application Z using message queueing. In this system, A does not explicitly send messages to a remote application but rather to a remote queue. So in the example application A sends a message specifying the destination as queue β rather than application Z. The remote application later extracts the message from the queue for processing.

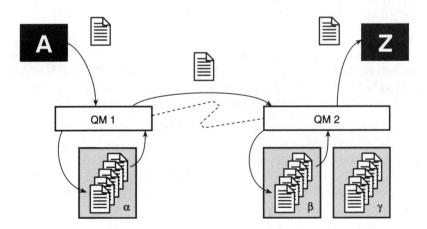

Figure 5.5 A to Z with queueing.

Each machine forming part of the message-queueing system hosts a queue manager (the 'QMs' in the figure). To send a message an application hands its parcel of data to the local queue manager specifying the destination queue. The queue manager places the message on a local transmission queue (α in the example) and then contacts the appropriate remote queue manager. When communication has been established it transfers the message and the remote queue manager adds the message to the matching local queue. As you would expect, each queue manager looks after a number of logically distinct queues.

Message-queueing systems can support the same sorts of message types – one-way, query–reply and relayed – as the message-passing systems we have already described above. In the case where all application components are up and running and ready to service messages as soon as they are delivered then the behaviour of the two types of system is practically identical, although the overhead of the enqueue–dequeue operation will probably make the queue-based system slower. However, queueing offers a richer set of possibilities than the pure message-passing model.

Time independence

The first piece of added value comes from the fact already mentioned above that the act of an application reading a message from a destination queue is logically separate from it being written to the source queue. It may be separated spatially – across local and remote machines – but it can also be separated in time.

A failure to deliver a message immediately is not considered to be an error condition in message-queueing. The delivery may be retried many times until the remote system can be contacted. There are usually mechanisms to control the total number of, and interval between, retries and there may also be a message 'drop dead' expiry time. These are needed in order to stop the system being clogged up by messages which have no prospect of successful delivery.

Message queueing is robust not only in the face of the destination's unavailability. Usually queues are also maintained on persistent storage. So if the sending system fails its transmission queue can be recovered on restart. This ability to complete operations in the face of network failures, machine downtime and other factors is one of the most important and useful facilities offered by queueing.

As well as being a means of achieving greater robustness the 'time independence' of a queued message can be exploited as a feature in its own right. Some queueing systems offer the ability to schedule the time at which messages will be dequeued and delivered. So you might say 'deliver this message to system Z but not until midday tomorrow'. In many ways this is very close to the traditional 'batch processing' mode of operation common on mainframe systems. There is a fine distinction between 'send a message to initiate job X at 21:15' and 'perform job X at 21:15'!

Immunity to system failure is not the only reliability feature which message queueing offers. The transfer of messages between queues is usually done so that a message is not removed from the source queue until it is guaranteed to have been added to the destination queue. The use of unique message identifiers as in message passing allows duplicate transfers to be detected and positive or negative acknowledgements to be generated.

Message dequeueing

It may not be immediately obvious, but sending messages to queues rather than specific applications allows for a number of interesting variations on the normal point-to-point flow of data.

The first possibility is selective dequeueing based on the purpose of the message. If messages are being held by the system within a queue there is nothing to stop the queue being read and processed by more than one application. So it might be simpler to split a large, single application able to handle any incoming message into a number of smaller applications tailored to handle specific requests.

To do this, however, requires that some sort of description or tag is agreed between sender and receiver and attached to each message. The tag is meaningless to the queueing system except to allow an application to request a message with a matching tag value. (Message tags are also supported by some message-passing systems but there the role is more one of providing a 'switch' value to select the correct processing strategy.) An explicit tag is needed because otherwise the queueing system would have to know the meaning of the data contained within all messages in order to determine the type.

We have already touched on the second major way of dequeueing messages, that of having multiple recipients. A simple form of load balancing could be achieved by having a number of processes ready to read messages from a shared queue as they arrive – the message will be handled by the first available process.

The operation of reading a message from a queue does not have to be destructive, it can be a 'copy' operation which extracts the contents of the message but leaves it on the queue for another application to process.

There are many possible ways in which this facility can be used. It might be used to provide a form of 'hot standby' where a second instance of an application reads all the messages destined for the primary instance. The backup could immediately take over processing with a fully consistent view of the application state if it detects the failure of the primary. The main difficulties in having shared access to queued data are ensuring that messages are processed consistently and that some application is responsible for finally removing the message from the queue.

5.2.4 Why use messaging?

Even leaving aside the many 'home-brew' systems there are a large number of messaging products in existence. The broad categories of 'message passing' and 'message queueing' described above are not always quite so clearly defined in practice and particular products may support elements of both styles.

A customized, handcrafted messaging system may provide the optimum solution to the needs of a specific application. However, it is unlikely that the same system will best serve the needs of a number of very different applications.

In general, the commodity messaging products are strong in the following areas:

● they provide a very simple interaction model and usually have small, easy to learn programming interfaces;

● they are often relatively small in code size and resource requirements;

● they are good at handling asynchronous communications requirements;

● they provide an easy means of dealing with networks composed of many different protocol links;

● message queueing provides good resilience in the face of system and communication failures.

Some of the typical uses of messaging have already been described. It is probably no coincidence that the best and most impressive examples using this sort of technology share some common features. These include:

● a high volume of simple, well-defined, short interactions;

● a large number of systems running a small set of applications;

● a high degree of asynchronous, unsolicited communication;

● widespread heterogeneous networks.

With such a repertoire it may seem that messaging should be the technology of choice for distributed processing. However, if we look back to RPC with its contrasting complexity it should be apparent that the facilities offered by messaging are at a fairly low level and still leave a lot of issues to be handled. Some of the most important of these include data marshalling and interface definition.

Desirable extras

Most message systems provide the ability to transfer an arbitrary packet of binary data, but few systems provide the facilities for conversion between different data representations and for the transmission of complex data structures. All of this has to be managed by application code – data marshalling has to be layered on top of the facilities provided by the messaging system.

The messages exchanged between applications (effectively the operations that make up the interface) are a private matter for agreement between application designers. An application interacting with a number of different remote partners may have to manipulate messages in many different formats. The messaging system does not provide any support for expressing these interfaces in a common manner. Similarly, all issues of version negotiation and compatibility have to be explicitly coded into the application.

To handle issues of data conversion and message-set definition many application designers end up implementing a set of routines and tools to smooth the process. Some programming libraries, for example some of the more widely used C++ class libraries, provide facilities for converting data structures into a format suitable for storage and transmission. Whatever the mechanism, however, much of this effort is, in effect, implementing the features of an RPC system! In fact, it is possible to build RPC systems over a message-passing virtual network infrastructure. The authors are aware of at least one case where this has been done commercially.

Reliability

As already described above, message-queueing does provide some good guarantees of eventual message delivery in the face of system and network reliability. These facilities do, however, bring with them some difficulties of their own. In particular, if messages are delayed then there is a likelihood that their contents may well be 'stale'. Intervening changes may make the data within the message inconsistent with the current state of the system by the time the message is delivered.

Stale messages are misleading if carrying the results of queries and cause even bigger problems if the messages cause updates to the state of the system. For this reason applications have to be able to detect stale messages and handle them appropriately. An example of how stale messages can be detected is described in Chapter 8. Unfortunately, this still leaves the potentially difficult problem of what to do with stale messages once they have been detected!

Asynchronicity and event loops

Message-based applications fundamentally process a series of asynchronous messages. Synchronous interactions are implemented as two operations: a send followed by a blocking receive. Although there are many potential ways of implementing message-based applications a very common mechanism is the 'event loop' style. This will probably be familiar if you have developed graphical user interface windowed applications. At the core of the application is a loop which continually reads an incoming stream of 'events' and invokes appropriate code to handle each one. The structure is as shown in Figure 5.6.

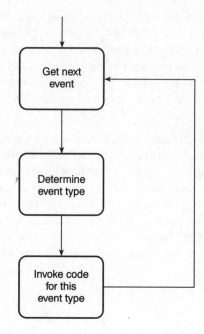

Figure 5.6 An application event loop.

Exactly the same strategy can be used to cope with incoming messages rather than 'events'. This is a very straightforward and easily understood mechanism. There is, as with every programming discipline, a set of pitfalls. The most common is to ensure that the routine handling an event does not block and so bring the whole application to a halt. However, this mechanism works well, particularly on single-processor machines. The model does become less attractive in a multiprocessor system or where the most natural course of action in a handler routine would cause the application to block. In this case multithreading is a more appropriate technique.

5.3 Transactions and groups – coping with failure

Messaging and RPC are very useful technologies but both suffer from a problem which is the bane of many distributed systems – coping with unexpected failures.

The completely bug-free piece of software is a rarity. Even with correct application logic things can go wrong – memory can be exhausted and disks can fill up. However, in these cases you can usually determine precisely what succeeded and what failed. Unfortunately, in a distributed system there is a much greater element of uncertainty. Did the network fail before or after your message was delivered? Is it the network that has failed or did the remote host crash?

In this section we will look at two different strategies for coping with failure. The first, distributed transaction processing (DTP), provides programmers with a simplified view of the world in which operations either succeed completely or fail completely. The second, process groups, takes a rather different approach and provides an environment where operations are impervious to the failure of individual processors or network links.

5.3.1 Distributed transaction processing – DTP

Transaction processing (TP), distributed or not, is a computing discipline in its own right. In ordinary business terms a transaction usually involves an exchange of some sort, for example of money for goods or services. Other examples of transactions include making an airline seat reservation, taking an order for a new telephone line, electronic funds transfers and stock control.

Over the years the use of computers for commercial data processing of such transactions has led to the term 'transaction processing' being associated with a particular set of qualities. These include a high degree of integrity and assurance.

The qualities commonly associated with a transaction within TP systems are atomicity, consistency, isolation and durability – which, for obvious acronymic reasons, are known as the 'ACID' properties. The meaning of each of these properties is described below.

Atomicity

Atomic literally means 'cannot be cut or divided'. As far as TP is concerned a transaction is an operation or sequence of operations which either succeed as a whole or fail as a whole.

The usual example of such an atomic operation is that of a credit–debit funds transfer. If I transfer £1000 from my account to yours the first step of debiting from my account must be accompanied by the second step of a credit to yours. If the first step succeeds but the second fails I will be £1000 out of pocket and you will still be hounding me for payment. If the credit operation is done but the debit fails then we will both be happy but a bank as sloppy as this is likely to be heading rapidly for financial disaster!

A transaction processing system ensures that either all the steps in a transaction are completed or that none are. In contrast to the 'at most once' semantics of RPC it provides 'exactly once' semantics. If all steps complete then a transaction is said to be committed. If any of the steps fail then it is said to be aborted. When a transaction is aborted any partially complete operations are undone or 'rolled back' to leave the state of the system the same as it was before the operation was attempted. (Perhaps a better term than 'atomic' for those with a background in the physical sciences would be a 'quantum' of processing – the smallest, step-wise change which can occur in the state of a system.)

Consistency

The property of consistency is closely related to atomicity. Particularly in the case of failure and 'roll back' there is a need to ensure that data is left in a consistent state. This usually involves the use of journalling – making a log of the operations performed and the changes caused – at key points. This provides a means to return the system to a consistent state if necessary by undoing failed sequences of operations.

Isolation

Transactions are isolated in the sense that the atomicity and consistency measures allow the transaction to execute by itself, without interference from any other work. In practice the transaction may well be executing in parallel with others but the key property is that the effects of one transaction should not be visible to another until the transaction commits. If the transaction aborts it will have had no discernible effect on the system because of the guarantees of atomicity and consistency. In order to obtain isolation one of the key facilities employed is that of resource locking: preventing other transactions from modifying a resource while a working transaction holds a lock.

Durability

Durability is all about ensuring that once a transaction has committed, the effect of the transaction is permanent and immune from network, system, disk or other failures. Once again, journalling plays a large part in this.

The X/Open model

In order to understand how the ACID properties are provided by transaction processing systems we will start by looking at the X/Open transaction processing reference model (X/Open Guide G307, 1993). This model applies both to distributed and non-distributed applications. The elements of this model are shown in Figure 5.7.

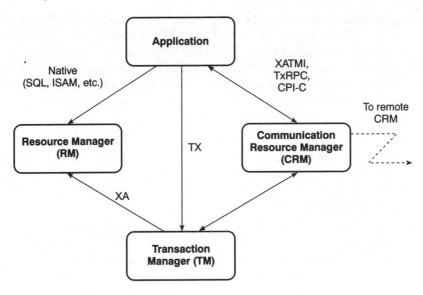

Figure 5.7 The X/Open TP model.

The basic components of the model are as follows:

- Application. The application code is the program provided by a user to solve whatever the problem at hand may be. The application draws on the services of the transaction manager and any number of resource managers to do its work.

- Transaction Manager (TM) (not to be confused with a transaction processing monitor. A TP monitor is a common component of a TP system which performs transaction management but has a number of other functions too) The TM is responsible for performing all the necessary coordination necessary to maintain the ACID properties of a transaction. When an application wishes to start a transaction it informs the TM. It calls the TM again when it wishes to end the transaction by committing or aborting. X/Open specify a simple programming interface (known as the TX or transaction demarcation interface) to perform these functions. It consists of operations such as tx_begin() and tx_commit().

- Resource Manager (RM) is responsible for maintaining a recoverable resource. A recoverable resource is one which can journal its state and perform commit and roll-back operations. The most common RMs are databases such as Sybase or Oracle but they could also be other resources such as file systems or print queues.

  Each RM has a native interface used by applications for performing operations on its resource. For example the native interface for many databases is SQL. The RM also has an interface to the transaction manager. When the application informs the TM that a transaction is starting the TM contacts each RM to inform it of the fact. The RM can then associate subsequent actions performed through its native interface with that transaction. Similarly on commit or abort it is the TM which contacts each RM to inform it of the end of the transaction and performs the coordination necessary to maintain the atomicity property. The interface between the TM and RM is specified in the X/Open 'XA' interface (X/Open CAE Specification C193, 1992).

● Communication Resource Manager (CRM). All of the components described so far are present on a single, non-distributed system. To extend the transaction to another system requires a special resource manager called a communications resource manager.

The CRM is informed of new transactions by the TM like any other resource manager. However, the CRM is also capable of communicating with another, remote CRM to inform it of the start of a transaction which will draw on remote resources. The remote CRM propagates the transaction to its local TM which then informs the local RMs of the new transaction.

There are a variety of standard interfaces to CRMs. The interfaces between CRMs are generally proprietary.

As you might by now have realized the hard work of providing the ACID guarantees falls to the transaction manager. If an application uses only a single resource then the facilities provided directly by the resource will be sufficient and there is little need for a TM. For example a database will provide commit, abort and roll-back commands. However, to maintain the ACID properties across updates to multiple RMs, and particularly across multiple systems, requires the use of a so-called 'two-phase commit' protocol.

Two-phase commit

It is not essential to understand how two-phase commit works in order to employ distributed TP technology. However, some appreciation of the underlying process may help in recognizing the benefits and limitations of the technology. (You may find the following explanation rather like the proverbial Chinese meal – satisfying at the time but you feel in need of another one a couple of hours later!)

To understand how two-phase commit works we first need to introduce the notion of local and global transactions. A local transaction is whatever native unit of work an individual resource manager may handle.

When a request is made to the transaction manager to start a new transaction it generates a new identifier for a global transaction. This identifier is guaranteed to be unique. The TM then communicates the global identifier to each participating

RM so that it can associate subsequent local transactions with this identifier and hence make them part of the global transaction.

To participate in the two-phase commit as well as being able to recognize a request to begin a global transaction an RM also has to be able to handle requests to prepare for commit, commit and abort such transactions.

When an application indicates to the TM that it has finished a transaction by calling tx_commit() the TM first informs each RM that the specified global transaction has ended and that subsequent native operations should not be associated with it. If any errors are detected at this stage, such as not being able to contact an RM, all the other RMs can be asked to roll back their work.

The TM then continues with the first phase of the protocol in which it asks each RM to prepare to commit all the local work associated with the current global transaction. The preparation consists of writing all essential information to stable storage. This is done to guarantee the durability property. When the information has been stored it must be able to survive system and communications failure.

The TM collects the responses to the prepare request from each RM. It may be that an RM is unable to guarantee the durability of its information, for example if disk space has been exhausted. In this case it will reject the prepare request. The TM will then ask all the RMs to abort the transaction and roll back. Similarly, if any RM is uncontactable, subject to retry and time-out strategies, the transaction will be aborted.

Only if all the RMs reply successfully to the prepare request will the TM issue the final commit instruction.

Once the prepare phase has been passed it is guaranteed that any final request to commit will succeed. If an RM crashes after completing the prepare phase it will be able to contact the TM as part of the recovery process when it restarts to discover whether it should continue committing the transaction or if it should abort it. Similarly, the TM will also have logged sufficient information such that if it crashes it will be able to complete the process on restart.

TP systems in practice

All that we have described so far is independent of any particular distributed processing technology. It could be implemented in a number of different ways, for example as a message-based system or as an adjunct to RPC. It should be no surprise to learn that both these and others exist as widely used products.

Novell's Tuxedo system is one of the longest established TP products in the open systems market. (Tuxedo was formerly produced by UNIX System Laboratories (USL) before they were bought by Novell. USL itself was spun off from AT&T. At the time the final revision of this chapter was being made there were reports that it was going to be sold on to yet another company.) Tuxedo supplies the ATMI interface (the basis for X/Open's XATMI specification (X/Open CAE Specification C506, 1995)) which is basically an asynchronous message-passing type interface. It does, however, have some RPC-like features. For example it provides for synchronous calls to named services with input and output parameters. It also supports the use of 'typed' buffers for the parameters that the system can automatically translate between different machine representations. However, the use of these features still requires a fair amount of effort by developers and the cooperation of the system administrator to configure them.

A more modern system is Encina from Transarc Corporation (now a wholly owned subsidiary of IBM). Encina is built on top of the DCE RPC mechanism and services. The basic Encina facilities themselves have been taken by IBM to build a UNIX version of their mainframe CICS system. This provides the same programming interfaces (CPI-C, also standardized through X/Open (X/Open CAE Specification C419, 1995)) as the mainframe system and can interoperate with it.

To further complicate matters X/Open also have a 'Transactional RPC' specification (X/Open CAE Specification C505, 1995) derived from Transarc's which provides for interfaces to be defined in a superset of DCE IDL. This specification has been implemented by Novell – effectively giving an IDL compiler that produces code using ATMI calls to implement the stubs. This gives a measure of application portability, but not interoperability, between DCE-based and Tuxedo environments.

The reliability features offered by message-queueing have made it an attractive complement to other distributed computing technologies, particularly distributed transaction processing products (see Section 5.3). So, for example, the Tuxedo system has the so-called /Q product and Encina has RQS (Reliable Queueing System).

The pros and cons of DTP

Distributed transaction processing offers many advantages to an application developer: a consistent model, a clean mechanism for handling failure conditions and good integration with database systems. At one time DTP was seen as the panacea for distributed computing problems. It has its place, but it has limitations too.

The single biggest problem facing the use of TP in a distributed system is that of locking. In order to preserve the ACID properties of consistency and isolation it is usually necessary to apply some form of exclusive locking mechanism. This protects resources against potentially conflicting, simultaneous updates. A transaction is only allowed to modify a resource when it alone has access to it. Other transactions needing access to the same resource are locked out and have to wait for the transaction currently holding the lock to complete its work and release the lock. (This is known as 'pessimistic' locking. We will return to the subject of locking again in Chapter 8.)

The main issue that arises from locking is the potential to grind a system to a halt. While a resource is locked all other transactions needing access to that resource have to wait. If the lock is held for too long by individual transactions – or worse, accidentally never released – a queue of waiting transactions can build up and response times grow without bounds. There are also the difficulties of avoiding deadlocks or 'deadly embraces' where two transactions are each blocked waiting for a lock held by the other to be released.

When only a single resource with fine-grained locking is used, for example a relational database capable of performing low-level locking, performance problems are relatively easy to avoid. However, as the number of resources involved in a transaction grows the opportunities for bottlenecks rapidly increase.

To begin with, for a transaction to operate it must first acquire locks on all the resources it will use. If each of these is on a different system then a response will be needed from each system before the transaction can proceed. Even if all systems can honour the lock request immediately, which again becomes less likely as more systems are involved, the delay will almost certainly increase linearly with the number of systems.

An even worse aspect of the 'multiple distributed resources' problem is the greatly increased opportunity for deadlocks. Within a single application deadlocks can be avoided reasonably easily by following simple conventions such as always acquiring locks in a set order. However, in a distributed system with resources being accessed by largely autonomous applications such conventions are unlikely to be workable.

The final difficulty with DTP is how to handle components that cannot 'play the game'. If one resource in a transaction cannot participate in locking or a two-phase commit then there is no way the ACID properties can be maintained for the transaction as a whole.

Given these problems you may be questioning whether TP is useful at all. The answer is, of course, that it is – but it is a tool that needs to be applied carefully. In situations where only a small number of components are involved and absolute guarantees of success or failure are required, such as in financial transfers, then TP is probably *the* best solution.

It is perfectly possible to have 'pockets' of TP performing critical operations within a larger non-transactional distributed system. However, TP should not be seen as a general cure-all for the difficulties of distributed system development. It can be expensive in terms of resources and performance but, like all expensive tools, it can bring great benefits when used correctly.

It can also be difficult to answer the question 'do I need a TP system?' because most TP products offer considerably more than just support for transactional semantics. For example they often provide facilities to start services automatically on their first use or to balance requests across a number of machines. They may also provide enhanced management and security facilities. Until relatively recently it was rare to find such capabilities in other distributed computing technologies. For this reason some people advocate using TP systems to develop distributed systems even when they have no critical need for the ACID properties.

5.3.2 Process groups

Distributed transaction processing simplifies the handling of partial failure in a distributed system by ensuring that if one component fails, the whole operation fails. It also copes with potentially concurrent actions by serializing them through the use of locks. However, these are not the only possible approaches to providing failure and concurrency transparency.

If a process participating in a distributed transaction crashes then the whole operation must be aborted. It may be possible to retry the transaction with remaining processes or the failure of a critical component may bring the entire system to a halt. However, for some applications it would be better to make the system virtually immune to the failure of any one component. In particular, if components are replicated on different processors then it should be possible to provide uninterrupted service even if whole machines or portions of the network are lost. This is the province of process group technology.

The basic idea is very simple. Separate processes, potentially on different machines, join together to form a coherent group to provide a single service. The group can be treated as a single unit by 'outsiders' and the fact that it is a group at all may be completely transparent. There are a number of different ways in which the group can behave. Not all of these are concerned with providing fault tolerance but can also provide greater levels of performance. Some of these group behaviours are shown in Figure 5.8.

- Hot standby. In a group providing 'hot standby' each member of the group is a complete replica of all the others. Every time a member processes a request there is a transfer of state information to other group members so that if it crashes any of the others can continue in its place. This is the primary means for providing fault tolerance.

- Divide and conquer. If there is a pool of processes available within a group it might be possible to divide up processing among them to increase performance. For example a database search might be best implemented by having a 'master' process divide the database into evenly sized chunks and allocating a separate chunk to other members to search in parallel.

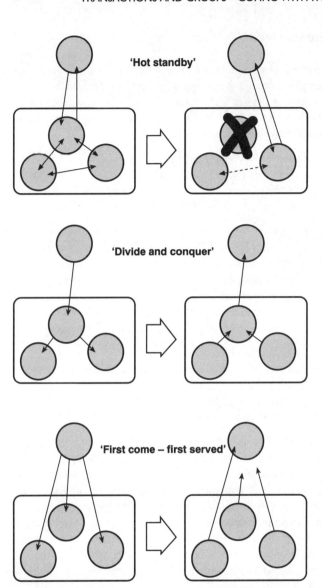

Figure 5.8 Group behaviours.

- First come – first served. Another approach to increasing performance through the use of groups is to send a request to all members of a group simultaneously. The first response, from the fastest or least loaded member can then be taken and the other responses discarded.

The idea of process groups is very attractive. It might also appear very simple to implement. Unfortunately there are a number of obstacles to overcome.

Who's the master?

The first problem is to maintain and communicate with the membership of the group. A simple approach is to appoint a single process as the master. All communications with the group and all changes in membership are mediated by this master process. Unfortunately, this master then becomes a single point of failure and a potential bottleneck for communications.

It might be possible to devise some form of hot standby for the group master, but then the problem arises of how to know when the standby should take over. If the standby cannot see the master still in operation is that because the master has crashed or is it because the network link to the master has been lost?

This problem is one that arises frequently in distributed systems – how can you tell if a remote system has died? Absence of messages received does not tell you that the messages have not been sent. The usual solution is to apply some form of 'time-out' period. If no reply is received within a set time then the remote system is declared 'missing, presumed dead'. The selection of an appropriate time-out value is a delicate compromise between maintaining good overall performance and avoiding the unexpected resurrection of the recently deceased!

The communications bottleneck is also problematic. If requests are sent to a single master which then propagates those requests to group members there is no easy way to increase throughput. Also, if the master crashes how does a client know where to reroute its requests?

These problems tend to lead towards a solution in which group membership is determined and maintained by the group as a whole. The problem of how to know when to carry on in the event of a network break can be solved by a quorum system. If a group has $2n + 1$ members then the group can continue to operate provided that at least $n + 1$ members can still communicate with one another. If a member discovers that it can only see n members or less (including itself) then it stops operating. It also calls for a communication scheme where requests are *multicasted* to the group – that is each request is sent to all members of the group. This multicast should also be able to share the knowledge of the group membership maintained by its members.

Consistent crashes

Assuming requests can be directed effectively to all members of the group the next problem is knowing when members of the group come and go. Adding a new member to a group is relatively easy. It needs to announce its presence and all the other members need to acknowledge its existence. It is also easy to amend the group membership if a process notifies others that it is going to leave. However, there is still the tricky problem of detecting and eliminating failed processes. If a process cannot be contacted is that because it is really dead or is there some temporary network break or congestion?

A relatively simple approach that works well in reliable networks is to adopt a 'fail-stop' model. If a member of a group appears to be unreachable then it is assumed to have failed completely and is dropped from the group. Even if it turns out to have suffered only a temporary absence it must explicitly rejoin the group and catch up with any interactions it may have missed.

Keeping in step

By far the hardest problem in implementing process groups is the problem of synchronization. Some of the potential problems that can arise are illustrated in Figure 5.9.

In Figure 5.9 processes **S1**, **S2** and **S3** are servers and members of a group. Processes **C1** and **C2** are clients that send messages (**m1**, **m2** and **m3**) to that group. **C1** and **C2** send messages at roughly the same time. However, because of network topology, processor load or any number of other reasons message **m1** is delivered before **m2** at processes **S1** and **S3** but after **m2** at process **S2**. Depending on the meaning of these messages that could leave **S2** in an inconsistent state with respect to the other two members of the group.

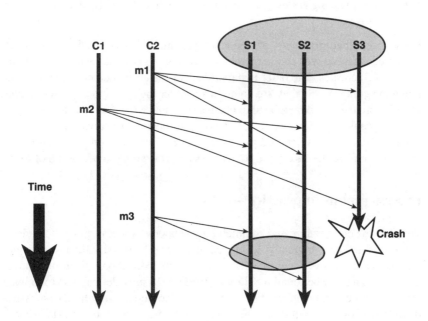

Figure 5.9 Synchronization problems.

One solution to this problem which might be considered is the use of timestamping. If each message contains a timestamp then messages could be processed in chronological order rather than in the order of delivery. However, there are some major problems with this. The first is the practical difficulty of synchronizing time accurately across a number of machines.

Even if adequate clock synchronization can be achieved there is then the question of how messages with the same timestamp, but originating from different machines, should be handled. It is possible to have the system march forward in lock-step – every member must agree and acknowledge each message before the next can be delivered. This may be the desired behaviour in some circumstances but could have dire performance consequences – the system will have to proceed at the pace of the slowest member.

Back in 1978 Leslie Lamport published a paper (Lamport, 1978) which considered the problems of using timestamps to capture the ordering of events in a distributed system. He proposed an alternative way of describing ordering based not on timing but on *causality*.

The issue to consider is not whether two events actually occur simultaneously but whether a system is sensitive to their respective ordering. If it is then there is a dependency or causality relationship between them. If it is not then, for all intents and purposes, they can be considered to be concurrent. So, back in Figure 5.9 if there is no dependency between messages **m1** and **m2** then it should not matter that they are delivered out of sequence to **S2**. In fact the expression 'out of sequence' is meaningless in this context because there is no sequencing between these messages.

Even given that problems of sequencing, timing and causality have been addressed, there is yet another problem lurking. This arises when one of the servers (**S3**) crashes. The other two members of the group detect this and reconfigure the group. While they are doing this another message is sent which arrives at **S1** before the group membership change was noticed and at **S2** after. This can cause a problem if, for example, the group is operating a divide-and-conquer strategy. **S1** could have started processing on the basis of it only having to perform one-third of the task while **S2** will assume it is going to perform half of it.

Process groups in practice – ISIS

Probably the most mature and commercially supported process group technology is the ISIS system, originally developed at Cornell University by a team under Ken Birman. An overview of ISIS and a much more thorough discussion of process groups can be found in Birman (1993). ISIS provides support for a wide range of group interaction styles and offers solutions for all of the issues described above. It builds on the causal ordering model to provide what it describes as *virtual synchrony*.

ISIS has found particular favour with users wanting a very high degree of fault tolerance such as finance institutions and the telecommunications industry. (In fact ISIS Distributed Systems, Inc., the company set up to market ISIS, is now owned by Stratus, a vendor of fault-tolerant hardware systems.) It has also been attractive to a number of people developing interactive 'groupware' applications where operations need to be replicated between a large number of workstations.

It is probably fair to say that process group technology is still seen as a 'niche' solution. There are signs that the technology is now making its way into the wider field. Efforts have been made to integrate ISIS with new operating system technologies to provide support for groups at a fundamental level, which is where it can provide most benefit. There is at least one example of ISIS being integrated with an ORB system (see Section 5.4) to provide distributed object groups. The reliable multicast protocol (RMP) project (http://research.ivv.nasa.gov/projects/RMP/RMP.html) is also providing similar facilities to ISIS.

5.4 Distributed objects – objects of desire

Just as object-oriented techniques have gained currency in the design and programming worlds, so distributed object systems are emerging as a force in distributed computing. In many ways object technology is the ideal partner for distribution. The notions of strict interface definition and enforced encapsulation that are fundamental to distribution are also the bread and butter of object orientation.

There have been a number of interesting developments in this field over recent years. However, the pace of change and innovation is still great and a large number of vendors are jockeying for position. This means that while there is great scope for new and exciting applications of the technology there is also scope for some spectacular disasters!

5.4.1 Objects on speaking terms

Before distributed objects could become a reality there was a more fundamental problem that had been troubling the users of object-oriented technology. In essence the problem was this – what is an object anyway?

Computer scientists may define an object as something that has characteristics of encapsulation, inheritance and polymorphism (see Section 4.5). However, in practice an object tends to be whatever it is that your current development tool implements. So within, say, a Smalltalk environment there is a very clear notion of what its kind of object is, how it behaves, how you communicate with it and so on. There is also a very concrete implementation of these objects within software. Similarly the C++ programming language implicitly defines a similar (but different) model of what constitutes an object.

While working within a single environment there is not really any problem with the fact that different object models exist elsewhere – you just ignore them! However, things are different as soon as you want to mix objects from different sources. A Smalltalk object cannot just be 'plugged in' to a C++ program or vice versa. Even when it is possible to make some sort of call out to a 'foreign' object it almost certainly will not behave in precisely the same manner as a local object. Inheritance, for example, will probably not be possible between mixed objects.

So it was that the developers of object technology found themselves in a difficult position. Objects should provide the ideal software component – well-packaged through encapsulation and designed for easy and extensive reuse. Unfortunately the lack of a common model left objects in a worse state than traditional, procedural software libraries. It is perfectly possible to call Fortran library routines from a C program or Pascal from COBOL, subject to obeying certain conventions about how function parameters are passed about. What was needed in the object world was a general interaction mechanism, a means for binary code objects to interwork with each other without losing their 'objectness'.

A number of different companies and organizations recognized this need and set about defining the necessary models and rules. IBM, for example, developed its system object model (SOM) which allowed object components to be used together within a single system. Microsoft's object linking and embedding (OLE) technology started to address the same issue, although perhaps from a different perspective.

OLE started life more as a 'compound document' technology where different standalone applications could be used as components to construct and present a document. (The non-Microsoft world has, by contrast, built up towards compound document technology starting from lower level objects. The rival to OLE in this area is a technology jointly developed by Apple, HP, IBM and others called 'OpenDoc' although this may be overtaken by 'applets' – see Section 5.7.) So a memo created in a word processor might contain data tables which could be manipulated through an embedded spreadsheet. The word processor does not have to have the functionality of the spreadsheet program but rather uses it as a very richly featured subcomponent. This coarse-grained reuse of whole applications as 'objects' led on to the definition of a more coherent and explicit object model to underlie OLE version 2. This is known as the component object model or COM. We will look again briefly at OLE in Section 5.4.5.

An industry consortium, the Object Management Group (OMG), was also formed with the intention of developing vendor-independent, consensus standards for object interworking. (The group grew out of the HP 'NewWave' users group. This was a proprietary object technology – now largely defunct.) The OMG has been highly influential and we will return to their contribution shortly.

5.4.2 Indirect objects

Many of the object interworking technologies were not primarily aimed at creating distributed object systems. They were intended to solve the problem of different object components cooperating within a single process or a single machine. However, it soon became clear that the same techniques that were needed to solve these problems would open up the prospects of interworking with remote objects.

The fundamental principle adopted by all of the technologies is 'indirection'. (There is a joke that every problem in computer science can be solved by adding another level of indirection. Except the problem of too many levels of indirection ...) Requests between objects are made indirectly through a common intermediary. Interfaces to objects are expressed in a commonly agreed form which allows objects on either side of the intermediary to translate that form to its own internal mechanisms.

Within a single program the intermediary can be as simple as an in-memory table of functions. The 'target' object populates the table with functions that it provides which handle each of the operations on the object and cause the internal mechanism to be invoked. A client object invokes the functions indirectly through their position in the table without knowing or caring about the implementation behind it. Whatever the intermediate mechanism the impact for distributed objects is clear. Once the invocation of an operation on an object is hidden behind an intermediary the operation could just as well be performed remotely as locally.

5.4.3 OMG, ORBs and CORBA

The most widely used term for the 'intermediary' described above is an object request broker or ORB. This was popularized as a result of the work of the OMG. In 1990 they produced their *Object Management Architecture Guide* (Object Management Group, 1992). This contains a diagram similar to that shown in Figure 5.10.

The main components are the object request broker itself and three different categories of objects.

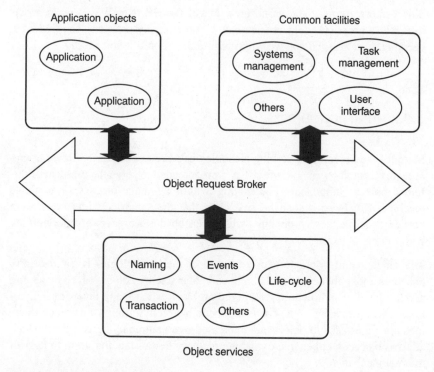

Figure 5.10 The OMG architecture.

The ORB

The ORB is the 'backplane' which mediates communications between all objects. From the diagram it may appear that the ORB is the pipeline through which all interactions flow, rather like the hardware bus in a computer. In a logical sense this is true but such a physical implementation is not required. The ORB may act rather like a stockbroker and mediate all requests between parties. Alternatively it may act more as a marriage broker – handling the initial introductions but then leaving the parties to get on with it!

Application objects

These are the objects built by the users of an ORB. The ORB and all its associated services and facilities exist so that application objects can be built. However, because the OMG's purpose is to define a common object infrastructure it has little to say about them other than to acknowledge their existence explicitly.

Object services

Object services are fundamental building block services needed by virtually all applications and which should form part of every ORB implementation. These include facilities such as naming, event notification, transactions, persistence (the ability to save the state of an object onto long-term storage in such a way that the object can be 'reincarnated' later) and security. Over 25 separate services have been identified. The OMG have developed definitions for a number of these and more are being worked on all the time.

Many of these services are not new but one of the key features of the OMG model is that all of the object services should themselves be packaged as objects just like any other. Much of the work of defining object services has been in figuring out how to wrap existing services so that they fit cleanly into the object world.

Common facilities

The common facilities are also collections of objects that provide general, reusable services. However, these are facilities that are not necessarily applicable to all applications. They may be thought of as optional packages which supplement the core ORB services.

Some common facilities are intended to be independent of any particular application area. These include user interface and systems management and are known as 'horizontal' facilities – having broad applicability. Others are 'vertical' facilities applicable to a particular application niche such as finance or telecommunications.

CORBA

The original OMG object model is good for talking about object systems at a high level. It does not, however, give any clue as to how such a system would really be built. Most critically it does not specify any way of defining the interfaces and properties of objects. So it was that in late 1991 the OMG published the Common Object Request Broker Architecture (CORBA) specification (X/Open Ltd, 1991). The term 'CORBA' is often used as a shorthand for much of the OMG's work and indeed it is central to it.

The CORBA specification defines an interface definition language (again just known as 'IDL') with which to specify objects. This language is closely based on C++ syntax but is purely declarative. This means that while you can describe the syntax of an interface you cannot write a program in IDL itself. It provides full support for key object-oriented features such as inheritance.

CORBA also describes the structure and principal components of an ORB. This is illustrated in Figure 5.11. This diagram is based on the latest CORBA specifications which differ from the earlier versions of this structure primarily in the introduction of the dynamic skeleton interface.

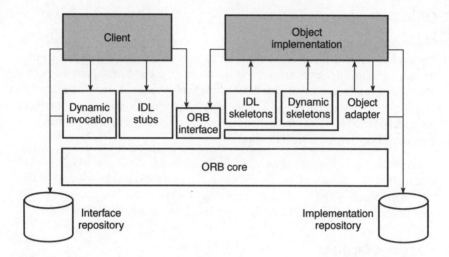

Figure 5.11 Structure of an object request broker.

Although the structure may look complex, many of the concepts are identical to those we have covered in previous sections. Before describing the elements, however, we need to highlight a crucial difference between ORBs and other client/server technologies. The difference is mainly one of granularity.

In conventional client/server technologies there is an implicit assumption that the services called on by a client will be provided by a relatively small number of fairly 'heavyweight' servers. There may be facilities such as dynamic startup and shutdown of servers to balance load but there are still reasonably few server instances in existence at any one time. In this world a company's database of customers, for example, may be accessed through two or three main servers. The database may contain tens or hundreds of thousands of customer records but these are all accessed through a few interfaces.

CORBA talks about clients but not servers. Instead it uses the term 'object implementation'. The interfaces defined in CORBA IDL describe a class of objects. A client may need to interact with thousands of objects in the system which conform to the definition of that class. In object-oriented terms, there may be thousands of instances of the object class.

The property of encapsulation means that each object instance is effectively seen as a mini-server, providing access to its unique parcel of functions and data. In the ORB world the customer database described above may be modelled as a collection of customer objects. Each of the traditional database records might be represented by an individual instance of a customer object.

Objects are addressed in CORBA through the use of 'object references'. The structure and content of an object reference is a matter for an individual ORB implementation but it has to contain sufficient information for the ORB to route any requests using it to the place where that object is implemented. As far as a client is concerned every object could be implemented on a different machine. It is the job of the ORB to hide all of this. In practice, many object instances may be handled by a single server program, but you can not assume this to be the case.

The ORB core and object adapters

We have just described the basic function of the ORB core to resolve object references and mediate requests between clients and object implementations. There is a standard interface to the ORB to provide basic facilities such as duplicating object references and 'stringifying' them into a form suitable for storage.

We have also just hinted at one way objects themselves might really be implemented – many objects contained within a single server process. There are others, for example every object instance might be implemented by a separate program or even by the facilities of an object-oriented database. To allow the ORB to work with any or all of this range of possibilities the CORBA architecture contains the concept of an 'object adapter'. This forms part of the glue between implementations and the ORB core. Object adapters are responsible for a number of functions including:

● generating and interpreting object references;

● mapping object references to the corresponding implementation;

● automatically activating (and shutting down) implementations when necessary;

● invoking operations on the object implementations.

Object adapters provide a standard interface to object implementations so that they can perform tasks such as registering themselves as ready to receive calls. The OMG envisage that there will be relatively few types of object adapter. This is wise because portability of object implementations across ORBs depends on having well-defined interfaces to the adapters.

The CORBA specification identifies three likely adapters: the so-called 'basic object adapter' or BOA, a library object adapter and an object-oriented database adapter. The BOA is the adapter that corresponds to starting up a server program or programs to service requests, much along the lines of the other distributed computing technologies we have discussed so far. All CORBA ORBs must support at least a basic object adapter and the interfaces to this are defined in the CORBA specification.

Stubs and skeletons

There are two components, the 'IDL stubs' under the client and the 'IDL skeletons' under the object implementation, identified in Figure 5.11, which correspond very closely to concepts already covered under the discussion of remote procedure calls. These are effectively client and server stubs very like those described in Section 5.1.2. They are automatically generated from the IDL description in precisely the same manner as for an RPC system. The server-side skeleton is dependent on the object adapter to direct calls to objects up through it.

Dynamic invocation

When the original CORBA specification was created one of the most contentious issues was that of static versus dynamic invocation. The stub-code method is static. Before an object can be used by a client the necessary stubs must be generated and linked into the client program. However, if a client could somehow obtain an object's interface definition it should be possible to interpret that definition and dynamically construct a request identical to that generated through stub code and then send this to the server. This is dynamic invocation. As communications are mediated by the ORB an object implementation could not tell which method was used to invoke its services.

In the end the CORBA specification accepted both methods as being useful and has the Dynamic Invocation Interface (DII) in addition to the stub method. This flexibility has its price and the DII is fairly complex and difficult to use. However, there are some applications, such as class browsers and certain types of management application, which would be very difficult to implement otherwise.

The story of the production of the first CORBA specification gives an interesting insight into the OMG processes. OMG made a request to industry for product-based specifications. OMG tried to operate by consensus and after an initial sifting process there was no clear, outright 'winner'. So various submitters were encouraged to collaborate to produce joint proposals. However, the proposals polarized into the 'dynamic' and 'static' camps. In the end, people from the companies providing the main competing specifications – DEC, HP, HyperDesk, NCR, Object Design and SunSoft – were pulled together to produce a unified document. This team was nicknamed the '90 days condemned team' because they were locked away and given 90 days to sort it out or else the CORBA effort would founder. They made it. But only just in time!

The latest version of CORBA has introduced the server-side counterpart of the DII in the Dynamic Skeleton Interface (DSI). A major motivation for this is to support ORB interworking by providing a means of fielding requests, identifying them as being destined for an object supported by a 'foreign' ORB, and forwarding them on.

Repositories

The two remaining components that we have not yet described are the repositories. The interface repository is an essential companion to the dynamic invocation facilities. Objects supported by the ORB register a description of their interface in the interface repository. This allows programs to retrieve those descriptions and build matching dynamic requests. The information in the interface repository may also be used by the ORB itself in performing operations. Although the primary role of the repository is to store interface descriptions there are also interfaces defined which allow other related data, for example debugging information, to be stored.

The implementation repository contains the information the ORB needs to locate and start up the object implementations. When a new object server is introduced to the ORB environment its details need to be added to the implementation repository. How this is done varies across different ORB products. ORB implementations may also use the implementation repository as a place to specify such facilities as security and resource controls.

CORBA 1, CORBA 2 and interoperability

The OMG is still an active body and new specifications are continuing to emerge. The first version of the core CORBA specification (version 1.1) appeared at the end of 1991. Although there have been some minor modifications and additions since that time this core document has remained largely unchanged in substantive content.

CORBA 1, as it is now usually known, was a good starting point but suffered from a number of limitations. The first and most major limitation was one of scope. The aim of CORBA 1 was to define a common architecture for ORBs. It also aimed to specify interfaces to give source code level portability of clients and object implementations across ORBs. In this it was successful in that other IDL variants and ORB architectures present in the industry have generally faded away and been replaced by CORBA-compliant versions, although the term 'CORBA-compliant' is a hard one to pin down since a wide range of systems claim some form of conformance to OMG specifications.

The degree of application portability achieved as a result of CORBA 1 is less clear. While CORBA IDL has become widely accepted and interfaces were defined to some core ORB services many other issues were left unaddressed. For example there was no standard way for a client to obtain its first object references, only 'placeholder' security interfaces and some uncertainty about server-side dynamic memory management. Also, although being intended for object-oriented application development the first published mappings from IDL were to the C language. As C has no direct support for object concepts this mapping was rather clumsy.

Despite these limitations a number of CORBA implementations appeared and vendors filled the gaps in the specifications with their own (non-standard) facilities.

Probably the most crucial element outside the scope of the CORBA 1 effort was inter-ORB interoperability. ORB implementations became available on a number of different platforms. Those from a single vendor happily interworked among themselves. However, there was no guarantee and very little hope of ORB implementations from different vendors interoperating.

Interoperability was a major focus of the phase of OMG's work which has become known as 'CORBA 2'. After a long and quite difficult process the OMG produced the Unified Network Objects (UNO) specification and Internet Inter-ORB Protocol (IIOP) at the end of 1994. The IIOP is a fairly simple TCP/IP-based protocol that defines a number of common message formats and exchanges. These allow CORBA IDL data-types, object references and operation invocations to be passed between different ORBs. This message set is independent of the underlying transport mechanism and is also known as the general inter-ORB protocol (GIOP).

As often happens in consensus-based standards making, commercial and political pressures can conflict with technical discussions. The OMG have made it clear that they consider that the IIOP was the best solution balancing a number of technical considerations. Some of the complexity of the problem can also be gleaned from the blizzard of new acronyms the work spawned.

The IIOP is the *lingua franca* of the CORBA world. ORBs may – and probably will within a single-vendor environment – talk to one another using other protocols. However, to guarantee interoperability with other 'foreign' ORB implementations they must be able support the IIOP or at least have access to a 'bridging ORB' which can.

Part of the contention in arriving at the IIOP specification was the proposal by some vendors to use DCE RPC as the basic transport mechanism. Although this was not ultimately accepted, DCE was specified as the first of potentially many optional interoperability protocols. These protocols are known as ESIOPs (environment-specific inter-ORB protocols).

Having a DCE-based protocol does not mean that standard DCE clients can instantly access ORB objects or that ORB clients can communicate directly with DCE RPC servers. In fact the protocol just uses DCE as a transport mechanism for GIOP messages. However, this does mean that different DCE-based ORBs can interoperate and make use of DCE facilities such as the security and directory services.

Although the IIOP has been seen as the major feature of CORBA 2, a number of other new and enhanced specifications have been developed at the same time. These include a wide range of object services and IDL mappings for the C++ and Smalltalk programming languages. Taken together this moves CORBA towards being an ever more comprehensive distributed computing environment.

CORBA realized

As we have already mentioned there are a growing number of CORBA implementations available. Some, like IBM's DSOM (Distributed SOM) are based on ORB-like products that predated the OMG's work but have now been given a CORBA-compliant facelift. Others, such as Orbix from Iona Technologies have been implemented from scratch to the CORBA specifications. Yet others, such as HP's ORBplus, have been built on top of DCE or other existing distribution technologies.

Unlike OSF DCE or Sun RPC there is no common code base from which vendors implement their ORBs, only a common set of specifications. This means that different products not only provide different value-added features but also a range of varying qualities such as minimum code size or maximum security. This has its advantages, for example you stand more chance of finding an ORB that exactly meets your needs. It also has disadvantages – you might end up with an unnecessarily diverse range of slightly different products. Such is the price of pure standards-based development.

5.4.4 COM – the alternative?

In Section 5.4.1 we mentioned Microsoft's Component Object Model or COM. This was originally developed as a basis for object interworking within a single machine. However, COM did not address the issues of intermachine working. To do this Microsoft worked with Digital to develop the Common Object Model (also, confusingly, known as COM) specification. (At the time of writing, this specification had not been finalized. There is, therefore, a possibility that some of the information in this section may have been superseded.) The full distributed COM implementation is expected to form part of a future operating system being developed by Microsoft, code-named 'Cairo'.

The common object model has many similarities to CORBA – and some big differences. We will look as some of these now.

Binary or source?

The first major difference is that COM is primarily a binary and network interoperability standard. That is it specifies exactly what code execution mechanism is used to invoke object operations and precisely what the network protocol exchanges are. This is rather like specifying the details not only of an ORB's interfaces but also its implementation. Of course, in the context of a proprietary standard this is entirely reasonable.

In COM the fundamental interface definition between a client and object is in fact a data-structure that sits between the client's code and the object's. (The data-structure in fact looks remarkably like a C++ 'virtual function table' – which is no surprise because C++ seems now to be Microsoft's language of choice for application development.) The client makes requests to the object indirectly via the data-structure. Having said that COM is a binary standard, it does also specify an interface definition language. COM IDL is an enhanced version of DCE IDL – the COM network protocols are also heavily based on DCE RPC.

One interface or many?

There is also a divergence between COM and CORBA at the level of the basic object model. COM has somewhat different interpretations for the concepts of class, interface and object.

CORBA follows a 'classic' object-oriented model where an object is an instance of a class. The class is the 'mould' from which object instances are created. In CORBA the concepts of interface and class are virtually synonymous. Interfaces may be defined by inheritance from one or more parent interfaces. One of the consequences of this model is that an object is fully defined by its interface – and it has one and only one interface. (This model is, perhaps, stretched a little by some of the concepts in the event services specifications where objects 'conspire' to provide a number of interfaces to a single service.)

In COM objects are also instances of classes. However, in this case a class is merely a convenient grouping of a number of related, but distinct, interfaces. So rather than an object being fully defined by its single interface it is defined by the set of interfaces it supports. Because of this aggregation facility COM makes far less use of inheritance than CORBA. In fact it only supports a limited form of inheritance of interface definitions from a single parent.

It is largely a matter of opinion as to which model is 'better'. The same end results can be achieved either way. If an object needs to provide the facilities of a **Foo** interface and a **Bar** interface in CORBA it will probably define a new **FooBar** interface inheriting from two parents. In COM the object will merely support both interfaces directly.

Objects great or small?

One of the examples given in the COM specification is of a spreadsheet program allowing a single cell from a spreadsheet to be embedded into a word processor document. This example is couched in terms of compound document technology but leads on to the question of how granular COM objects really are. Under COM would you model the cell, the spreadsheet or the spreadsheet program as an object?

Currently the answer would probably be the program – a fairly coarse level of granularity. One of the reasons for this is that the COM interfaces are basically defined and referenced at the level of a chunk of executable code. This does not really represent the same sort of fine-grained level of encapsulation of function and data fundamental to a CORBA object. Even if fine-grained objects, such as spreadsheet cells, are implemented within a COM server the basic mechanisms do not provide any way of referencing them with a unique 'handle'.

COM addresses this problem of object (as opposed to server interface) referencing through *monikers*. Monikers are persistent, intelligent object names. They are persistent in that they endure over time and provide a means of 'getting back to' the object they refer to. They are intelligent in that they encapsulate the details of how to locate and bind to whatever service can perform operations on the object they name. In a sense a moniker is a little like parts of the ORB core and object adapter functionality in CORBA.

COM + CORBA = ?

We have not discussed COM in any great depth, partly because it is still something of a 'moving target'. However, it should be reasonably clear that CORBA and COM both address roughly the same sorts of problems. Unfortunately they have somewhat different approaches to solving those problems. So what are the prospects for working between the two object worlds?

Digital itself straddles both camps. It is a very active member of OMG and also partners with Microsoft in specifying COM. It is providing COM on a non-Windows platform and integrating it using their CORBA-compliant ORB product, ObjectBroker.

Within the OMG there is an activity supported by Microsoft to define a standard COM–CORBA interworking strategy. Given the large philosophical differences between COM and CORBA this will almost certainly result in some reduction of facilities available through any gateway. However, it does look reasonably certain that COM and CORBA will be able to co-exist and cooperate – even if the relationship is based on a grudging acknowledgement that neither party is likely to shut up shop and disappear!

5.4.5 The end of the rainbow?

With the other technologies covered in this chapter we have tried to give some idea of where and when they are best used. It is hard to do this with distributed object technology for two reasons: maturity and ambition.

Object technology is the 'place where the action is' in the distributed computing field. That is not to say that all the other technologies have ceased to evolve and develop – far from it – but the field of distributed objects is certainly the one which seems the most active and rapidly evolving. Many vendors are investing huge amounts of time and effort in building newer and better products to support object interaction.

We have barely mentioned the technologies growing up around the basic object distribution mechanisms. Microsoft's OLE is one example of compound document technology. In the CORBA arena the rival specification is OpenDoc. This was originally developed by Apple but is now in the hands of a not-for-profit consortium known as Component Integration Labs. This was founded by Apple, IBM, Novell,

SunSoft, Taligent, WordPerfect and Xerox Xsoft. A number of companies are developing 'object frameworks' – class libraries and tools to speed object-oriented application development – on top of CORBA. Similarly the proprietary NextStep object environment is moving on to other platforms as the OpenStep toolset.

The price for all of this potentially exciting development activity is lack of stability and maturity. Some of the distributed object technologies are truly leading edge (if not 'bleeding' edge!) but not consequently that well-proven in critical applications. Many lack key facilities such as security and large-scale operability. However, ORB-based products are now starting to find their way into the 'hard' commercial environment.

While the maturity of this technology may be open to question its ambition certainly is not. OMG are making steady progress in providing 'objectified' versions of all the major computing services – transactions, security, systems management, persistent file storage and so on. Individual ORB vendors have gone further and provided integration with other technologies such as ISIS and DCE.

Similarly, the future direction for core operating system technology seems to be increasingly towards embracing object concepts at the most fundamental levels of the computing platform. Technologies such as Chorus, from Chorus Systèmes, Mach, originating from Carnegie-Mellon University and Amoeba, from the Free University of Amsterdam, are being adopted and adapted into mainstream systems. The stated direction for Microsoft's Cairo is also towards an object base.

In short, it looks likely that within a few years distributed object systems will have acquired the whole set of capabilities of other distribution mechanisms. This does not mean that distributed objects become some kind of panacea and totally replace other technologies. For a start, the technology needs to build on all that has come before it. It is inherently complex and may as a result not meet particular performance, robustness, resource or other requirements of some applications.

There is one major ultimate prize offered by distributed objects. There is a good chance that it will be possible to have a single, consistent environment providing as complete a range of distribution transparencies as possible. Maybe then the distributed world will be as comfortable as the single-system environment once again.

5.5 Neccessary infrastructure – the supporting cast

This chapter has so far been concerned with introducing the major members of the distributed computing family. However, there are some important friends and relations whom we have only so far mentioned in passing, if at all. These play a crucial role in helping the others to function. We will now take a brief look at some of the members of this 'supporting cast'.

5.5.1 Directories and name services

One of the fundamental problems in any distributed system is finding things. On a number of occasions in our discussions we have mentioned that it is the job of particular components to find services on behalf of a client. RPC systems, message queue managers, ORBs and the others all need this fundamental ability.

If you look back to Figure 5.3 you will see that a 'directory server' is used to help resolve the binding between client and server. Almost every distributed computing technology has a similar service either explicitly or implicity provided. The commonest facility is the ability to translate some form of symbolic name into an address. The address need not be a network address but rather is whatever information is needed to tie down the precise location of the service described by the supplied name. The most basic form of this facility is usually known as a 'name service' – you give it a name and it returns its translation, if any. In its simplest form this is little more than a straightforward look-up table.

Finding the finder

Even with the most basic name service there are several questions that need to be addressed for the distributed environment. The first is a classic chicken-and-egg problem: if you use the name server to find servers then how do you find the name server?

There are several possible answers to this. One might be to require that clients are supplied with the location of the name service directly, perhaps through a configuration file, start-up parameter or even by hard-wiring it into application code. This can work quite well although it does suffer from a certain lack of flexibility – if the name server crashes, or has to move, the client is stuck until provided with new information. This can, however, be alleviated by providing a list of fall-back servers.

Another solution is for a client to use a network 'broadcast' to find any listening name servers. This is particularly suited to a LAN environment and provides the ability to find another server in the event of failure. Unfortunately, network-wide broadcast beyond a LAN is usually prohibited because of the traffic volume it can generate. This makes such a scheme unworkable for wide area use or where any fall-back servers are sited beyond the current LAN. There are also some potentially sticky security issues – if anyone can reply to the broadcast request then they might pretend to be a name server and cause havoc.

It may also be possible to side-step the problem of locating the name server. In some environments the name service is not a separate entity but is completely integrated as part of the supporting infrastructure. If you can talk to the infrastructure at all then you have access to the name service. The Tuxedo TP monitor's 'bulletin board' is an example of this. It exists as a structure in memory and if Tuxedo is running at all then the bulletin board will be accessible. If it is not running then clients will not be able to perform any processing anyway, name service or not.

Keeping up to date

If you solve the problem of locating your name service the second main problem arises: how can you keep the information up to date? If there is a single, central server this is not too much of a problem. It is a reasonably straightforward task to maintain a single database. However, this is then a critical central point of failure. If the name server is lost the whole system may stop. In reality, you will want the name service to be resilient to failure. This is harder because you will probably need to replicate the data to other servers. (This is a common problem in a distributed environment, not just difficult for name servers.)

There are several options for tackling the replication problem. The easiest is to appoint some server as the 'master' and others as 'slaves'. Changes are only made to the master database and then copies are sent out to the slaves when necessary. Sun's Network Information Service (NIS) is of this master–slave type. (Formerly known as 'Yellow Pages'. It was changed after certain telecommunications companies objected to a conflict with well-established trademarks.) This works reasonably where there is well-defined central control and management of the whole system. Unfortunately it can suffer from delays in propagating changes out to all slaves. Also if control of the master is subverted then all slaves are subverted too.

A different approach to the master–slave mechanism is to have every name server remain in contact with every other and propagate all changes to each other. But as we have seen above in Section 5.3.2 this is not easy to achieve and veers into the realm of process group technology.

Hierarchical look-up

There is a more fundamental issue lurking beneath both the problem of locating the name service and updating its data. This stems from one of the reversed assumptions outlined in Chapter 4. In this case it is the move from unification to federation. A master–slave or even mutual update strategy can be made to work where there is a single database of information. However, these break down where there is a naming hierarchy with different branches owned by different people.

Probably the largest example of a hierarchical name service in the computing world is the Internet Domain Name Service (Mockapetris, 1987a, b). DNS is the service used to resolve textual names such as gatekeeper.dec.com and www.bt.net into the Internet addresses 204.123.2.2 and 194.72.6.51 respectively. There is no central DNS server for the Internet. Indeed such a server would be impossible to maintain as it would have to track the changes to potentially billions of network addresses. (In the beginning of the Internet (or ARPAnet as it was then) there *was* a single central source – a file HOSTS.TXT which was maintained at the Network Information Center and copied out regularly to every other site on the network!)

The way Internet addressing works is to allocate blocks of addresses and the responsibility for assigning them to particular domains. So BT, for example, owns a number of address ranges including the 132.146.xxx.xxx range. All of these addresses correspond to names ending in the suffix .bt.co.uk and are part of that domain. The domain names are hierarchical in structure. So BT forms part of the co.uk domain which in turn is part of the uk domain.

The hierarchical structure is used to direct the look-up process using DNS. A look-up request starts by asking a local server if it can resolve the name directly. It will be able to do this either if it is the authoritative source of the translation for the name or if it has already resolved it recently and has it in a cache. Each server is configured to know the addresses of several other servers and the domains which they handle. If a server cannot resolve the name then it will look at the structure of the name and tell the requester the address of another server more likely to be able to help. This process will continue until either a server with the authoritative data is found or all further possibilities are exhausted.

Directories

So far we have been fairly cavalier with the use of the terms 'name service' and 'directory'. Indeed the terms are often used synonymously but there is a valuable distinction which can sometimes be made.

A name service is something which provides a simple translation look-up. You specify a single key and return a single record of information. DNS is tailored to performing domain-name-to-address and address-to-name translations although it can handle other forms of data. NIS can be used for storing and retrieving arbitrary key-value pair information. In neither case, however, can you easily perform sophisticated matching or searching.

Directory services, by contrast, are usually meant to be considerably more flexible. They may allow sets of attributes to be associated with names and provide facilities for performing complicated searches and matches in addition to straight one-for-one look-ups.

Probably the most comprehensive directory service specification is the X.500 standard (ISO/IEC, 1990*b*). (The name known as 'X.500' comes from the equivalent name of the standard given by the CCITT (now the ITU-T)). This provides a fully hierarchical, federated directory service allowing some very sophisticated operations. Unfortunately, X.500 is also fairly complex, not widely implemented and has some difficult security and management issues.

The DCE cell directory service (CDS) is somewhere between a name service and full-blown directory service. It provides a very comprehensive hierarchical name space with facilities automatically to replicate and synchronize parts of the hierarchy. It can also store arbitrary attributes associated with each entry. CDS does not itself, however, provide full directory searching facilities although libraries layered on top of it add some of these features.

Sun's NIS+ is a development on from NIS that turns the name service into a full hierarchical directory service. NIS+ is not widely implemented, being a Sun proprietary product. It has, however, been influential in the creation of a general 'federated naming' programming interface standard. This is the X/Open federated naming (XFN) standard (X/Open CAE Specification C403, 1995). This allows many different naming and directory services to be accessed uniformly through a single programming interface.

Brokers and traders

Directories and name services are a necessary part of distributed computing infrastructure but neither is particularly 'intelligent'. These services allow information to be stored and retrieved based on some selection criteria. They have, however, very little knowledge about the meaning of the information that they hold.

The next phase in the development of directory services is to enable them to act rather more intelligently in responding to requests. ORBs are starting to move along this road. In an ORB the role of symbolic name translation is reduced and most resolution operations are of 'object references'. These are opaque structures to the programmer but serve as identifiers for objects known to the ORB. In addition, the interface repository facilities allow much more dynamic discovery and resolution of services.

Beyond this lies the concept of 'trading'. This idea came to prominence in the ANSA project and from there has gone forward to form part of the ISO Open Distributed Processing (ODP) standards. Both ANSA and ODP are described in Appendix A. A trading operation is more than just a look-up of information. Instead it is a more dynamic service which matches offered services with requests from clients.

The first step in trading involves ensuring that interfaces are at least syntactically compatible. This is similar to the facility of DCE and other systems to select a compatible interface based on interface identifiers and version numbers. A trader, however, may have more access to interface definitions and could determine for itself what is syntactically compatible. Trading goes beyond this in also allowing other aspects such as desired quality of service to enter the equation. These can also be negotiated such that a client would like, for example, response times under 0.1 seconds but could tolerate 0.5 seconds if no more suitable server was available. The idea of trading is not only to find a compatible service but also the most suitable service.

Ideally we would like to be able to ensure that not only are interfaces syntactically compatible – that is they support the right set of operations and parameters – but also semantically compatible – they perform the expected actions when those operations are invoked. To provide this sort of guarantee, however, would probably require validation 'on the fly' or a formal specification of a server's code. That would make an interesting research project but is unlikely to make it into product before the authors draw their pensions ...

5.5.2 Security

There are some fundamental security issues in distributed systems. This is a large topic in its own right and is discussed further in Chapter 7. This chapter would not be complete, however, without a brief discussion of some technologies used to enforce security in a distributed system. (If you are unfamiliar with general security concepts and terminology then you should probably read the section on security in Chapter 7 first.)

Encryption

Probably the most fundamental tool used within distributed security technologies is that of data encryption. Many people have devoted countless years to devising ever more subtle, sophisticated and effective forms of encryption. The basic function of encryption is to transform data into a form which hides its original content and meaning while being able to recover the original data when required. It is also usually a requirement for any reasonable encryption system that this reverse translation should only be possible by someone possessing the necessary secret key to unlock it.

Some form of encryption is the only way to guarantee confidentiality of data transmitted over an unsecure network. The strength of the guarantee depends on the degree to which the original data is concealed by the encryption mechanism and, vitally, the security of the secret keys. The most difficult form of code-breaking is to spot some form of pattern in encrypted data that might allow the coding to be 'reverse-engineered' back to the original data. Sometimes a more productive approach is to attempt to guess a poorly chosen secret key.

Most encryption algorithms, including the U.S. Data Encryption Standard (DES) and the International Data Encryption Algorithm (IDEA), are called *private* or *symmetric key* systems. The security of the encryption depends on a shared secret known only to the two communicating parties.

There is an alternative to private key encryption called *public* or *asymmetric key* encryption. In public key systems, such as the Rivest–Shamir–Adleman (RSA) system, a user has a pair of keys – a private key which is kept secret and a public key which is made widely available. A message encrypted using the public key can only be decrypted using the private key and vice versa. This means that you can receive encrypted messages from anyone who knows your public key safe in the knowledge that only you can read them. It also means that if you encrypt a message using your private key it can be guaranteed that it could only have come from you if it decrypts properly using your public key.

Public key encryption is a fundamental part of the widely used Pretty Good Privacy (PGP) program. PGP has an interesting history. The RSA encryption algorithm is patented in the U.S. However, some people do not believe that such techniques can or should be covered by patent law. The original creator of PGP – Phil Zimmerman – believed strongly that good cryptographic tools should be widely and freely available. So PGP originally used an unlicensed version of the RSA algorithm. Katz and PGP have since become involved in a series of legal wrangles but a version of PGP is now available which uses legally approved routines and is free for non-commercial use. However, this version can not be legally exported outside the U.S. ...

Encryption is usually only applied sparingly because a strong encryption algorithm usually requires many processing steps to implement. It is often used to protect only critical data, such as the digital signatures described below. Also, while public key encryption is very attractive for many purposes – you do not need to have managed to exchange secret keys before you can communicate in privacy – it requires even more processing than most private key systems. Public techniques are, therefore, often used to protect only the initial exchange of secrets keys which can then be used with more conventional, faster mechanisms. A good example of this is the 'secure sockets layer' (SSL) protocol (http://www.netscape.com/newsref/std/SSL.html) proposed and developed by Netscape Communications, Inc.

Hashes, digests, signatures and fingerprints

There is always a measure of uncertainty in any exchange of data between two parties. How can a recipient know that the data received is the same as the data sent? How can they know if it has been accidentally corrupted or maliciously tampered with while 'in flight'? A common aid to solving this problem is the creation of a sort of 'digital fingerprint' for messages which can easily be verified. This is often known as a 'hash' or 'digest'.

The principle of creating a message hash is simple. All the data in the message is fed into a procedure which mashes and scrambles the contents down to a string of, usually, 128 or 256 bits. This string of bits is the hash value – the message fingerprint. The key to creating a useful message hash it to devise a routine which makes it both very unlikely that two sets of input data will give the same hash value, and also extremely hard to construct a set of data that will generate an arbitrary hash value. Even if the input data differs only by a single bit the hash should be different.

Once a hash value has been calculated it can then be attached to a message. When the message is received the hash is recalculated and compared with that supplied with the message. If the communication channel is secure then this will suffice. Where the link is not secure then it is sufficient to protect the hash value by encryption to be able to guarantee the integrity of the message data. An encrypted hash attached to an unencrypted message is sometimes known as a message signature. With the use of public key encryption a hash can act very much like a real signature guaranteeing the origination of a message. The hash is encrypted using the signatory's secret key. If it can be decrypted and verified using their public key then the message can only have been signed by the holder of that matching secret key – the signatory.

There are a number of hash algorithms in widespread use. These include RSA Data Security, Inc.'s MD4 and MD5 algorithms (published in Internet RFCs (Rivest, 1990, 1992)) and the U.S. Federal Information Processing Standard secure hash algorithm (SHA-1) (Federal Information Processing Standards, 1993).

Authentication systems

Probably the most necessary security service for a distributed system beyond simple encryption is an authentication service. It is the job of such a service to help communicating parties to discover and verify each other's identity.

Kerberos

By far the best known distributed authentication service is Kerberos (the Greek name of the three-headed dog who in ancient legend guarded the entrance to the world of the dead). This system was first developed at the Massachusetts Institute of Technology (MIT) as part of 'Project Athena' which was a project to provide a campus-wide network of workstations and servers.

Kerberos is a 'trusted third party' authentication mechanism. It depends on having a central, highly trusted server which holds the secret keys of all users. It is the job of this 'key distribution centre' (KDC) server to issue 'tickets' which allow users access to all other services. Both clients and servers implicitly trust this server to issue valid tickets.

The basic operations of the Kerberos mechanism are illustrated in Figure 5.12. The process is roughly as follows:

1   A user requests a ticket for a service from the KDC.

2   The KDC sends back a packet of data that contains the ticket – but encrypted using the requester's secret key.

The only way to unlock the ticket is by knowing the secret key, it will be useless to anyone who does not. This means that a user can obtain a valid ticket without their password having to travel over the network.

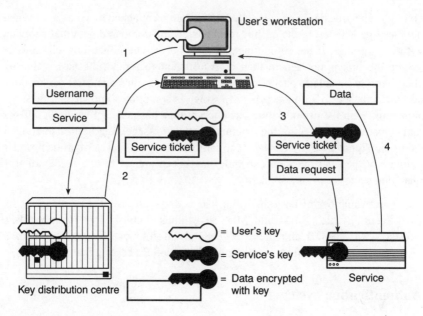

Figure 5.12 Simplified Kerberos protocol.

3   The user makes a request to the service and presents the ticket it has extract-
     ed from the KDC's reply.

     The ticket itself is a packet of data encrypted using the secret key assigned
     to the service. This too is known to the KDC which created the ticket. (In
     Kerberos it is not only humans who can be identifiable 'users' but also client
     or server processes. Kerberos uses the term *principal* to describe any entity
     which has a distinct identity that it can authenticate.) The ticket contains the
     requester's identity along with other items to guard against forgery and
     reuse.

4   If the service can decrypt the ticket it will decide whether and what reply to
     make to the requester.

In fact this is a rather simplified description of the Kerberos protocol. There are
a number of good references that explain the protocols in further detail (Steiner
et al., 1988; Schiller, 1994). The most important omission from our description
is the fact that the KDC itself only issues a user with a single ticket called the
'ticket granting ticket'. This is then used with another special and highly trusted
service called the ticket granting service (TGS). This exists to get around the
problem of the users otherwise having to use their secret key every time they need
to get a new ticket from the KDC. In all cases Kerberos tickets have a limited lifetime to prevent them from being stolen and reused.

MIT have made implementations of Kerberos freely available and probably for this reason it has been very widely adopted and used. Version 5 is, for example, at the core of the OSF DCE security services. There are also a number of other commercial products based on the MIT code.

Other approaches

While probably the most widely used distributed authentication service, Kerberos is not the only such technology. Others, such as IBM's 'Kryptonite' product have a similar model but differ in detail. Partly in recognition of this a system-independent programming interface has been specified. The Generic Security Services application programming interface (GSS API) is defined in an Internet RFC (Linn, 1993). It allows an application to obtain and verify credentials, encrypt data and perform other security-related functions in a manner independent of any particular underlying service.

The primary purpose of Kerberos is to enable parties in a distributed system to identify each other reliably. Based on that identification it is up to a server (or client) to decide what operations if any they will allow. One approach to this is to use access control lists (ACLs). These list which users or groups of users may perform particular operations. A server compares the identity in a supplied ticket with the membership of the ACL for the requested operation to decide whether to permit it.

A rather different approach is embodied by the 'capability' mechanism (Dennis and Van Horn, 1966) as used in environments such as the Amoeba operating system (Mullender et al., 1990). A capability is rather like a ticket for a service but, rather than identifying the user and then letting the server decide how to proceed, the possession of a capability actually confers the rights to perform operations. Effectively, a capability is like an ACL in reverse. Rather than saying: 'here is who I am, now what will you allow me to do'? it says: 'here is what I have been told I am allowed to do.'

The advantage of capabilities is that the burden of authorization checking is substantially reduced for servers. They are also easy to administer centrally. The main disadvantage is that a server loses a large amount of control. Not only must a third party be trusted reliably to authenticate users but it must also be trusted not to violate the server security by issuing over-empowered capabilities. As with many design issues there is a trade-off between flexibility, operability and security.

5.5.3 Timing

On a single system all processes share the same notion of the current time – they see the same clock. This is not so in a distributed system. In Section 5.3.2 we looked at some of the issues surrounding synchronization in a distributed environment. We said then that it is very difficult to support the notion of a common 'current time' across a number of systems. It is also virtually impossible to be able to say with certainty whether events with the same timestamp truly occurred simultaneously.

Having painted this slightly worrying picture there is still value in providing some degree of time synchronization. Not least among the reasons for doing this is to minimize confusion for the poor human users! Without reasonable synchronization some very disconcerting phenomena start to occur. Time skew between a client and a file server can lead to effects such as the creation date on files apparently lying in the future. This is off-putting enough for humans but can also cause applications such as automatic code compilation systems and backup programs to fail.

Timestamps also form a part of a number of security protocols, including Kerberos described in the previous section. The usual purpose of this is to provide limited lifetimes on tokens and tickets so that they rapidly become worthless if they are somehow stolen. Under these circumstances widely varied system times can halt interactions altogether if lifetimes are less than the difference in times.

There are several ways in which acceptable synchronization can be achieved. Software-based solutions include the Network Time Protocol (NTP) which is defined by Mills (1992). This is a master–slave system where a central server provides the authoritative time from which other systems take their lead. A slightly different approach is taken in the DCE distributed time service (DTS). Here there is not one master but a number of servers agreeing among themselves on a common time reference point. Both mechanisms can usually manage to maintain synchronization across a number of systems to within a few seconds and often much better than this.

For some applications it is desirable either to have even more precise synchronization or to ensure that systems are kept close to true local time. Under these circumstances it is common to employ an external time signal from a recognized source such as government-supported radio broadcasts or even Global Positioning Satellite (GPS) signals. Often these can be fed into the more conventional time synchronization mechanisms so that not every machine needs to be equipped with special hardware. (The author once had occasion to review a design for a truly globally distributed system. There was a strong requirement to have close time synchronization between all of the systems. The design proposed equipping each with a GPS receiver. This would give worldwide synchronization to within a few milliseconds. The design also noted a second benefit – if somehow one of the machines were ever to be misplaced or stolen it would be able to report its precise latitude and longitude!)

5.6 Other technologies – the motley crew

We have now covered the range of general purpose distributed computing technologies from message passing through to distributed objects. However, in many ways these do not necessarily represent the bulk of distributed computing technology deployed today. Over time a large number of specialized or *ad hoc* solutions to distributed processing problems have been developed. This has particularly been the case during organic and explosive growth of the Internet.

Before concluding this chapter we will take you on a whistle-stop tour of some of the most important and widespread 'custom-built' technologies. This will undoubtedly not do justice to them but will, we hope, at least set them in the context of the discussions of this chapter.

5.6.1 RFC822, MIME, HTTP and friends

RFC822 is the Internet standard for the format of electronic mail messages (Crocker, 1982). The basic structure of an Internet e-mail message is a plain text file consisting of a set of header lines, a blank line and then the text of the message. Each header line is of the form 'Keyword: some text' as shown in Figure 5.13.

This simple format has proved to be very flexible and has been adapted to a wide variety of purposes. The simple and consistent header format has allowed people to add extensions and to write a variety of automatic processing systems that do anything from generating automatic 'sorry, I'm away' replies to performing database queries. (RFC822 defines a standard set of headers but allows for user-defined extensions through the use of header lines beginning X-. So you will commonly see X-Mailer lines describing the originating mail system, X-MD5-Checksum to detect corruption and even X-Face-Data containing data for a picture of the sender!)

```
Received: by mail.axion.bt.co.uk Tue, 22 Aug 1995 22:15:10 +0100
From: "Neil Winton" <N.Winton@axion.bt.co.uk>
To: "Mark Norris" <M.Norris@axion.bt.co.uk>
Subject: Chapter 5
Date: Tue, 22 Aug 1995 22:10:17 +0100

Mark,

You asked about the progress on Chapter 5. It's nearly done.
My family will certainly be relieved when this is all over --
and so will I!

I'll see you on Saturday to put the whole thing together.
        Regards,
            Neil
```

Figure 5.13 Typical RFC822-format message.

The basic message format has been extended by the Multipurpose Internet Mail Extension (MIME) standard (Borenstein and Freed, 1993). This defines some additional headers but also imposes some structure on the message body so that it can cope with the inclusion of other forms of data than plain text.

Another offspring of RFC822 and MIME is the hypertext transfer protocol (HTTP) (Berners-Lee *et al.*, 1995) that is fundamental to the operation of the World Wide Web. The response received from an HTTP server is formatted in a very similar way to mail messages. There are a set of header lines, a blank line and then the data.

Not only is RFC822 the source of inspiration for many other applications but the Simple Mail Transfer Protocol (SMTP) used to deliver messages is one of a number of very similar protocols. These protocols are characterized by conducting a simple, ASCII-text dialogue over a stream-based connection between client and server. A typical control message consists of sending a line containing a short text string such as helo to announce the start of a new dialogue. The response usually contains a line beginning with three decimal digits, for example 200 OK or 400 Forbidden as a response code. This basic scheme is used by SMTP, FTP, NNTP, HTTP and many other protocols.

In some ways these protocols and messages are like a very simple RPC mechanism. An HTTP interaction in particular consists of connecting to a server, sending a single GET, PUT or POST command and some associated parameters, receiving a result and then disconnecting. In fact the ANSA project have done some work in integrating HTTP and CORBA IDL descriptions so that WWW forms and documents can be fitted into an ORB infrastructure (http://www.ansa.co.uk/ANSA/ISF/ANSAWeb.html).

5.6.2 X Window System

The X Window System (http://www.x.org/) is a client/server system for controlling bit-mapped graphical displays. An X server resides with, and has direct access to, the display hardware. X client programs – such as terminal emulators, editors and drawing packages – make requests of the server to display graphics and text and to receive input from the keyboard and mouse.

The X protocol consists of a large number of messages and data formats. These are designed to be capable of being transported over a wide range of network protocols or over local communications mechanisms within a single machine. The protocol is intended for use of high-speed links such as those provided by a LAN. Intensive graphical operations such as real-time animation can generate very large volumes of network traffic. Although it is possible to use X over a wide area network this is usually a fairly frustrating experience for users because of bandwidth limitations and network latency.

The X Window System is designed to be a flexible graphical display system but it is not intended to be used as a general purpose distributed computing mechanism.

5.6.3 Distributed file systems

One of the most familiar of all distributed computing technologies must surely be the distributed or networked file system. The basic premise is to make a portion of a remote system's file storage appear as part of the local file system. There are a range of such technologies which serve different operating systems and provide different levels of functionality.

Within the Windows environment the so-called 'network operating systems' Novell NetWare and Microsoft LAN Manager provide broadly similar facilities. They provide not only access to file storage but also to networked printers and devices such as CD-ROMs and tape streamers.

The most common distributed file system in the UNIX world is Sun Microsystems' Network File System (NFS). This is implemented on top of Sun's ONC RPC mechanism and is probably the main reason for the widespread availability of this technology. NFS has a number of weaknesses particularly in its security but it is ubiquitous – shipped as standard with virtually every UNIX implementation – and is in daily use by millions of users.

The DCE distributed file system (DFS) is, naturally enough, built upon the DCE RPC mechanism and services. It was developed from the Andrew File System (AFS) from Carnegie-Mellon University. DFS and AFS are more robust, secure and perform better than NFS. However, the penetration of NFS is so great that relatively few sites use either AFS or DFS.

Beyond the obvious purpose of providing shared access to data there have been some creative uses of distributed file systems to perform crude forms of distributed processing. One common ploy is to have a shared directory that is constantly monitored by one or more server processes. Clients deposit files containing work requests in this directory. These files are detected by the server processes which pick up the requests and act accordingly. They may then later write results back to the same or another directory. This is often how network printing works and is very similar to the way many batch processing systems operate within single systems. Some network file systems come with this sort of network batch processing facility as standard.

5.6.4 Distributed databases

A natural follow-on to distributed file systems is distributed database technology. Database vendors have long recognized some of the potential benefits to be had from splitting and replicating data across a number of machines. There is potential for performance improvements through parallel searching and access to more local copies of data, reliability may be increased by replication and there is also the prospect of having huge databases exceeding the capacity of any one machine to support.

Unfortunately, providing these facilities requires employing a large number of the techniques we have discussed in this chapter. Distributed two-phase commits are an obvious essential element for ensuring data integrity. Many data replication strategies effectively require reliable message-queueing. Location of remote database partitions requires naming services and security services are needed to guard against malicious interference with remote data. The difficulty of providing all of these facilities has meant that distributed database technology is only now starting to live up to its promise.

Most of the major vendors have addressed these problems by building their own proprietary mechanisms and protocols. However, there are now signs that at least some level of integration with other general purpose technologies is happening. A good example of this is the move by both Oracle and Sybase to allow DCE directory and security services to be used. CORBA recognizes a special form of object adapter to be implemented by databases to provide smooth integration into an ORB environment.

Regardless of whether the core database itself is truly distributed, nearly all databases provide support for remote clients to access a central server. This usually involves the transfer of 'raw' SQL requests from client to server. This has been described by some as 'SQL squirting'.

The term is intentionally somewhat pejorative because one of the disadvantages of this approach is that it is hard to control the effects of arbitrary database commands. If there are a million rows in a table and a query matches every one then the network will take a hammering while they are all returned to the client. (One approach to limiting this sort of damage is to allow access only to 'stored procedures' within the database which perform defined units of processing and do not allow uncontrolled access. In this case using the stored procedure is effectively equivalent to making an RPC call.)

There are a number of different remote access protocols in use although there are interfaces such as Microsoft's open database connectivity (ODBC) that allow the differences between databases to be hidden at the price of some flexibility. Although we will not go into greater detail here this is, in practice, a very widely used technology particularly for smaller scale and *ad hoc* client/server developments.

The proprietary nature of distributed database technology means that it is not, in general, possible to have a single distributed database made up of Oracle, IBM DB2 and Sybase nodes, for example. However, there is a mechanism which goes some way to supporting this. It is known as 'federated' database technology.

A federated database management system (FDBMS) sits above existing databases and uses their remote access interfaces. It provides a single, consolidated database schema where data items in different databases can be equated and tied to one another. The FDBMS does all the necessary translation between formats and access mechanism to provide a single, consistent view to its users. Federated database technology is still relatively new and, at present, seems most suited for query-only access owing to the problems of maintaining consistency between disparate underlying systems.

5.7 Internet terminals and mobile code – the future of distributed computing?

Computing in general and the distributed branch in particular is a rapidly evolving field. It is a measure of this that between the completion of the initial and final drafts of this chapter a technology has moved from largely academic discussion to a major 'hot topic' within the industry. The technology is 'mobile code' and the means by which it has become known is a World Wide Web browser called 'HotJava'.

The idea behind mobile code is quite simple. It reverses the normal nature of distributed processing we have discussed so far. Instead of sending local processing over to a remote program you bring a remote program to local processing. The model is one where a local processor downloads code – whole applications or fragments known as 'applets' – as and when needed from the network. The code could also be actively sent to a remote system to be executed there.

In a sense, there is little difference between the downloading of 'mobile code' and a machine loading word processor software, for example, from a central file server on a LAN. However, a conventional word processor program is distributed in a form compiled only for particular computer hardware, for example Intel processors. For true mobile code to be achieved then it must be capable of running on any sort of machine.

5.7.1 Scripts and virtual machines

There are broadly two ways of achieving the required degree of machine independence. The first is to transfer programs round in their source form and to have this interpreted on every machine. This 'scripting' approach works quite well, although it is not necessarily very fast. A major disadvantage is that for large and complex applications the size and slowness of the script becomes too great to make it viable. A second problem is that, if the source of the whole application is being distributed, it makes it very difficult for software authors to retain any ownership and control. Having said this, for small and *ad hoc* applications scripting is very simple and attractive. Examples of languages that have been used in this way are Tcl (Ousterhout, 1994) and General Magic's TeleScript.

The second approach is to equip different computing platforms with the same 'virtual machine'. A virtual machine is a software program which provides an execution engine for primitive instructions or 'byte-code' from which other programs can be constructed. It is essentially a software CPU. The beauty of this is that programs compiled to run on the virtual machine will run unchanged wherever the virtual machine itself has been implemented. This is precisely what is needed for mobile code.

A developer needs to perform slightly more work and have a few more tools to exploit a virtual machine. Programs have to be compiled from their source into byte-code meaning an extra step, another tool and some greater configuration management issues. However, the benefits are great. The speed of byte-code interpretation can approach that of 'native' compiled code and there is no need to publish the source code any more – only the byte-code is shipped around.

The virtual machine idea is by no means new. In the 1970s the UCSD 'p-system' was a fairly well-known environment used, among other things, for making a Pascal language compiler available across a wide range of machines. Smalltalk and other highly interactive language environments often use byte-code implementations. So why has this caused such a recent stir in the computing world?

5.7.2 Java and HotJava

In mid-1995 Sun Microsystems made a new World Wide Web browser called 'HotJava' freely available. In many ways it is a fairly standard browser with fewer capabilities than the market leaders. It is written in a new object-oriented programming language called Java which was compiled into byte-code and executed by a Java virtual machine (JVM). This of itself is not what makes the browser unusual. The most exciting feature is the ability of the browser to download Java byte-code from Web pages and execute them. This enables the pages not only to display interesting new forms of information such as animated diagrams but also allows the browser to be extended 'on the fly'. Why Java? Apparently the designers were fond of good coffee! Sun's Java logo is a stylized steaming cup. It may also have to do with the need for large quantities of caffeine to sustain the inveterate Web surfer ...

There are, of course, a large number of potential security issues associated with downloading code of unknown provenance. Not least is the potential for viruses to be imported. The Java virtual machine tackles a number of these issues by placing strict limits on what a program may do. The Java language itself tries to make it impossible to write 'unsafe' programs. The measures adopted address many, although probably not all, of the major problems.

Many people have now seen the potential for the use of Java and a number of companies, including Netscape Communications and Microsoft, have licensed Java technology. Netscape 2.0 incorporates Java support along with a scripting language, JavaScript. In fairly short order a very large community of users have become 'Java-enabled'.

The definitive reference site for Java is http://www.javasoft.com/ although a large number of books are in preparation.

5.7.3 Internet terminals – the end of the line?

There has been an explosion of interest in Java and much speculation (some of it wild) over how such technology might be used as it becomes ubiquitous. One of the industry buzz-phrases of the moment is the 'Internet terminal'. The idea is to produce cheap but powerful boxes, with limited local storage but the in-built ability to download and run mobile code. All applications are provided through the network. There is no longer the problem of running obsolete or unsupported software – the latest 'killer' applications are just a download away. Distribution becomes a matter of shipping mobile code around.

So does this spell the end for all the other distributed technologies we have discussed? Does the future belong to mobile code? Unsurprisingly, the authors do not believe that it will ever be that black and white.

There is very little evidence that any computing technology, with the possible exception of paper tape and punched cards, has ever fully been displaced. Mobile code will add another strand to the tapestry. It is an elegant solution to a number of problems. For example, Internet terminals may become the devices of choice within office LAN environments where a high degree of sharing of common applications is required. They may also offer a good solution to the market for home information and entertainment devices.

Mobile code still has to face up to many of the same security, operability and integrity issues addressed by other technologies we have covered. Some of the problems will be worse in this environment. It is also not clear how it will fare while mobile communications do not reach the same data rates as the fixed network.

The future is likely to see yet greater fusion between all of the distributed computing technologies. Only one thing is certain, in the words of Francis Bacon: 'He that will not apply new remedies must expect new evils: for time is the greatest innovator.'

5.8 Summary

This Chapter has covered a very large number of topics and introduced a wide range of technologies and concepts. It is very difficult to provide a single summary that draws it all together. However, there are some common themes. Each technology aims to simplify life for application developers by providing one or more distribution transparencies. The various technologies also draw upon techniques and concepts from other systems. CORBA inherits much from the messaging and RPC worlds. Object transaction services add in TP techniques and so on. The 'new kid on the block' of mobile code adds yet another dimension.

Figure 5.14 tries to illustrate some of the evolutionary development of distributed processing technologies. This is not meant to imply that the later technologies are

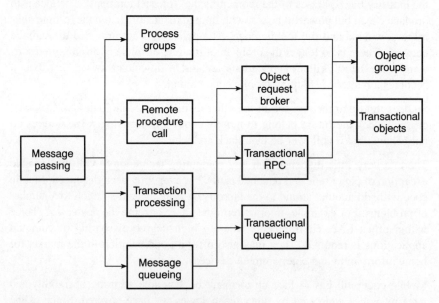

Figure 5.14 More transparency, greater complexity.

necessarily better than their predecessors. Sometimes greater transparency is worth the price of increased underlying complexity. On other occasions the simpler solution will get the job done more effectively and cheaply.

Problems that have many solutions are hard to solve. We hope that this chapter has equipped you with the knowledge to understand the range of options at your disposal and to choose the right tool for the job – or at the very least, to recognize the wrong one.

CHAPTER 6

Integration

'If the map and the terrain disagree...
Believe the terrain' – Swedish army motto

It is remarkable to observe just how many software-based systems have been deployed over the past decade or so. It also worth dwelling for a moment on how much we all rely on them. Most people are painfully aware of what happens when supermarket checkout or flight booking systems go down. Less visible, however, are the legion systems that support many a company's operations – those that maintain the payroll, generate and issue the bills, dispatch the orders and keep customer information (Software's Chronic Crisis, 1994).

To a large extent it is these less visible or glamorous systems that we rely on the most. They perform many of the basic processing functions required by any organization. Because of this, they tend to be well established (this is a common euphemism for 'old' or 'decrepit but too costly or difficult to replace') and they are often taken for granted. It is by virtue of their fundamental importance that these systems remain unaltered over the years.

Many organizations have an operational system base that has been built up over several decades. It will probably consist of all flavours, ranging from assembly language programs running on an old mainframe through to client/server applications running on the latest hardware.

The trouble is that they are rarely independent – they usually do complementary jobs, have to work together and form but two links in an organization's overall value chain. For instance, the data in older systems is often needed for the effective operation of the newer ones.

So they all have to work together and keep working together. The heart of the problem is that (at least) one of them is getting on in years and is getting rather difficult to maintain. Another is complex to manage and still dogged by the teething problems that afflict any new technology.

The basic 'building block' technologies that help in coping with evolution and integration have been explained in Chapters 4 and 5. The way in which they can be used to provide effective distributed systems has also been covered. However, constructing real systems from the components and principles built up so far raises another set of issues. In anything other than a completely 'green field' environment a number of ugly practicalities intrude.

This chapter considers some of the problems that arise and how they can be solved. Given the almost infinite variability of real world challenges, this chapter concentrates on the advisory rather than the prescriptive. The bad news is that the devil is in the detail (this is the U.S. version of the phrase – for some reason, the common UK version appears to be 'God is in the detail') when it comes to integrating a new-style system into the *status quo*. Fortunately, this can be set against the fact that many people have faced this problem before and there is a wealth of practical experience that can be drawn on. What follows later in this chapter is a condensed helping of what others have done to find a way forward. First, however, we look briefly at how we got here in the first place.

6.1 Differentiation explained

There are a number of reasons for the current situation, many of which have been caused by a very dynamic marketplace – the consequence of the progress outlined in Chapter 2. Some of the more important forces that are driving the sort of fragmentation described above are:

- Fast-evolving technology. The whole area of computing is a very fast-moving one. New ideas are coming on stream every year and today's state-of-the-art technology is likely to be tomorrow's item from the ark. An already rapid rate of change in computing is further complicated by its convergence with other technologies from which it was recently quite distinct. It is now very difficult to separate distributed computing from software engineering and high-speed networking. All three play a central role in delivering real distributed systems, yet each is a significant specialism in its own right.

- More on offer every year. The basic component parts of computer systems – processors, memory and the like – shrink in price and grow in capability every year. It is not that long since major concerns in engineering a computer system were its memory usage and processing requirements. These issues have become less important with the dramatic year-on-year advances in computer performance. Naturally enough, people want to take advantage of the best and most up-to-date technology.

So, with major advances on offer at low cost, it is not surprising that shelf-lives are short in the world of computing equipment. The trouble is that some system elements are somewhat slower to change. In particular, it is not easy to keep the software (the term software covers data and processes here) that controls complex or large-scale transactions (such as those mentioned at the beginning of this chapter) in step with a frequently changing platform. Upgrading the computers may look an attractive proposition but there can be hidden costs in integration. As with icebergs, there is an attractive and visible 10 per cent, a hidden and potentially destructive 90 per cent.

- Increasing pressure/desire to automate. People have, to some extent, become accustomed to 'computer magic'. They have seen the immense potential in the likes of the World Wide Web and have used computer systems that provide intuitive and friendly interfaces to complex utilities. Furthermore, they have come to expect that networked software will actually work first time, every time (this contrasts sharply with the incredulous reaction, of only a few years ago, when a software system actually did what it was supposed to do).

In short, customer confidence and expectation is now high enough to want the facilities they have on their own PC, their local LAN and the rest of the world, to be as one.

One particular aspect of this has become known as 'business process re-engineering'. This involves using (or, more often, bending) an organization's operational systems to support directly some part of its business process. So, for instance, a customer database would be treated as a component to support a business process (for example 'dispatch orders') rather than a system in its own right.

The real point is that this approach (and attendant expectation) sometimes makes change more difficult in that it mixes data and process. In this case, the order dispatch process is likely to be a lot more volatile than the organization's customers. The hope is that the support systems will be amenable to rapid and very flexible reconfiguration. The reality may turn out to be somewhat different.

- Need to build bigger, better. A follow-on from a couple of the above points is the belief that you can do it all if you have enough machines and programmers. There are many instances of 'total solutions', especially in the recent history of information technology (IT) projects (Norris *et al.,* 1993).

They tend to share two characteristics. First, a design that closely couples all existing data and processes. Second, the fact that nearly all were abandoned (usually after much expense) because they could not provide the flexibility to cope with an ever-changing world.

It would be unfair to suggest that the chosen design approach was directly responsible for subsequent failure – poor requirements, project management and variable funding all have an effect. Even so, the often overlooked aspects of complexity, scale and availability of data has sunk many a 'total solution'.

- Supplier lock-in. One last point that should not be forgotten here is that the marketplace has many players and that they need to differentiate their products if they are to compete. In many instances, vendors of computing equipment go to some lengths to ensure that their offerings interwork with those from other suppliers (Appendix A catalogues a number of 'standardization' bodies led by suppliers). Even so, there is (and always will be) heterogeneity in the distributed computing world. The onus of integrating the components, albeit compatible ones, lies with the user.

In addition to these market changes, the nature of the systems themselves has changed. The individual applications introduced in the 1970s have become more and more integrated. It is no longer acceptable to have isolated packages for word processing, mail and programming. Users (and this covers everyone from the desk clerk to the CEO) want access to all manner of information through the machine on their desktop (Atkins and Norris, 1995).

The general drift from monolithic platforms (that is the large mainframe secreted in the computer room) to more distributed options has not helped in realizing this aim. Few organizations run all of their applications on one platform. They tend to mix and match products from a number of vendors. And this diversity of platforms has driven a diversity of applications. The typical computing infrastructure for a large organization now comprises a number of domains of machine types, each running vendor-specific security, mail, database, access and other applications.

To provide the user's ideal of a coherent set of computing resources, you need to talk over all of these domains, pass information from one so that it can be used by another and so on. This is quite viable when only part of the overall problem is addressed. Tactical solutions (a true tactical solution is a short-term expedient designed as a step on a grand plan – in practice, it is often just a convenient fix that puts off the dreaded moment of evolution planning) that provide part of the answer are frequently implemented, pending a more enduring, strategic solution. Frequently, however, there is no convenient time to retrench – the pressure to deliver even an 'intensive care' solution is paramount. And so, the tactical solutions pile up on top of the legacy mountain, with the strategic options that are needed to exit the loop always in abeyance.

All of this has, in many cases, given rise to a layer of complexity, designed to fool users into thinking that they have a homogeneous system in front of them. And there is a problem that arises from this illusion. This is the plethora of conversion routines required to reconcile data-structures and naming conventions between different applications protocol convertors and so on, that are put in place to get everything to look as if it is working in unison. These pieces of 'system glue' are fine for the present setup but compound the task of further integration. By and large, the fixes, work-rounds and special configurations tend to be undocumented.

In toto, it has reached the stage where everything needs to talk to everything else to work properly but this is achieved in a piecemeal fashion. And, in practice, this means that a large part of the introduction of a new system is concerned with its integration with the many flavours of what already exists. But what, exactly, is meant by the term 'integration'? That is what we now aim to find out.

6.2 Integration explained

It would be nice to give a precise definition of integration. One that inspires confidence that a soundly based set of techniques to deal with it will be following shortly. For all of the reasons given in the previous section, however, it would be wrong to even aspire to this at the moment. That is not to say that it is a lost cause. Yes, it will be messy – a consequence of what is really in place – but some progress can be made towards systematic integration.

First, then, a working definition. In the context of computer systems, integration covers all aspects of getting the myriad components of a real system to work together such that it is fit for the purpose. In practical terms, this is just as difficult as mathematical integration – and considerably less well defined.

To some people, integration is achieved as soon as a number of components have been connected – rather like welding together two halves of a car. The result is about as satisfactory in both cases. To others, the job is not complete until there is seamless interworking between all of the various parts. Perhaps the best way to characterize the term, however, is to explain some of the challenges that ensure that the life of a systems integrator is never dull.

- Dealing with existing installations. This is usually called 'coping with legacy', is caused by technical evolution outstripping ability (or willingness) to build new systems and is characterized by 'graunching' – the use of excessive force – to make a collection of hardware, software, data and networks all work together.

Legacy has been accumulating for long enough that risk, cost and complexity are rising month on month. Research indicates that around half the companies in the high-technology sector have over 15 years' worth of legacy. The good news (although this is arguable) is that the nadir of legacy is past. Awareness of the issue and the development of the concepts explained in Chapters 4 and 5 have done a lot.

- Stovepipe designs. There are myriad choices to be made in designing a system. Some of them are internal and, although they may affect performance or efficiency, they tend not to have wider impact. Other choices are critical to the way in which the system can work in the wider community. In particular, the general structure of the system – where the data, the application logic and the presentation logic reside – is vital to its openness.

In the past, each computer vendor has tended to build systems their own way, a fact celebrated in a variety of proprietary architectures. There are a number of monolithic applications and architectures that work well – up to a point. As soon as you try to (or have to) work with applications that do not fit this structure, there are potential problems.

By way of illustration, the use of a personal computer (PC) as an X Window System Terminal (see Section 5.6.2) leads to the use of a very low-level protocol between client and server. This requires high bandwidth to work and usually provides poor response times for the user. It does work but it is far from ideal.

There are other cases of mismatched structure that cause implementation difficulties. SQL-squirter products, such as Oracle forms, move a lot of the application functionality onto the PC client (see Section 5.6.4). This means that an SQL database query protocol has to be provided between client and server. This factor, if compounded with other similar requirements, would quickly sink the system in complexity.

In both cases, extra effort is required to get two ends of the same, supposedly cooperating, system to work together. This general problem is illustrated in Figure 6.1. Two systems that need to interwork are shown as autonomous 'stovepipes' that have to reduce interactions to an unnecessarily low level.

Figure 6.1 represents a situation illustrated later – that of trying to get differently architectured systems to cooperate on a single task. In an ideal world, this would be achieved by accessing the necessary resources from each system via common processes. In practice, however, this can demand a lot of specialist crafting.

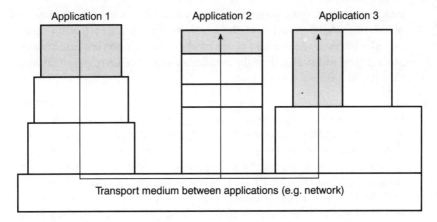

Figure 6.1 Stovepipe systems – communication, the long way round.

- Multiple access requirements. Despite all the changes that have happened in the computer industry over the years, one of the few things to remain constant is the need to know the identity of the user who is requesting service, and for this information to be gathered most systems require the user to provide their name plus a password before access is allowed. This process of authentication is usually referred to as 'logging-on' and normally takes place when the user first connects to the computer.

  The problem is that further logons are then required if the user wishes to access other computers or services. In a distributed environment, with information and computers all over the place, multiple logons are required nearly all the time. The basic problem is compounded when user-codes and passwords are not coordinated across computers leaving the poor old user trying to remember dozens of name/password combinations in a variety of formats.

  There are ways of providing an authentication scheme that operates in a multiprocessor, client/server system (see Section 5.5.2). The trouble is that each legacy system has to accommodate this scheme ... and there is always unwillingness to change from the *status quo*.

- Closed interfaces. Most established computing systems are set up to do things in a particular way. This includes the way in which they talk to peripherals, control user access and interconnect to other systems. Yet most real-world computer environments are composed of a variety of diverse elements of different vintages and from different manufacturers.

  Given the desire to organize a computing environment so that it looks like a single resource, there has to be some provision of routing and translation services so that a user can see what is out there and can negotiate services, wherever they originate. People do not want to change the way they do things, however – not surprising when you consider how much time and money they have invested in their system. So interfaces tend to remain closed with each requirement being handled with a different tactical work-around. The accumulation of these make maintenance increasingly difficult, thus fuelling the desire to rework.

- Diverse data. Information that once resided on one machine is now scattered to the four winds. Typically, a customer's identification will reside on one system, their current orders will be in a separate physical and logical location and their market behaviour will be somewhere else again. Yet all these pieces of data may need to be assembled for a particular session and often need conversion functions before they can be brought together in a usable format. The problem is akin to a network composed of many subnetworks, all connected with a plethora of protocol convertors. What the system user wants, and views as a single logical entity, may have to be gathered from many diverse sources. This point is worth labouring a little as it is generally the data that binds systems together, not its electrical or logical interfaces. Explicit plans for data integration are an essential part of coping with legacy.

A corollary on this point is that any two systems with similar data (variants born of a common ancestor, perhaps) may well disagree. With information becoming the currency of many businesses, consistency of data becomes increasingly important. Getting data formats agreed and cleansing of data held can be a huge task. And not cheap either – even at 10 cents a record, the cost to many companies would be very significant.

- The assumed user. Just as there is no such thing as a green field for new computer systems, neither is there a typical system user. It is unrealistic to assume that anyone will be sitting at a terminal at any particular time or for any assumed duration. Applications that take a long time to assemble even the most complex record will not be perceived as helpful. Neither would a UK-based query that has Eastern Standard Time embedded in the response.

Distribution brings with it all manner of access patterns. Add to this the host of (sometimes long forgotten) configuration files, macros and the like that cause an application to execute in a particular way and there is considerable potential for unwitting error.

One particular aspect of the assumed user that is becoming more prevalent is that more non-human users are accessing systems. The use of robots, knowbots and data miners has shot up over the past few years. They tend to hit systems very hard, with high volumes and rates of transactions. The need to extract information from vast pools of data will, inevitably, increase the use of these intelligent agents.

- Loose and tight integration. The extent to which two systems or applications have to work together should determine the way in which they are integrated. Some applications need to appear as a natural extension of the systems to which they have been added. Others can be added as a separate facility. The former (for example an address-driven switch) requires tight coupling, which, for all its attractions, usually requires a considerable amount of low-level work and, potentially, reduces future flexibility. The latter (for example file-based interactions) may entail extra user configuration and may be seen by those users as collections of piecemeal elements but there is at least some scope to change a part of the system without resorting to wholesale redesign. The choice of integration style needs to be carefully considered.

The bottom line that follows from all the above is that the integrator just has to cope with all these difficulties. Some of them may turn out not be a problem, either by chance or by design. Others, almost inevitably, will be.

With around 50 per cent of all operational computer systems between 10 and 15 years old, so legacy is something that the integrator has to live with. This section has, at least, highlighted some of the areas where integration difficulties are likely to lie and what issues need to be attended to. Later in this chapter we explain some of the strategies that can be adopted in dealing with the problems raised here. To put all of these issues into context, it is worth identifying two key roles. These are:

- The designer. This role is concerned with specifying a system that works together as well and as fast as needs dictate. Designers need to take all of the above issues into account but should be more driven by the concepts introduced in the previous chapters. The key objective of this role is to design with integration in mind.

- The integrator. This role is more focused on delivering the specified system so that it works *in situ*. Integrators need to validate and verify the designers' work by showing that it operates within actual environmental constraints. The key objective of this role is to deploy the system so that it operates as desired.

Usually, these two roles are separate people (or groups of people). In practice, they need to work closely together. In both cases, there are some specific guidelines – these come later. First, however, we reinforce the points made so far with an example.

6.3 The beleaguered user

As already indicated earlier in this chapter, it would be virtually impossible to explain what is involved in integration through one example – the topic is too diverse and ill-formed to be treated so poignantly. In view of this, the following example aims to illustrate the challenge facing the integrator by focusing on just one aspect of putting together a practical distributed system from diverse components.

It should be apparent from the range of design decisions that need to be considered in this constrained example just how much planning and analysis would be required to meet more wide-ranging needs.

Here we look at a case where a new site (see Figure 6.2 on p. 172) is to be added to an established set of computing resources (see the top left segment of Figure 6.3 on p. 174). The new site is intended to provide a focus for the existing distributed computing network and is designed as a client/server installation. (The example is based directly on a real project that aimed to explore the practicality of various strategies for integrating disparate computing elements. As with most projects, the tactical was usually preferred to the strategic.) The major requirements to be met in adding the new site were:

- to allow easy access to all data held on the various systems currently being used;

- to minimize disruption to the existing facilities;

- to preserve system security.

It should be fairly apparent that there is some tension between the first and last of the above requirements. Ease of access often implies lack of security. In this instance, the value of data held on the systems was very high and security was seen to be the prime driver. The challenge facing the integrator, therefore, was to meet the other requirements without compromising it.

Given this background, we now turn to its solution. Perhaps the first thing to note is that there is a potentially heavy usability penalty with the variety of information sources distributed across this network. This lies in the fact that each requires (usually) a separate user/host session and proof of identity. A security overhead that impeded user access to all of the information they required would not be acceptable. Some trade-off between restriction and responsiveness has to be designed.

The usual way of implementing the security requirement is to force the user to declare their user name (the identity that the computer recognizes as referring to that user) and password (known only to the user and the computer). The computer checks the password is correct before allowing the user to gain access. This authentication process always takes place when the user first connects to the computer with further logons required if the user wishes to access particular applications, services or specific disk areas.

The trouble with this is that users of the system need to access a large (and ever-increasing) number of computers in order to gain the information they need to do their job. So their perception of repeated authentication changes from one of acceptance to one of frustration as they have to go through it so many times. This problem is compounded when (as is typically true in practice) user-codes and passwords are not coordinated across the computers, leaving the user to remember half a dozen or more user name/password combinations. The *coup de grace* comes when local security practices require each password to change every month or so! (This is typical but suboptimal. A three-month cycle is better in practice.)

The advent of client/server computing actually compounds this problem as the user no longer knows which computer is hosting the service that has been requested. Also, the inevitable consequence of more and more information being held on a range of different systems is that there will be an increasing frequency of connection requests.

An example of this might be the provision of a directory look-up service. In our new system, a dialogue starts from the client side which allows the user to formulate a query (tell me about Neil Winton?). It then automatically connects to the server that hosts the most relevant database, identifies the user (logs-on) to the server, sends the query, receives any replies and displays them to the user. Finally, at the end of the session it disconnects from the server.

This way of working has the benefit of only using the server resources when they are actually required (rather than holding open a session until the user logs-off from the client) but does mean that the authentication process has to be performed for each of the separate queries that the user initiates.

By way of contrast, a straightforward connection under the control of the user (who has to use a terminal emulator to access the database) allows repeated queries during a session but holds the resources for the duration of that session.

For a simple query, there is little to choose between the client/server and direct access options. If the user's query is more complex, the picture is different. Let us say that you are trying to build a report that includes financial information, some narrative and some performance statistics. The first item resides on a remote spreadsheet, the second is locally stored text and the third is in the form of a set of graphs maintained by regional offices. In terms of the above choice, we are looking at multiple sessions or lots of client/server interactions.

As hinted at earlier, it can be taken for granted that the existing systems in this example are unlikely to undergo very much change – the main responsibility for secure access to them lies with the external user. The external user here is taken to be a user's terminal coupled to a processor unit working in client/server mode. So, to provide a structure that allows computers of different types to work together requires you:

- to provide an architecture that supports a single logon for user access to a variety of information systems without compromising the existing level of security;
- to hide the details of the network from the user requesting service, in much the same way that the World Wide Web shields the user from details of the route taken to get from one page to the next;

● to develop front-end integration facilities that allow information from a number of disparate sources to be compiled as the user wishes.

The above are but a few of the key challenges that the system integrator has to meet. They derive from (and are a refinement of) the requirements stated at the start of this section. And so to a way for the designer to at least start tackling this problem.

Let us start by taking a look at the new bit of the system. As already stated, it is designed to be a client/server setup based around a local area network (LAN) - in Figure 6.2 the clients are on the left, the servers on the right. This is a fairly well-understood arrangement and some of the more standard elements (for example the file server) are not shown. The critical components that do need to be high-lighted in Figure 6.2 are:

1   The Access Control System (ACS)

2   The communications facilitator (Comms)

These are the elements that have been added to meet the requirement for a secure single logon to a variety of information sources. Taking each of these elements in turn:

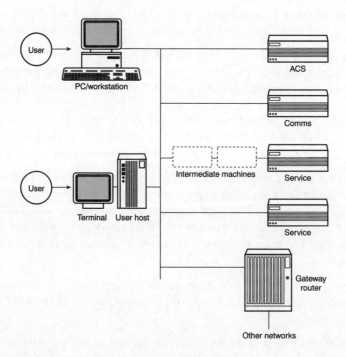

Figure 6.2 The local resources.

- The access control system controls access between the client and any of the services that it needs. This can be achieved by the issuing of authentication tickets that guarantee the identity of the user (this approach is embodied in the DCE's security technique, Kerberos, explained earlier in Section 5.5.2). In practice this strategy requires that both the client and the destination service be made 'aware' of, and can deal with, such tickets.

  In a network where more than one type of access controller is used, as may be the case when multiple 'levels' of security are implemented, it would be necessary to ensure that the client requests the correct type of ticket if the destination service is to understand it. For this example, one ticket type is enough.

- The communications facilitator is the collective name for the other components that are needed by the process of a client gaining access to a service. These include the availability of services and where they can be obtained from on the network, the type of authentication ticket that the service requires, how that ticket is to be presented to the service (ASCII, binary, with preamble and so on), the type of client required to connect to the service and information on the front-end integration script to run (for example to filter out intermediate screens or connection messages).

  Access to the communications facilitator would not require an authentication ticket since its services will be required in order for a user to gain the first tickets. Information about which services are available for use by particular individuals would have to be implemented as a particular service on the network since the identity of the user would be needed.

This covers the key elements at the new site to enable effective integration. Let us now take a look at the wider picture – the new site and the legacy with which it needs to work.

The top left of Figure 6.3 represents the new site (the collection of personal computers, workstations and servers linked by a local area network, as already described). The other domains in the figure are the various legacy systems. Each has its own specific characteristics.

The IBM mainframe in the bottom right is the source of customer records. The machine serves a set of dumb terminals and is protected with a proprietary remote access security facility (RACF).

The VMS environment shown on the top right (this refers to an operating system popularized on Digital's VAX and MicroVax computers (see Chapter 2)) is the source of project and finance information. It is a distributed system in its own right and has several levels of authentication that the user has to clear before getting access to all the data they could want.

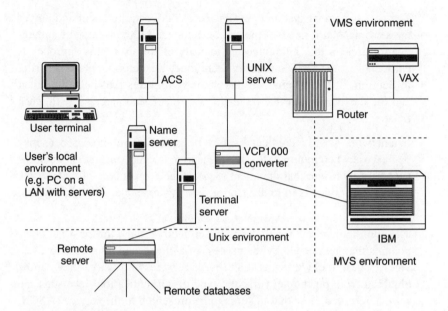

Figure 6.3 The separate enclaves in a real distributed system.

The UNIX environment in the bottom left corner has minimal access restrictions and is used to import various pieces of market data.

Altogether, the system illustrated in Figure 6.3 has all the perils that the integrator has to face. Each of the systems domains is a separate stovepipe but the user expects to have uniform access across the whole thing. Some of the interfaces are proprietary, data formats vary and there is a range of operational and deployment issues undefined.

So what has to be done to get it all working as per the stated requirement? There are several key areas:

• Connections. Since the VAX enclave is on a LAN, the connection to the new site can readily be effected with a router. Getting to the IBM is a little more difficult but can be achieved via a data link over the public telephone network. The link is connected to a specialist communications controller which also connects to the Ethernet LAN. This is a very useful piece of equipment since it behaves as a TCP/IP device on the LAN but looks like a 3270 cluster controller on the modem side (that is to the IBM machine) and also converts 3270 protocols to VT100 in the process.

Specialist devices such as this can be a tactical godsend. In this instance it made connection between the IBM and the LAN easy and avoided the problem of having more than one emulator built into the Telnet client on the PC. The point, however, is that it provided a tactical fix here and deferred the need for a more strategic solution. Nonetheless, the aim of this section is to illustrate reality by exposing what really happens, rather than an idealized view of what should happen.

- Access. In the above, the user terminal was equipped with a Telnet client (a virtual terminal emulator with TCP/IP networking) running on a PC. This client had to be modified to understand ACS tickets and to send them to the required host, thus performing the logging-on function. This client type is common to many platforms and enables connection to each of the legacy systems in the above network. There is, therefore, basic access to any applications or services that have been modified so that they are aware of authentication tickets

- Unified view. The ultimate aim of the exercise described here was to provide a user with secure and easy access to a range of information. To achieve this, the modified client was constructed so that remote resources were seen by the user as extra icons on the screen. This allowed a straightforward process from the user's point of view to be easily carried out. For instance, to incorporate information held on the IBM, the user only had to open their local spreadsheet application (Figure 6.4). And then select the relevant icon for accessing remote data (Figure 6.5).

This would set in motion an interchange of tickets between the user's PC and the remote mainframe. This would all be taking place without the user having to break off to identify and validate him or herself. The required information would be incorporated into the user's work, ready for subsequent processing and the import of more remote information, if required (see Figure 6.6).

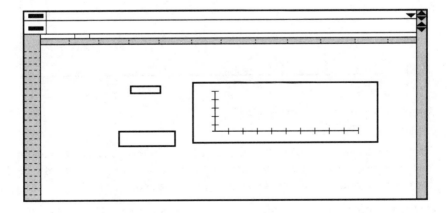

Figure 6.4 Local information.

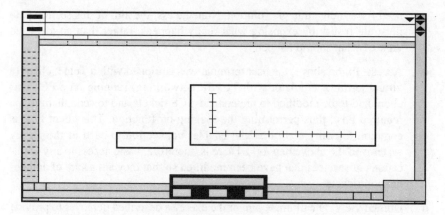

Figure 6.5 Direct access to a remote machine.

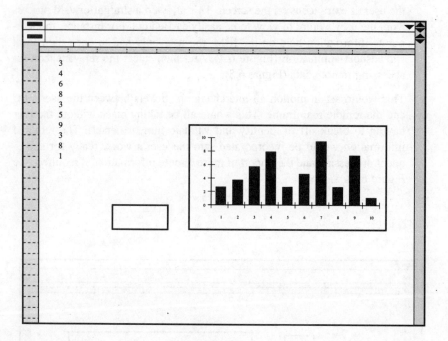

Figure 6.6 Incorporation of remotely held data.

This example majors on one aspect of integration – in this case, the key requirement was easy, secure access. As indicated earlier, there are a number of other important integration challenges that may have to be addressed.

Awareness of the issues is a first step in dealing with them. The practicalities, however, usually defy any sort of prescription or recipe. Indeed, some of the choices made in the above example were convenient and may result in more integration problems further down the line.

Over the next couple of chapters, we give some guidelines that should ease future integration. For the illustration given in this chapter, there are a number of lessons that only really come through experience. Some of the more useful in this instance were:

- Each type of target machine (MVS, VMS, UNIX) requires the ACS ticket to be presented to it in a different way. This was owing to the way the authentication had been implemented and the method of connecting to the machine. The UNIX implementation actually modified the standard login mechanism and so it could cope with a binary ticket that was passed to it as the first piece of data after the connection had been established.

  The MVS and VMS implementations, however, both required that the ticket be passed as character strings since the machines expected nothing more than a fixed function terminal at the end of the connection. The MVS system had the ticket passed as part of the initial connection request while the VMS system required that the user-code be sent as the first piece of information once the connection had been established and then the ticket. The devil is in the detail!

- An implication of the first point is that it is usually necessary to know the type of machine providing a service in order to present the ticket in the correct format and at the right time. A further implication is that if user-codes (or user names) are not standardized across an organization, as is typically the case, the user-code to use at a particular system needs to be known. Since the user is too shielded from this, some sort of look-up table needs to be provided. It would be easier to have standard user-codes across an organization – easy to say, difficult to implement.

- There are many ways of retrieving data from distributed sources. The details of this were glossed over in the above example but this is an area that usually requires more attention than it gets.

  One option is to minimize the level of integration by making the user responsible for retrieval as soon as the remote source is accessed. Supplanting this level of interaction may require specific details of the format and location of data on the remote machine. There is therefore a balance that needs to be struck between flexibility for future extensions and fulfilment of the specific current need.

- Following on from the above point, there is a need for flexibility in the architecture to allow for the automatic access of fallback services in the event of a failure – in this example the role is performed by the communications facilitator and so, in general terms, the clients only need to be aware of all the communications facilitators available for use.

- Many of the management processes have yet to be fully thought through – for example if one-time passwords are used in conjunction with a PIN, does the PIN need to be changed regularly in order to maintain security? What should be done with all the auditing records and so on. There are a host of management, maintenance and administration details that have to be put in place to support whatever flavour of solution is implemented.

- Without careful systems planning, protocol converters tend to abound. A little time invested in analysing and structuring the information to be passed from one domain to the next is usually worthwhile. For instance, a basic character-passing facility can be used with a variety of formatters to replace a large number of specialized converters. This point (raised earlier as the 'tactical solution today with strategic jam tomorrow' approach) is not a one-off decision but rather a whole set of issues, each of which needs to be duly considered.

- The match of communications links between the various elements of the distributed system needs to be thought out. There is little point in buying unnecessary bandwidth from a public network operator unless both client and server are capable of taking advantage. The chosen style of interaction between two distributed machines needs to be taken into account. In general, performance issues have been glossed over in the example. In practice, this can be a vital factor.

- Most distributed systems will require changes to the existing as well as the new parts. These need to be socialized as soon as possible as even the best solution will not work unless it is implemented system-wide.

- The front end that is presented to the user needs, inevitably, to adapt to information from a variety of different sources. Some facilities (for example to cut and paste between different windows) should be provided across all applications. The basic aim here is that user operations should be consistent, predictable and reproducible.

- Finally, as a general rule, it is worthwhile putting a strategic front end onto even a tactical solution. This provides early feedback on the overall system suitability and minimizes user reaction to any subsequent, behind the scenes changes.

This list could be extended as the range and variety of pitfalls in real systems integration is impressive. The aim here, however, is to illustrate the problem – not to proffer an all-embracing solution. Many integration tasks have to be dealt with as one-off challenges; the result of earlier design decisions not suited to the current need. This reinforces the need to get things right at an early stage.

We now move away from the specific back to the more general. Abstracting from the instances in the example, we aim to provide a set of basic principles for integration. In the next section, we look at the basic strategies that can be adopted and then, in the following section, how they can be implemented.

6.4 The good citizen

Given that you have to live with history, there are choices in how you deal with this. Here we explain some of the strategies for integrating systems, from the basic fallback of screen-scraping upwards. Each strategy has its pros and cons. Which one is adopted should be considered on the basis of overall business benefit. After all, there is little sense in elegantly integrating a system just before it is removed from service! Likewise, a cheap and cheerful patch to access important information may well prove to be a false economy.

Anyway, here are five basic strategies that might be considered for coping with basic system integration. There may be others but those below illustrate most of the cases that occur in practice:

- Scrap. Throw it away. Build a new one if you need it – it will be cheaper and easier in the long run. This strategy has to be driven by commercial judgement and based on the longevity and importance of the legacy system balanced against cost of replacement or alteration. The judgement of replace or reuse is a complex one, well covered in the literature on business planning (Ward *et al.*, 1993). Even so, the operational cost of an inappropriate or ineffective system is rarely counted.

- Trap. Keep the legacy system but avoid perpetuating its use. In this case, integration all takes place within the client that uses the legacy system. This could be a mix of screen-scraping (as the name suggests, this entails the retrieval of data from the point at which it is presented to the user; even a small change in the screen layout means that the screen-scraping has to be revised), file transfer and so on. It traps the client with the legacy system, making it expensive to build and difficult to change. The likely next step is to scrap both legacy system and the client that allowed it to remain operational a little longer. The downside of this option is that it may result in a bigger problem later on.

- Map. A front end is provided to the legacy system. This is the first level of real integration (as opposed to the two strategies described above – they simply avoid, delay or work around the problem). In this strategy, a proxy interface is provided (usually hard-coded in a server) to allow clients to communicate with the legacy system. Again, techniques such as screen-scraping are required (usually).

- Wrap. As above with the legacy system also being re-engineered to some extent. The aim here is to pull the legacy system apart and reassemble it into more maintainable chunks. This is some sort of attempt to integrate the legacy system, usually by reworking the more problematical areas (or, at least, easy to change) areas.

● Unwrap. The legacy system is fully integrated. This follows on from the above, with the legacy system being completely reworked to allow a client direct access. In effect, the old system is rebuilt to modern architectural guidelines.

There are methods and techniques that could be explained for each of these: business analysis methods to place value and strategic importance on systems, tools that can be used for screen-scraping (for example Desqview-X) and software suites for re-engineering (for example the Bachmann toolset). The main thrust of this text lies elsewhere, however, so these aspects will not be dealt with further. In any case, they merit lengthy coverage in their own right, mostly because they are not readily prescribed.

Figure 6.7 is a general view of the various types of legacy system that surround most new developments. The point here is that whatever strategy is adopted for interfacing, there are four main types of legacy function that need to be considered. These are:

1   User PCs, where each person tends to look after his or her own work and attend to individual security requirements. In terms of technology this group use OLE and the like to share information.

2   Systems administration, where specialist units are required to look after service and network management. The technology used here is guided by the network management forum (see Appendix A).

3   Information services, where a huge amount of data is collected in warehouses and these are managed to service routine reporting requirements (for example monthly sales returns).

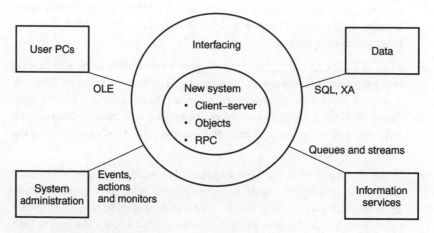

Figure 6.7 A general template for systems integration.

4   Data, which is similar to the above, with the exception that requests are *ad hoc* and need to be serviced quickly. Direct database queries (for example via SQL) and transaction processing are relevant here.

The aim from here on in is to look at ways of building distributed systems that can readily integrate without resorting to delicate surgery. So we now move on to give a few of the tried and tested tips for avoiding future legacy – separation of concerns, standard interfaces, parameterization and so on. – before giving some guidelines for planning the integration activity.

6.5 Right next time

This section focuses on the designer's role introduced earlier in the chapter. The aim is to highlight some of the more effective approaches for getting designs that can be integrated.

The first thing to say is that, to some extent, there is always going to be a problem: today's new system will be tomorrow's legacy. Even with the best planning in the world, systems from the 1960s are unlikely to fit readily with modern equipment. The variable that can be controlled, however, is the time it takes for a particular system to become legacy. This should very much be a conscious choice, taken in the light of local circumstance. It may be that freedom of action is so important that any attempt to constrain diversity is unacceptable. In this instance, systems can be purchased and developed to no set plan, the cost of subsequent integration (if, indeed, this is relevant) being accepted. The only observation to make here is that the anarchic approach should be selected and not happen by default!

For most enterprises, some form of control is seen as desirable. The rest of this section outlines the main areas where control can be exerted. A few of the choices in each instance will be mentioned. By and large, however, these are the primary subject of the rest of this book.

6.5.1 Get a strategy

This sounds rather grand but can be very straightforward. For instance, 'only buy IBM equipment' was a strategy adopted by many computer operations managers in the 1970s (for the very good reason that, at that time 'no one ever got the sack for buying IBM'). The key point about establishing a strategy is that it lays down some ground rules – usually in the form of a limited set of options for the purchaser, designer and planner.

An effective strategy can be driven by a number of considerations. It may be that a cross-company alliance motivates a particular choice, or a technical suitability may give rise to a preferred choice, or bulk discount from a particular supplier may win the day. Either way, the aim of a strategy should be to reduce overall (that is, whole-life) costs. And this can be achieved by defining, among other things:

- key design options that allow for future flexibility,
- technology choices that ease integration (see Section 6.5.3),
- purchasing considerations that minimize cost.

In practice, many of the organizations that have a strategy are driven either by purchasing requirements or by technical preference. Explicit integration strategies are few and far between. Indeed, in many instances, the cost of integration is considered as no more than a minor feature of stated strategy. The huge investment in computing infrastructure and the ever-accelerating rate of change is causing this balance to shift, however.

6.5.2 Define an architecture

This builds on the above in that it covers the 'how' as well as the 'what'. An enterprise architecture should go beyond stating intent – it should map out how systems are put together and which components are to be used. The level of detail tends to vary from one instance to the next. For example, the distributed systems architecture contained in the ANSA reference manual (ANSA, 1988) gives a host of formal concept definitions and object specifications.

In contrast, the more general 'three-tier' model of computing (usually attributed to the Gartner group (but difficult to say for sure as there does not appear to be a readily available reference to prove the matter!) provides a simple but elegant structure for system planning, as illustrated in Chapter 4.

Some organizations, especially large multinationals and information-intensive businesses, need to have their own, in-house enterprise architectures. In addition to cataloguing existing systems and showing how they are likely to evolve, they often provide design guidelines for developers. Many of the issues covered earlier in this chapter (such as the need for separation of presentation, application and data) are included, either as recommendations or as mandates.

6.5.3 Prescribe technology

There are many technology choices that can be made in constructing distributed systems and Chapters 4 and 5 should certainly have shed some light on the wonderful variety that is available! At some point, however, it is expedient to decide what the preferred set should be. For example there are two basic distributed processing technologies – remote procedure calls (RPCs) and transactional remote procedure calls (T-RPCs). The former is well suited to real-time applications and office automation, the latter is usually associated with data processing and batch applications.

Within each of the two basic categories, there is a further raft of technologies, for example for RPCs there is Sun's ONC, Microsoft's NT/RPC and so on, and for T-RPCs, there are Encina, Tuxedo and IBM's CICS. Time spent devising what you actually need and what constitutes a coherent set can be time very well spent. Once this is done, it becomes possible to constrain choices sensibly.

Diversity is nice but can be costly and (with the devil residing in the detail) is a good way of storing up problems for the future. Quite apart from being able to cope more easily with change, there is significant financial motivation in constraining choice (for example less evaluation, retraining, support and integration cost)

With a little informed planning, it is possible to avoid many of the integration blues and prolong the active life of a system. The authors know of at least one PDP-11-based system, introduced in the mid 1970s, still providing a worthwhile part of an organization's service.

There are certainly many options for building a distributed system – the length of Chapter 5 is testament to this. A reasonable set of decisions for one organization might be to opt for a three-tier structure with NT/RPC providing a PC client for the user terminals, NT advanced server on the mid-range server and an IBM mainframe running MVS with NT/RPC. Of course, this might be ideal in one circumstance, totally unsuitable in another. The key is to map out the route that best suits the needs of the enterprise. This is rarely easy but always worthwhile.

There are also a number of useful guidelines to inform appropriate choices. For instance, Spirit (an initiative to define consistent system profiles – see Appendix A) is one of a number of useful pointers.

6.6 Making it happen

So far we have concentrated very much on what to do to achieve integration, rather than on how to actually implement it, once you have something to integrate. In order to create operational distributed systems you need to attend to both. They are quite different in nature – the former is very much to do with strategic design and analysis, the latter is more focused on the organization and planning of testing. The one thing that both do have in common is that they are both far from extensively documented. The issues raised in this section are intended to apply to the integrator role, identified earlier in the chapter.

Effectiveness in this area seems to rely more on the competence and experience of individuals than on the diligent application of a well-tried and tested formula. Nonetheless, there are some procedural guidelines that have stood the test of practical application. This section outlines what they are and how they came to earn their repeated adoption.

Perhaps the first thing to do here is to highlight some of the known problems – those issues that tend to be either overlooked or take the most time and energy to resolve. Those that have proved to be most telling when looking back at many practical instances are:

- Overlooked data. Time and again, the integration of system data is not adequately heeded. The format, volumes and location of data all need to be attended to as part of the integration exercise. It is also important to discriminate static data from dynamic data and to consider how the data needed for test harnesses or generators can be created (in practice, this entails identifying, accessing, and using (perhaps, after modification) existing data).

- Timing skew. No matter what the plans say, the component parts of a distributed system always seem to arrive out of step with each other. Integration plans fixed around a set sequence of deliveries are doomed. Contingencies need to be prepared for.

- The traditional test ploy. Having independent teams to exercise a component and then pass it on to another team when it has passed its tests does not necessarily transfer well into integration testing. Ownership and familiarity are valuable when trying to integrate a component.

The above lessons of experience give some sort of shape to the guidelines needed to deal with them. Here are the main steps that have proved effective in minimizing the practical perils of integration:

1   Organization. There are various stages of integration that should be explicitly recognized and planned for. At the lowest level is basic interworking. The aim here is to get two components in contact with each other (for example a workstation that can ping a server). Once this is established, the next check is for data passing (c.f. the workstation logging-on to the server). At the next level is functional operation, where the two components can cooperate effectively on a task. Finally full system integration is achieved, when useful end-to-end testing can be carried out.

2   Roles. The whole aim of integration, that of having a set of components that work one with another, goes against the well-established testing independence philosophy (at least to some extent). Ownership matters when trying to integrate systems, as does continuing familiarity with the components to be integrated. In practice, traditional independent test roles need to be supplemented with a number of roles that provide continuity.

The most important of these are data ownership and function ownership. The former focuses on how data is created, moved and processed within the system. This role often 'owns' the systems data model and is responsible for test data. The latter is analogous and tends to own the functional specification.

3   Teams. Just as top level continuity is provided with specialist roles, so working level continuity can be effected by assigning ownership to test teams. This means that the same people carry a component through integration test and on to system test, rather than having separate integration and component test teams.

4   Scheduling. Given that some system components will be available before others, the main focus of integration testing should be on functional areas. This entails assembling the components (or stubs, drivers and test generators, if they are not available) required to provide a particular system function. This approach is sometimes described as 'side-to-side' testing and contrasts with 'end-to-end' in that it takes the business requirement's point of view, rather than that of the technical proof of concept. The important point is that components based on key system functions should be grouped as soon as possible to allow early localized tests to be performed.

5.   Support and procedure. The complexity of integrating distributed computing systems means that particular attention should be paid to the support and control of the whole exercise. In particular, formal procedures for configuration, change and problem control need to be established (Norris, 1995). In addition, handover criteria, exception conditions and quality gates are well worth defining. With, typically, a live target environment not available for trials, a considerable amount of effort is usually required in setting up a reference environment in which partial system builds can be evaluated.

These guidelines are no guarantee of success but they have proved to be effective in reducing risk. The overall approach is integration-led with functionality and data consistency being key drivers. This contrasts with (and, in reality, complements), the well-established independent test approach which deals, in the main, with internal consistency.

One final aspect of integration remains. Once a system has been designed, tested and assembled, it has to be deployed. The deployment of distributed systems to a waiting audience is what we now look at.

6.7 Legacy people

Just as there are legacy systems, so there are legacy people – those who have become so expert in one area that they cannot (or will not) move to another. In many cases, individuals want to dabble with new technology but they possess skills so rare that they are bound to the design, support or operation of a particular type of system, and as it becomes a legacy, so the associated person or people go the same way.

The basic problem is that many people stop evolving at a certain era. For many, open systems, client/server and the like have come as a surprise. This is not just prejudice, either. This can be nicely illustrated by paraphrasing two definitions of mythical airlines that have been conjured up within the computing fraternity:

- UNIX Express, where all the passengers bring a piece of the aeroplane and a box of tools with them to the airport. They gather on the tarmac, arguing about how the pieces should fit together. Finally, in frustration, they split into groups and build several different aircraft but give them the same name. Some of the passengers actually reach their destination, some do not. They all believe that they got there, however!

- MVS airlines, where the passengers gather at the airport to watch hundreds of technicians check this huge luxury plane that has 10 engines and 1000 seats. The claimed cost per passenger is lower than for any other plane, unless it is you who has to pay for the ticket. The pilot has never seen or flown any other type of aircraft.

The results of having legacy people, or rather, legacy thinking, in an organization are far reaching. It is not uncommon to find that new ways of doing things go against good practice that has been built up over years of working in the old way. For instance, the dyed-in-the-wool relational database designer might be very keen on normalizing the data to be stored. Experience has taught him or her that this is an important part of achieving the required speed of operation. This concern is not shared by the object database designer who focuses attention elsewhere. The rules of thumb that worked in one instance do not necessarily transfer to a similar activity when different technology is used.

As stated at the very start of this book, distributed computing requires many people to re-evaluate the way they look at the world. At the same time, much of their accepted wisdom needs to be re-examined (we take wisdom to be 'information with attitude'. Part fact and part opinion born of experience). Examples of this abound. For instance, when working to develop a new system with a national bank, the authors found that they had a support system that required all information to be fed through the existing (monolithic) processing system as another job type. It was assumed that the new application would be implemented as an addition to this existing load. The suggestion that the new application could be built faster and cheaper on a set of networked PCs, was greeted with blank stares. The option had never been considered, simply because none of the in-house team had any idea that it might be an option.

Active steps need to be taken to cope with this sort of thing. They are primarily the responsibility of organizational management, as the consequences of remaining still are:

1   New systems do not work, when designers and developers fail to capitalize on the sort of offerings that are available in the marketplace.

2   Deployed systems do not work properly, when field staff are not familiar with the technology adopted by the designers of the systems that they are expected to support.

3   Deployed systems are not used effectively, when users find that the system they are using does not accord with their model of the world.

Getting everyone into the same technology era is only one part of the story. Ownership is just as important as technology and people who regard a system as their own are not always open to change. It is not unknown for attempts to integrate two systems to degenerate into a battle between two competing approaches. Integration usually implies change and this will only be viable if the hearts and minds of the system owners are won over. The alternatives are to hack a solution around pockets of intransigence thereby storing up greater problems for the future, or to sit and plan the ultimate solution without ever moving towards its implementation.

Distributed systems are built by people so that other people can use them. The human element is central and persistent. It should be treated with as much importance as the technical and commercial aspects. Some of the key aspects that need to be attended to are:

●   Retraining in new skills. The software engineer has to know about communications technology and the telecommunications engineer has to appreciate computing concepts and software design methods.

●   Education and rotation. New systems should be developed with user and support engineers' involvement at the earliest possible time. Administration and management are two vital aspects of a distributed system (more of this later). Typically, neither is assigned priority.

●   Collaboration. No one can do it all these days. It is important to plan what is bought in, what is developed and what is outsourced.

Given the fast-moving and complex nature of distributed systems, it is far from easy to define a clear evolution path. This is as true for people as it is for the systems they use, build and maintain. Nonetheless, there is a real risk in being overly conservative and some measures to minimize this risk are required. The message of this section is that planning needs to cover people as well as technology, networks, software and systems.

6.8 Summary

Change is inevitable. Computer systems are far from immune and there is always going to be a mix of the old and the new in any organization, just like the furnishings in the average house. The consequence of this is that you either have to replace everything (which is usually prohibitively expensive) or blend the new items in with the old (which is tricky but manageable). The only trouble is that the home furnishings challenge of matching colour and style becomes a lot more complex when distributed computer systems are the object of attention.

The challenge is not one that can be shunned, however. There is little doubting the central role of computers in business these days. They are an essential element in supporting many of an organization's basic operations. Further to this, the way in which they are deployed is becoming a key differentiator as we enter the information age – a source of competitive advantage. So it is desirable to be faster and better than the rest.

The extent to which this can be realized, however, is constrained by history. There are now some 30 years' worth of computer systems in place. To a greater or lesser extent, they do the job for which they were built. In some cases, investment has been recouped. In many others, it has not. When newer ideas – such as a move to distributed systems – come along, the installed base has to be taken into account and this means that the new has to be integrated with the old. In practice, this is a major problem for many organizations.

This chapter explains some of the reasons why integration has become such a major issue. The challenges that have to be faced when designing in a constrained environment are explained and the key point illustrated with reference to a practical (that is, messy and inelegant) example. The main message that emerges from the example is that integration is a complex and, often, messy exercise for which there are precious few prescriptions. That said, there are some useful guidelines and strategies, borne of experience, that can minimize the challenge:

- Architecture. Akin to the building regulations that allow progress while preserving the beauty of an old town.

- Constraint. Paring down the range of options to an approved set; one that gives enough scope but not too much rope.

- Strategy. A broad direction to follow.

The last part of this chapter deals with the actions that can, and should, be taken to help integrate new systems into an established environment. This is not limited to the immediately apparent design aspects, but also covers the process and people issues. The former is essential in managing change consistently, the latter in ensuring that the right skills and experience are in place to allow effective and continuing evolution.

CHAPTER 7

Common concerns

'Tender-handed stroke a nettle,
And it stings you for your pains;
Grasp it like a man of mettle,
And it soft as silk remains' – Aaron Hill, *Verses Written on Window*

The fastest, cheapest, most secure and reliable components of a system are those that are not there. There can be a large amount of extra baggage associated with distributed design and technology. One of the greatest challenges in building and using distributed systems is to ensure that the baggage is packed with essential supplies rather than ballast.

In our discussions so far we have covered a wide range of different concepts, technologies and techniques. The extensive catalogue in the previous chapters may seem very daunting. All of these together provide a rich set of tools with which to construct a wide spectrum of distributed systems. However, technology is not an end in itself. For an implementor or an end user the make-or-break issues in distributed processing are often the so-called 'non-functional' aspects of the system – its overall qualities. This chapter highlights some of these issues and discusses how they can be addressed.

7.1 Security

The 'network is secure' is a popular, implicit assumption. However, for many users this statement is no more than a comforting myth which belies harsh reality. Distributed computing security would be so much easier if all communication was conducted via dedicated channels immune from eavesdropping and interference. Unfortunately such mechanisms are far too expensive for all but the most privileged or paranoid users. Modern shared local and wide area networks have brought highly productive communications capabilities to a huge number of users. They have also brought a whole new raft of security issues along in their wake.

7.1.1 What do we mean by security?

When people talk of computer or network security the image often conjured up is one of defence against pale-faced, teenage hackers hunched over their personal computers and modems in darkened rooms. (There are those in the computing field who deeply resent the usurping of the term 'hacker' – which was originally a term of respect and distinction applied to skilled programmers – as a label for miscreants. They have tried to encourage the use of the alternative term 'cracker'. Unfortunately that linguistic battle appears to have been lost some time ago.) The detection and prevention of such activities is indeed an aspect of computer security but it is by no means the whole story.

Computer security is about safeguarding the operation and preserving the integrity of a system in the face of accidental damage or deliberate attack. There are many aspects to security. Some of the most important are outlined briefly below.

Integrity

Maintaining the integrity of a system is largely a matter of ensuring that the system remains in a consistent state. This first requires the ability to prohibit unauthorized actions which might leave the system in an inconsistent state. It also means having the ability to detect if such inconsistencies occur and being able to return the system to a previous, known 'good' state. Most commonly this is done by taking regular snapshots or backups. Other techniques for maintaining integrity in the face of application or system failures were covered in Section 5.3.

Privacy

Privacy is about the ability to keep secrets. Nearly all multi-user computer systems have the ability to protect users' data from unauthorized access. The use of some form of read or write permission on files is a common example of this. Privacy can go beyond just data access permissions. For example, many secure systems can even stop you finding out which other users are logged-on to the same machine.

Identification and authentication

In order to enforce any sort of controls on the usage of a system or its resources a usual prerequisite is the ability to determine who (or what) is trying to make use of the system. This means that all consumers of services, be they human or machine, must be uniquely identifiable. Commonly this identity is expressed as a user name or user-ID.

A user could claim to have any valid identity known to the system. In some cases, where the user community is completely trustworthy, it may be sufficient to believe what the user says. However, most systems require that users prove their identity in some way. This process is known as authentication. The most familiar authentication process is that of specifying a user name and a secret password to logon to a system. Other more exotic examples of authentication mechanisms include fingerprint or voice recognition and 'smart-cards'. In nearly all cases the basic principle adopted is to prove your identity either by something you know (such as a password) or something you possess (such as a smart-card).

Establishing and verifying the identity of a remote party in a distributed system is not easy. Some of the ways in which this can be achieved were covered in Section 5.5.2.

Authorization

Having established a user's identity, authorization is the process of deciding exactly what actions that user is or is not allowed to perform. In many cases such decisions are fairly straightforward and it is a simple case that a user can either perform an operation or not. So, for example, rebooting the system is an operation that system administrators can perform but ordinary users may not. Similarly, authorization may be based on data being accessed rather than the operation being performed. So you might be able to access all of your records from a personnel database but nobody else's.

Some authorization decisions, however, can be far more subtle. There may be some operations that are permissible for a user in some circumstances but not in others. For example, someone handling account queries may be permitted to issue credits for amounts less than £100 whereas credits for greater amounts could only be issued by a supervisor. (In practice there would probably be an additional constraint that whatever the amount, a person couldn't issue credits against their own account!)

Auditing

If detection of wrongdoing were completely assured no one would ever drop litter or break the speed limit let alone commit more serious crimes. One of the main purposes of auditing is to provide accountability for and traceability of actions. Auditing is the process of collecting a record of actions (both successful and failed) and associating these actions with their instigators. The second purpose of auditing is to be able to detect anomalous activity which may indicate a threat to the integrity of the system as soon as possible – preferably before any real damage has been done.

Availability

People involved in computer security have been known to comment that the only truly secure computer system is one that is inside a steel vault, in a building patrolled by armed guards, with no connections to the outside world – and is turned off. While this wry observation may have an element of truth it is hardly helpful. The most elaborate mechanisms able to enforce authorization decisions completely, detect intrusion immediately and maintain the consistency of the system in the face of all attacks are worthless if the system cannot be used to perform its primary functions.

'Denial of service' attacks are those which do not breach the security mechanisms themselves but which render the system otherwise unusable. Examples of this include consuming all available disk space and flooding networks with junk traffic. An important aspect of security is, therefore, maintaining the availability of the system particularly in the face of attack.

7.1.2 What are the threats?

Before deciding upon the appropriate security measures to be applied to any system you must first assess the risks and threats to the system. By their very nature distributed systems tend to introduce a number of threats which do not apply to standalone systems. We cannot describe all the possibilities here but there are some common problems that afflict many systems. Most of them stem from a matter of trust, or rather lack of it, in the networks, systems and users 'out there'.

Eavesdropping

An obvious problem on open, shared networks is that of eavesdropping. Common local area network protocols make it very easy for any machine connected to a LAN to observe all the traffic on the network without leaving any trace. This process is often known as network sniffing. This is not necessarily a flaw in the network design. There are many occasions when sniffing is useful and valid, for example in gathering network usage statistics or in tracing problems.

Many people do not realize that every interaction they make with a remote system may be silently recorded and analysed by someone else connected to their LAN. This means, for example, that if you logon to a remote machine then your user name and password are very likely to be open for everyone else on the LAN to see. Another slightly more subtle example is the problem of remote file access. Files stored on a file server may be strongly protected and the file server might apply rigid access control checks. Unfortunately, as soon as the data from the files reaches the network it is open for all to see.

So far we have only talked about LAN sniffing. Wide area networks are not usually so susceptible to interception as WAN links employ more tightly controlled communications mechanisms such as lines leased from telephone companies. Telephone tapping is the world of espionage and is in a rather different league from LAN sniffing! However, this does not mean that wide area networks are immune from eavesdropping.

Many large networks, including the Internet itself, are composed of a large number of interconnected LANs and WANs. Each interconnection is made through some sort of gateway. Someone who gains control of a gateway can monitor all traffic that flows through it. The increasing use of radio links and cellular telephone technology as part of the mobile, extended wide area network opens up yet another opportunity for snooping.

Eavesdropping is not only a problem at the network protocol level. Electronic mail, for example, is often delivered using a store-and-forward mechanism. This can involve a series of transfers along a chain of intermediate routing machines. Each machine can read the contents of all messages that pass through it. For this reason many organizations adopt a policy of 'never write anything in an e-mail message that you would not be happy to write on the back of a postcard!'.

Connectivity

It is very useful for many organizations and individuals to have the ability to be able to connect to machines on the other side the world as easily as the machine down the corridor. The global Internet provides access to millions of machines and users. Corporate networks provide links to central resources from even the most far-flung outposts.

Total connectivity has become the order of the day. However, the down side of this is that there are many, many more places from which an attack on a system may originate. Most of the remote systems will be outside the control of local administrators. In this sort of environment the only safe assumption for providers of services is that everybody and everywhere outside the local environment is potentially hostile.

Related to the issue of connectivity is that of traceability. It can be very easy to hide your tracks in a complex web of systems and networks. Much of the difficulty in halting security breaches comes in tracking down the source of the problem in the first place. A very entertaining account of this sort of tracking being done 'for real' can be found in the book '*The Cuckoo's Egg*' (Stoll, 1989).

Forgery

There is great potential for forgery in a distributed environment. Counterfeiting paper currency may require a great degree of skill, painstaking work and access to specialist materials. It also carries a high degree of risk in printing and distributing the forged currency. Very little equipment, by contrast, is needed to produce a stream of fake bits and bytes. If the bits and bytes represent an electronic funds transfer between banks, the attraction of such forgery is obvious.

There are less serious examples of forgery. The U.S. government has become more accessible via the Internet in recent years. However, the ability to e-mail the President has resulted in a regular crop of spurious messages purporting to originate from president@whitehouse.gov!

Occasional forgery is probably an inevitable consequence of the openness that characterizes the Internet.

Unforeseen use

Many pieces of software get used in ways that their original designers never envisaged. 'Prototypes' get deployed for live use. A 'handy little utility' may be so useful that it suddenly spreads to a wide community of users. Such unforeseen usage can stress the original software beyond its limits. This problem is bad enough in a standalone environment. In a distributed system, where usage may be uncontrolled or uncontrollable, it can be disastrous.

An example of unforeseen, and malicious, use was the infamous 'Internet worm' (Spafford, 1988). (It is probably worth noting that while the potential of a 'network virus' that spreads from machine to machine in a distributed system has often been discussed, with the exception of the Internet worm, it does not seem to have happened much on a widespread scale ... yet.) Among other attack strategies this program exploited a number of design flaws in common remotely accessed services which were not robust enough to cope with unexpected input.

Unforeseen use is not only a threat in providing potential unauthorized access to a system. It is a threat to the availability of a system if some component becomes overused and overloaded. Without the ability to monitor and control usage this will always be a danger.

Complexity

Complexity is the enemy of security. In any complex system it is easy to over-look things which might compromise the overall security. The potential failures which might harm the integrity of the system multiply with increased complexity.

Distributed systems are almost inherently more complex than their standalone counterparts. At the most basic level there are more components involved, both hardware and software. The distribution technology itself can introduce further layers of complexity and potential security weaknesses. Einstein's exhortation to 'make things as simple as possible – but no simpler' applies as much here as in any other field.

Another aspect of complexity is its effect on users of the system. If a system is overly difficult to use then people will very likely find ways around the com-plexity – perhaps by taking unnecessary risks. If it is too hard to understand then the maxim that 'foolproof systems usually underestimate the ingenuity of the average fool' comes in to play!

In a sense simplicity can be an enemy on occasions too. It is all too easy to choke a network when someone can unintentionally send a 2Mb file to 5000 users simultaneously at the touch of a button!

7.1.3 Tackling the threats

So what can we do about the threats to the security of distributed systems? Fortunately, there are solutions to all of the problems we have raised. Some of these solutions come at a cost, others are more matters of good design and effec-tive training. Deciding on the appropriate cost to protect a given system has to be a key design decision.

Avoid the problem

It may sound trite but the easiest way to solve security problems is not to have the problems in the first place. You can avoid many difficulties by careful system design. For example, if you are processing large amounts of sensitive data then it is not sensible to continually transfer that data around an unsecured network. Instead it would be better to move the processing to the same place as the data rather than the other way around.

Security, like many other non-functional aspects of design such as manage-ability and performance, is not a 'bolt-on' extra which can be added to a system later. It usually has to be designed in from the beginning. So it is probably better to assume potentially hostile use rather than a completely trustworthy user community when designing a service for a distributed system. It is far easier to turn off controls that are not needed than to turn on those that do not exist.

Firewalls

One of the most effective and widely used strategies for preserving security is to use a 'firewall' system. Just as a real firewall is a specially built barrier which stops the spread of a fire within a building so a computer firewall tries to limit the extent of damage to computer security. The basic idea is as follows. Machines and networks on the 'inside' of a firewall are trusted, those 'outside' are generally untrusted. All communication between machines inside and outside goes through the firewall. It is the job of the firewall to monitor and filter all traffic passing through it and only to allow through known communication corresponding to certain well-defined services or to trusted external systems.

Machines on the inside of a firewall have a reasonable degree of trust of other machines within the firewalled network and so have to apply fewer controls themselves. Sections of the internal network may themselves employ firewalls to restrict the domain of trusted machines even further. This is illustrated in Figure 7.1.

Firewalls are most often applied at the level of network transport. However, the same idea is also applied to higher-level services with good effect. A service may be shielded by a *proxy* server. The proxy presents the same interface to the outside world as the real service but instead of performing the requested operations itself it filters out undesirable requests and only passes 'good' requests on to the real server. (Proxy servers have many other uses than just security screening. For example a WWW proxy server may fetch remote documents on behalf of clients and then add them to a local cache for subsequent faster access by other clients requesting the same information.)

Further detail on the subject of firewalls is beyond the scope of this book. A good starting point for further reading on the subject are the World Wide Web pages of Trusted Information Systems, Inc. (http://www.tis.com/) and the excellent book (Cheswick and Bellovin, 1994).

Encryption

Encryption is the process of encoding messages so that they cannot be understood without possessing the appropriate secret key to unlock them. There are many ways of performing data encryption. These range from trivial, easily guessable schemes to complex algorithms which can only be broken (if they can be cracked at all) by applying vast amounts of computer resources.

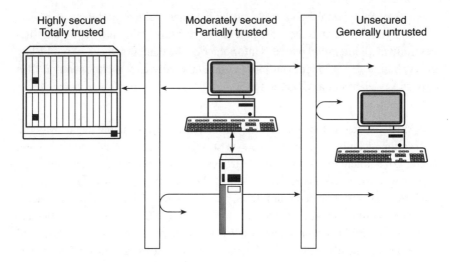

Figure 7.1 A firewalled network.

It might seem that widespread use of data encryption can solve many of the problems of distributed system security. Confidential data can be transferred across public networks without fear of disclosure. Servers can protect themselves against malicious use by only allowing properly encrypted requests from trusted clients. These are real possibilities. However, data encryption is by no means a panacea for at least three reasons: cost, management and law.

Encryption is usually a computationally expensive operation. (We talk only about encryption here for simplicity but encryption usually has to be paired with an equally expensive decryption process to be any use!) A reasonably secure algorithm such as the U.S. Data Encryption Standard (DES) gains much of its strength from applying a large number of different transformations to its input data. This requires a significant amount of processing time. Encrypting all data flowing onto a network could prove far too costly in terms of overall system performance. There are hardware devices, such as 'DES chips', which remove much of the processing burden but these are expensive and may not be available for all types of machine.

Section 5.5.2 outlined the two most commonly used encryption technologies – private key and public key encryption. Private key encryption is the easiest, fastest and most widely used. It depends for its operation on two parties having a shared secret – the private key. However, this begs the question of how the two parties acquire that secret in the first place. The problems of key distribution and management escalate rapidly, particularly as a separate key is required for each pair of users or applications that wish to communicate.

Public key encryption solves many of the key management problems of private key encryption although there are still issues of propagating the public key successfully to all interested parties. Unfortunately, the main drawback of public key encryption is that it is an even more computationally expensive operation than private key encryption. Generating the initial keys is, in particular, a very time-consuming operation.

The final barrier to the use of encryption is not technical but legal. Modern encryption techniques have become ever stronger and more resistant to cracking. Some governments view the use of strong data encryption with suspicion. The U.S. government, among others, restricts the export of much data encryption hardware and software, including DES, as 'munitions'. (This is viewed as patently absurd by many people both outside and within the United States – particularly as the algorithms themselves are freely published and widely known and implemented outside the U.S. To illustrate the absurdity a 'munitions T-shirt' has been designed which has the software for a restricted algorithm printed on it in machine-readable bar-code form! This is just one example of where legal systems are struggling to cope with the information age.) Even the use of encryption by non-government agencies is severely restricted within some countries, for example France. There are arguments both for and against the 'right to encrypt' but whatever the reasoning the restrictions that exist do limit the ubiquitous use of encryption.

In practice full encryption of data is usually used only when confidentiality is of the utmost importance. More commonly it is used only to secure critical steps in interactions. These include establishing the identity of a caller or in applying 'digital signatures' to messages to ensure either their authenticity or that they have not been tampered with.

7.2 Manageability

There are far too many examples of applications which have been built and tested by a development unit and then 'thrown over the wall' to the people who actually have to figure out how to deploy, operate and fix the system in a production environment. An application is no use if it cannot be managed – and the hidden operational costs can often far outweigh the more visible costs of development.

Distributed systems can make this perennial problem far worse. This section explains what the difficulties are, what can really be done now and the 'grand idea' of DME – distributed management eventually!

7.2.1 What is so hard about it?

So what is so difficult about the management of distributed systems? To start to answer this let us consider the fairly well-understood problem of backing up a system. The purpose of taking a backup is to record a snapshot of the current state of a system such that it could be restored at some later time. In order to maintain a consistent view of the state, backups are often performed when the system has been partly shut down or late at night when there is little system activity.

Suppose now that the system to be backed up is an application distributed across machines in London, New York and Tokyo. Each machine may be in use 24 hours a day servicing remote requests – there will be no 'quiet time' during which it can be taken out of service to perform backups. Also the question arises as to what it means to back up 'the system' anyway. Should a completely consistent snapshot be taken across all three sites? How can this be achieved without locking out current tasks? Can each machine be backed up separately? What happens if the application is distributed across 300 sites rather than just three?

The problem of distributed backup is just one example of some of the difficulties facing the administrators of distributed systems. Some others include:

- Autonomous domains. In a large distributed system, particularly one spanning organizational boundaries, different parts of the system are likely to be managed by independent groups of people using a variety of policies and tools. This imposes a need to negotiate and agree the boundaries between administrative domains and often requires additional components (such as gateways and firewalls) which themselves need to be managed.

- Getting the 'end-to-end' view. Components of a system are often built to be managed as isolated units, if at all. This and the 'autonomous domains' problem described above can make it very difficult to get a complete picture of the behaviour of a distributed application. For example, you may find an application responding poorly to your input at a workstation. But the single application you see from the desktop may involve a number of separate distributed components. If the individual components do not supply performance information which can easily be correlated and cross-checked it will be very difficult to determine where the bottleneck may be.

- Problem location. In a standalone system if a program fails the whole program stops. There is often a reasonable record of the failure, such as a stack trace or error log information. This can be examined by the administrator of the system, the problem determined and appropriate action taken.

  Even within a simple client/server interaction between only two components of a distributed system it can be difficult to pin down the source of a problem. An error in a server may cause a failure in the client. Both server and client may fail at roughly the same time indicating a likely cause and effect.

The server may, however, be more robust and continue to run apparently without any problems long after the client crashes. If the server error-logging information is not available to the administrator of the client system it may be very difficult to prove that the real source of the error lies in the server rather than the client.

- Configuration control. One of the biggest management headaches in a distributed system is its dynamically changing configuration. Unless the administrative regime is draconian it is very difficult to stop machines and software being introduced into any large network in a fairly haphazard manner. There is a basic problem in just discovering 'what is out there' on the network. Even if you can somehow get a view of the overall state of the whole distributed system then that picture will only be valid for a very brief period before new changes invalidate parts of it.

Getting a good snapshot of current system configuration is hard enough, managing and controlling it over time is an even greater problem. In Chapter 4 we saw that the change from static to dynamic configuration is one of the 'reversed assumptions' that come with distributed systems. Management strategies that depend on having a system in a precisely defined state are almost certainly doomed to failure.

- Information overload. A single application will probably have a fairly well-defined and straightforward error-handling mechanism. For example all errors may get reported using a library function which writes messages to a single log file. A distributed system, however, is made up of a number of autonomous but cooperating components. A single error may affect a number of components each of which may adopt its own error-handling and reporting strategy. For example the loss of a network link between a single client and server might cause a message to the end user saying that the server has apparently gone away while the server might record the loss of its client in a log file. At the same time the network elements themselves might be signalling a failure in an entirely different way.

Error reporting is just one example of the potential for information overload. If a system administrator is going to be able to manage a distributed system without needing a brain the size of a planet then facilities to collect, filter and correlate information from a wide range of sources are essential.

7.2.2 Where are we now?

Distributed systems management is not a solved problem. We are still a very long way away from the dream of having a single administrator, sitting at a single workstation who can monitor and control a complex distributed system involving hundreds or thousands of machines. So what can we do now?

If you want to understand how you might manage distributed systems in general a good place to start is to look at how the underlying networks themselves are managed. Network administrators have had to tackle many of the same problems that afflict more general distributed systems and network management techniques are relatively mature. In particular we will look briefly at two major network management technologies: the Internet Simple Network Management Protocol (SNMP) and OSI network management. (SNMP is really just the name of a protocol but is often used as a shorthand for a set of related protocols and standards. Similarly OSI management involves a large number of standards which are often bundled under the label of CMIP – from the Common Management Information Protocol.)

Managers, agents, objects and MIBs

The SNMP family of standards is described in a series of Internet RFC (Request For Comments) documents (SNMP Version 1, 1992; SNMP Version 2, 1995). OSI management is defined in a set of formal international standards (ISO/IEC, 1990). Despite having come from very different cultural and ideological backgrounds, both SNMP and OSI management share a broad range of fundamental concepts.

The basic facilities needed to manage networks are the abilities to monitor and control the operation of remote components such as modems, routers and communications links. Many network hardware devices have comforting flashing lights on them to indicate their health or otherwise. They usually have switches to toggle to control their operation. In a small network and with sufficient staff it is possible to keep things going by having people manually inspect the status lights and push the right buttons. (In fact it is possible to keep very large networks going like this as well – and that is precisely how things were done in the days before digital telephone exchanges! It should be no surprise, therefore, to learn that telecommunications companies have been at the forefront of efforts to provide good network management standards.) Obviously to perform any sort of remote management this kind of physical intervention is impossible. So as we have already touched on in Chapter 4, this leads to the concept of management *agents*.

An agent is effectively a special kind of server which provides a view to any interested clients, or *managers,* of a particular resource. A resource is basically anything which can be managed. It might be a modem, or a printer or even a whole computer. It can even be purely a software artefact, such as a print queue.

It is important to realize that the agent is only concerned with management operations. It provides the management interface to the resource. The functional interface – the operations concerned with really doing the useful work of the resource – will likely be completely separate. For example, the function of a network router is to take an incoming data packet and route it on to its destination. This happens through a very specific interface. However, the management interface to the router might let you configure routing tables and packet filtering rules through a completely separate mechanism.

It is not unknown for some resources to have a set of management operations which greatly outnumber the set of functional operations. For example, a print queue really only has a single basic function – take a specified file and print it on a specified printer. The management interface to the queue, however, might provide operations to enable and disable accepting print requests, cancel print jobs, reroute them somewhere else, reprioritize jobs in the queue and so on.

We have described the agent as providing a management interface onto a resource. This is not strictly accurate. Agents provide a standardized view of resources to the outside world. They usually do this in terms of a set of one or more *managed objects* which encapsulate the resource. (The term 'managed object' comes much more from the OSI network management camp than from Internet management. SNMP talks about 'tables' and 'variables' rather than 'objects' and 'attributes'. However, the same basic concept is common to both domains.) It is a purely internal issue as to how the agent actually interacts with the 'real' resource. A set of such objects for a resource or group of resources is described as a Management Information Base or MIB. A MIB is effectively the collection of interface definitions for the managed objects.

The relationship between managers, agents, objects and resources is shown pictorially in Figure 7.2.

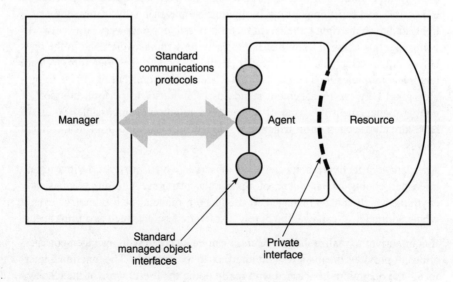

Figure 7.2 Managers, agents, objects and resources.

Managed objects have a series of *attributes* which describe their characteristics. So a print queue might have an attribute which describes the number of currently queued print jobs or whether the queue is currently enabled or disabled. Managers can perform remote *operations* on objects and their attributes. Commonly a *get* operation reads the value of an attribute. Some, but not all, attributes may be remotely *set* – which usually causes some resulting change in the behaviour of the resource. So to carry forward the print queue example changing the status from 'enabled' to 'disabled' should cause the queue to stop accepting requests.

Some purists object to this – if you will pardon the pun – on the grounds that a 'true' object-oriented interface would encapsulate all elements of internal state (attributes) and provide instead *enable* and *disable* operations. The example has been used of the 'nuclear missile managed object'. The object-oriented interface has a 'launch' operation which you invoke as opposed to the attribute-based view in which you change the status attribute from 'in silo' to 'launched'. Those on the receiving end might be moved to observe that from their point of view it doesn't really matter which method was used to launch it – the end result is pretty much the same …

Polling, events and filtering

Having described the basic components of management systems, the next issue is how they interact with one another.

The first problem comes in trying to answer the question 'what is the current state of a component?' Assuming that the component has an associated agent a manager can just ask the agent for the necessary information. To find out the overall state of a complex distributed system a manager may have to ask the question of many different agents. This is fine if the purpose is just to get a rough snapshot picture of the state of the system. Unfortunately, it suffers from a major deficiency in that it may take an appreciable amount of time to contact all the components of the system. By the time the last results have been obtained the earliest may be completely out of date.

Being able to obtain a view of the overall state of a system at a particular moment in time is useful – even if it may be somewhat inconsistent. However, system management is a full-time job and it is far more useful to have a continually updated picture highlighting changes as they happen. So how can this be achieved? The easiest solution – and the one most commonly used in SNMP management – is *polling*.

Polling is basically the process of repeatedly asking agents for their current state. So a manager which polls its agents every 60 seconds should have a picture of the system which is reasonably accurate – provided that the rate of change within the system is not too high. Changes between the current and previous states can be detected and highlighted as necessary.

Polling is analogous to sending someone down to the computer hall every few minutes to walk around and inspect all the machines then report back on their states. This is very easy to do and does not require very sophisticated facilities on the managed machines. Unfortunately, it is also rather wasteful in terms of resources and becomes unworkable on a large scale – the time to visit all machines becomes too great. Exactly the same problems afflict automated polling. So if polling has problems is there another mechanism?

The usual alternative to a polling model, and that favoured in OSI management, is the use of events and notifications. When an agent finds that the state of a managed resource has changed it sends out an unsolicited message called a *notification* to 'interested parties'. The notification contains information about the *event* which occurred. So a printer running out of paper might cause a notification of an 'out of paper' event to be generated and sent out. Managers looking for 'out of paper' events can then take whatever action they desire, for example denying further print requests until a 'paper added' event is detected. (The equivalent in SNMP terms to an event notification is a so-called 'trap'.)

Event notification is a much more attractive model in many circumstances. No resources are wasted in continually asking for status reports when nothing has changed. Information is also likely be more timely and fresh because events are processed as they happen rather than at the next poll cycle. On the other hand, without any control over event generation it can be all too easy for a manager to get flooded with a rush of notifications, particularly if a catastrophic failure – such as a major network link being lost – causes a large number of agents to generate events simultaneously.

The solution usually adopted for the event overload problem is *filtering*. We said rather boldly above that an agent sends notifications to 'interested parties'. The usual model adopted is that when a manager establishes communication with an agent it specifies what types of event notifications it would like to receive. Only events of the selected type are then sent to the manager and others are discarded.

The event-based management view is very powerful, particularly when combined with other techniques such as correlation and escalation. For example an occasional 'glitch' in a network may be insignificant, but a fault that occurs repeatedly could be much more serious. Administrators would like not to be bothered by the former case while being confident that they will be alerted of the latter. The main disadvantage of event-based management is that it usually requires somewhat more sophisticated and complex manager and agent implementations.

7.2.3   Where would we like to be?

Both SNMP and OSI management work well within their domains. SNMP is very widely used, particularly for LAN-scale monitoring. (One of the reasons SNMP is less used for control is its relatively poor security. SNMP version 2 goes some way to addressing this.) OSI management has received a great deal of support from the telecommunications community, for whom large-scale network management is of obvious concern! We have not even really mentioned the so-called 'network operating systems' such as Microsoft LAN Manager (or its successor 'Hermes', now officially known as SMS) and Novell NetWare which also provide management for PC-based environments. So is there any need for yet another solution?

The first issue is the fact that both SNMP and OSI management address the problem of network management. Distributed systems are more than networks and add a whole new degree of complexity which the existing technologies may not easily be able to address. However, there is a more fundamental issue. Network management is really a distributed computing problem.

In order to tackle the problems of network management SNMP and OSI management have had to invent customized solutions to what are really more generic problems. For example, OSI management has its own interface definition language called GDMO (Guidelines for the Definition of Managed Objects). Both the common technologies effectively define a form of RPC protocol and a format for data on the wire. Event filtering and other event handling services are found in the CORBA object services (see Section 5.4).

The Open Software Foundation recognized that a more generic solution was required when it embarked on the development of its distributed management environment (DME). It was envisaged that this would be based on more mainstream distributed computing technologies. The DME project has since largely foundered for both commercial and technical reasons – it was basically too ambitious and too far reaching. However, the central idea has persisted and been widely accepted that distributed management should be solvable using the same technologies as any other distributed computing problem.

The best hope for the management systems of the future seems to lie in the distributed object technologies described in Section 5.4. X/Open have played a leading role in recent years in trying to push forward systems management standards. The X/Open systems management reference model (X/Open Guide, 1993) positions these and existing network management technologies against an overall framework. Progress is difficult for several reasons: there are many problems to be solved, most of them are hard, vendors all have their own solutions and no one has the complete answer.

7.2.4 Can we get there from here?

Ideally, one day we may be able to have a single distributed framework into which all our applications fit. A fundamental part of this framework will be management facilities and components will be managed in a single, consistent and simple manner. Many people are working towards this goal, but there is a long way still to go.

So what can we do in the mean time? The first and most fundamental rule is to consider what needs to be managed and how it will be done as an integral part of system design. As with security it may be possible to 'design out' management problems before they occur. For example, if there are to be a number of copies of a server which all need essentially identical configuration data it will be far easier for them all to draw that data from a single source rather than to have to keep each separately up to date manually.

The second rule is to use whatever facilities are already available. Today's technologies are not ideal but they are a great deal better than the alternative – do-it-yourself anarchy. If a system is already being managed using SNMP then a new component that provides an associated SNMP agent will be likely to be much more welcome than one that does not. Picking a technology and living with its deficiencies is much more productive than waiting around for the ultimate solution.

7.3 Performance

Many people are worried about the performance of distributed systems. How can a system running on widely separated machines, strung together by networks of limited bandwidth ever perform better than its single-system counterpart?

There is no simple answer to that question. The greater parallelism and concurrency of distributed systems offers the chance of increased throughput – subject to the constraints of Amdahl's law as described in Section 4.6. On the other hand, there is significant complexity and processing in providing much of the distribution transparency that developers and users want.

There can, however, be far too much of a fixation on the properties of technologies. The authors' experience has been that performance problems, in distributed or standalone systems, are almost always the result of poor design. Most often the designers have sinned by omission rather than commission – they have failed to give the issue sufficient consideration rather than made overtly bad decisions.

There are, of course, some additional pitfalls in designing distributed systems. Most of these stem from a failure to acknowledge the 'reversed assumptions' described in Chapter 4. In some ways the better the distribution transparency a technology provides, the easier it is to make mistakes. For example a good RPC system can magically transport a complex linked list data-structure across the network. A programmer might want to search through the list for a specific item. It is attractive to obtain the list and then walk through it locally using normal language constructs. However, the list could consist of megabytes of data which needs to be transmitted across the network only for the majority of it to be discarded. A much better design would be to provide a remote search operation which returns only the desired element.

Concurrency is another source of potential difficulty. In particular it is all too easy for an application to bring a distributed system to a standstill by making the assumption that it is the sole user of resources. When two or more users try to access the same resource at the same time there is a danger that their actions might interfere with one another. In order to protect resources from multiple potentially conflicting accesses it is usual to employ some form of locking mechanism. There are a number of different mechanisms including semaphores and mutual exclusion locks or 'mutexes'. In all cases the effect is the same – only the user holding the lock is allowed to perform the operation on the associated resource while other potential users are forced to wait.

There are, however, a number of potential performance problems that arise from the use of locking. The classic deadlock or 'deadly embrace' is the most extreme form of this. In a deadlock two users each hold a lock that the other needs before it can proceed. The result is a stalemate while each waits for the other to release its lock. Deadlocks are usually fairly obvious when they occur but rather more subtle problems arise when locks are taken correctly but are held for too long before being released thus holding up all other users. One possible strategy for coping with this is so-called 'optimistic locking' which will be covered in Chapter 8.

So how can performance problems be avoided? Yet again it is really a matter which must be addressed up-front in the development life-cycle. Performance tuning and optimization by, say, employing faster network links, may be possible in deployed systems but the greatest gains will almost always be from having a sound design in the first place.

One possible supplement to the design process is the use of modelling techniques. The discipline of predictive performance modelling is still underused in the software industry. The basic idea is to be able to predict the performance characteristics of a design before implementation. In many ways it is even more vital to the success of distributed systems. Reasonable results which at least indicate if a serious problem exists in a design can often be obtained from fairly rough models.

7.4 Reliability

The concept of reliability for a distributed system is different. In Chapter 5 we looked at some techniques for obtaining reliable, predictable behaviour from distributed systems (see Section 5.3). In many ways, however, it can be more productive to let go of the notion of absolute success or failure. It may not be a case of 'all or nothing' but rather 'almost working or not quite failed'. Shades of grey are the order of the day.

7.4.1 The myth of reliability

There are a number of ways in which we can interpret the term 'reliability'. In these discussions we will leave aside issues of whether application logic is correct. The field of 'formal methods' by which programs can be rigorously specified and proved correct is one which is independent of issues of distributed computing, although some of these methods do address issues of particular relevance such as the impact of concurrent processing. Instead we will consider more the resilience of a distributed system in the face of the failure of one or more of its component parts.

In some ways we have come to expect more of software in terms of reliability than almost any other type of system. We do not stop using a car when it has a dent in the bodywork or just because it is not running very smoothly. Offices may operate at reduced efficiency if one or two people are off sick but they do not usually shut down completely the moment someone stays in bed with flu!

There are probably several reasons why we are intolerant of failure in computer systems. One of these is that many applications have a very crude way of handling failure – they bail out at the earliest opportunity and come to a grinding halt. It is also the case that the closely coupled nature of a single application usually means that there is no opportunity for part of the program to be taken out of service. The notion of 'sorry, that subroutine is temporarily unavailable' just does not enter most programmers' minds!

There are also some psychological effects at work too. We have become sold on the idea that as computers operate on 'pure' logic their output should be precisely correct. In some cases this is justified – you do not, for example, want the automatic teller to inform you that that your bank account is 'approximately in credit'. In other cases it is not.

7.4.2 Defining reliability

So what exactly is reliability anyway? A common way of expressing it is in terms of availability figures. These are the proportion of time during which a system or service is available for use. So an availability of 99 per cent means that the system is only unavailable for a little over one and a half hours a week. To put this in perspective, the availability target for the telephone network is 99.999985 per cent or around three minutes unavailability in 40 years! Availability figures can be rather misleading. They often exclude 'planned downtime' such as the time out of service for maintenance. So a system may claim 99.99 per cent availability but require an hour's downtime each day for backups – which gives a real total of 95 per cent availability.

If a whole application is contained in a single machine then the machine availability is often the limiting factor on reliability. But what happens when an application is distributed over a number of machines? On the face of it the situation rapidly deteriorates. If a single component has a probability of being available of p then the likelihood of n such similar components all being available simultaneously is p raised to the power n. In other words if a component has an availability of 99 per cent then the chance of a group of 10 such components all being available is 90 per cent and the chance of a group of 100 all functioning is only 37 per cent!

Obviously if a distributed system can only function when every component is available then any reasonably large-scale system will almost certainly never work. Given the target availability figure for the telephone network – which is achieved in a system with hundreds of thousands of components – then the notion of reliability needs to be redefined. The positive aspect of the availability calculations above is that if there is only a 37 per cent chance of all 100 components being available then the chance of none of them working at all is only one in 10^{200}! If a system can function with only some of its components in service then the potential availability is vastly increased.

There are a large number of applications where partial service is more than adequate. A hotel booking service may draw on a number of data sources to provide pricing information. If you ask for details of hotels in London costing less than £75 per night you will probably be satisfied provided that the system can supply you with a list of some, even if details of every possible hotel are not available at that point.

Another case where total success is not an issue is where information or processing has a limited lifetime. For example, the event notification services described in Section 7.2 fall into this category. It would be foolish and wrong to apply 'all or nothing' constraints to notification delivery. If a single manager is temporarily unable to receive notifications from an agent that should not stop other managers from doing so.

There are at least three main parameters that can be used to define reliability in a distributed system:

- the proportion of the user population to which a service is available;
- the degree or quality of service provided;
- the proportion of time the service is available.

This trio of space, time and quality can be balanced against each other. So in the hotel booking example above it might be reasonable to provide a service that was available 99.99 per cent of the time to at least 99 per cent of users and guarantee access to at least 50 per cent of the potential data sources. Alternatively, access to 90 per cent of the sources might be guaranteed 90 per cent of the time for 75 per cent of users. Achieving these targets might mean different implementation strategies with different costs. You generally get what you pay for – the temptation is to want it all and then to resent the bill!

7.4.3 Obtaining reliability

In Chapter 5 we covered a number of technologies that provide different guarantees of reliability. Some, like distributed transaction processing, give very good guarantees but are 'heavyweight' technologies and require significant amounts of resources to implement. Others, like message queueing and basic RPC, are lighter weight but give fewer guarantees. In a large distributed system different technologies may need to be deployed to solve particular problems. So it might be appropriate to employ DTP to preserve the integrity of some data while using simpler mechanisms elsewhere.

The most fundamental shift of attitude necessary to gain reliability in distributed systems is to recognize that if a single component fails this should not necessarily cause the whole system to fail. Identifying which components can fail and what strategy to adopt if they do is a key element of design. Sometimes automated mechanisms can handle this. For example, many failures of 'lookup' operations which do not alter the state of a server can be handled by searching for and rebinding to another server. Message queueing can be used to complete update operations in the face of temporary server unavailability. On other occasions the only appropriate strategy is to employ human intervention to sort out complex failures.

There is no single 'right' strategy to adopt. In truth the situation is really no different than with standalone systems but once again distribution merely throws new light on problems which have always existed.

7.5 Scalability

Which distributed system is more complex, one made up of 10 machines or one made up of 1000? The answer is that it depends entirely on what those machines are doing! A system which consists of a single server and 999 identical clients is probably far easier to understand, test and manage than one made up of 10 different, cooperating but largely autonomous elements.

Scalability of distributed systems is a hard issue to pin down. There are many factors that can define what it means to build a 'scalable system'. These include:

- the number of users;

- the number of machines;

- the number of application components;

- the number of different services;

- the volume of network traffic;

- the rate of interactions;

- geographic dispersal.

A scalable system is one that can handle a wide variation in one or more of these factors. It is quite possible that a single system may have good scaling properties with respect to a number of such factors. It is highly unlikely that a single system can ever provide complete flexibility in all dimensions. For example the desire to be able to operate a system at a truly global scale across multiple continents will probably adversely affect the volume of traffic which can be handled because of relatively slow and expensive wide area links.

For these reasons scalabilty is not an absolute concept but instead a complex balance of competing requirements. It is also worth noting that, although scalability is often talked about in the context of being able to grow a system, the ability to be able to scale down a system can be very advantageous on occasions too.

7.5.1 Know your enemy

All of the non-functional aspects of design share a common feature – it is very hard to 'bolt them on to' existing systems. Scalability is no exception. A large number of systems (not only distributed systems) have foundered once pushed beyond their design limits. (Many very large corporations invest great amounts of money in developing apparently standard business applications, such as finance systems, in house. One of the reasons for this is that many off-the-shelf applications are designed for 'large' companies of hundreds or maybe a few thousand employees. Unfortunately, this definition of 'large' leaves something to be desired ...)

The traditional approach to providing scalability has been to buy a 'bigger box'. Unfortunately, throwing resources at a problem is a very expensive solution and may, in practice, be neither practical or desirable. There may simply not be a bigger box to buy but even if there is a lone machine supporting an entire enterprise it becomes a very vulnerable single point of failure.

Distributed computing potentially offers a number of ways out of this situation. In fact, distribution is almost inherently about working on a large scale, be it in terms of physical size or numbers of machines. Some of the potential scaling benefits include:

- load balancing across machines;

- replication for resilience;

- true parallel processing for some problems;

- processing partitioned to reduce network traffic;

- easy addition and removal of extra resources.

Each of these may be applicable to a particular problem. However, each of them will also carry a cost in, for example, difficulty of implementation, complexity of management or a penalty on performance. It should be a part of initial system design to determine what the ultimate scalability of a system needs to be and to recognize what other trade-offs may need to be made to achieve that.

7.5.2 Some key questions

It should be no surprise that there is no simple technique for achieving the 'perfectly scalable' system. Not only that, but there is no such beast anyway. However, here are some key questions which can be asked of any system.

- **What are the limits of the design?** If a system is designed initially for use by 10 users it is unlikely to work adequately in support of 10 000 unless that possibility has been allowed for. The limiting factors in a system, for example network bandwidth or numbers of machines, need to be identified.

- **How are other aspects of the system affected?** As we have already said, achieving scalability will probably require trade-offs to be made. It is likely that all of the non-functional requirements discussed in this chapter – security, manageability, reliability, performance – will affect one another.

- **Will the infrastructure cope?** Sometimes it is the obvious things that get overlooked. For example, there is little point in designing a system that could support a network of 1000 machines on high-speed LANs if the buildings in which it is be deployed cannot physically be cabled up to provide that. A project for the UK National Health Service was delayed by 6 months while they laid extra power lines for the computers.

- **Are the tools available to build it?** In order to build and test a large-scale system equally scalable tools are also needed. Unfortunately, it often seems to be the case that 'nice tools do not scale'. For example, some graphical tools which provide on-screen maps of the interconnections between components can be fine for tens of elements but fare badly when asked to display hundreds or thousands.

- **Can it be managed once it is out there?** We have already discussed the
issues of management. However, it does seem to be the case that of all the
aspects of design affecting scalability it is the one that designers and developers often consider least. Real systems defy hobbyist management.

7.6 A cautionary tale

Even when all of the non-functional aspects of design have been separately and
carefully considered, things can go unexpectedly wrong. Here is a story from the
motor industry that illustrates how.

A certain well-known manufacturer had spent literally millions of pounds to
develop its new flagship mid-range saloon. The company previously had a fairly
poor reputation for security so this was addressed by providing central locking,
an alarm system and high-security locks. Also, as customers have been demanding ever higher standards of safety it was fitted with a number of safety features,
including an airbag, as standard. It was generally considered by the trade to be the
one of the best vehicles the company had ever produced – a real world-class car.

Unfortunately, it did not take the criminal fraternity long to discover that these
two excellent sets of features had an unforeseen interaction. A swift blow with a
hammer to the right spot on the front of the car triggered the impact detection system, the airbag inflated and the doors were automatically unlocked to allow any
trapped passengers – and radios, tape decks and CD players – to escape …

7.7 Summary

The non-functional aspects of a system design are often those that make a difference between mediocre and magnificent – for standalone as well as distributed
systems. All of them are to some extent hard to pin down. Many are interrelated
and any design must make trade-offs and compromises between them. However,
in all cases these decisions need to be addressed right at the early stages of system design. Adding security, management, performance, reliability or scalability
'after the fact' will almost certainly be a costly operation – if it is possible at all.

CHAPTER 8

A route map

*'Long is the way
And hard, that out of hell leads up to light'* – John Milton, *Paradise Lost*

In distributed computing, as in software-based endeavours as a whole, there is no 'silver bullet'. An increasing number of suppliers claim to have the tool that can 'do client/server for you automatically'. Some of these tools will surely help. However, just as distributed computing is not the solution to all problems, neither is there a simple formula that will make it work for all cases.

This chapter provides some basic guidance for users and for developers of distributed systems. It is based on the experience of the authors and others in defining, building and using distributed systems. It is not a complete or formal set of procedures or checklists. Instead it is an attempt to help you to think about some of the high-level design issues as well as providing a little advice on some of the things the manuals do not always tell you.

8.1 Architecture – the big picture

One of the terms in the IT industry which has been frequently used, abused, misrepresented and misunderstood is the word 'architecture'. It has been employed for anything from the most detailed technical description of hardware and software components to a convenient banner for a vendor's set of almost totally unrelated and apparently competing products. With that strong note of caution in mind we are now going to tell you what we mean by an architecture and why you need one!

The job of conventional, concrete, glass and steel architects is to design buildings. In doing this they often first arrive at the overall shape and feel of the building and try to ensure that it will be fit for its purpose. They also show how it will fit into its surroundings. Architects usually decide on the primary construction materials and ensure that they can be used together. They then draw up the plans that can be used to communicate these ideas clearly to the construction team. These blueprints show the key dimensions and materials and may specify the construction of critical elements of the design in some detail. However, the builders, electricians, glaziers and other workers will have considerable latitude in deciding exactly how large parts of the building are constructed.

In the same way a distributed system needs an architecture (a blueprint) before it can be built successfully. (You may find it difficult to distinguish an 'architecture' from a 'high-level design'. If so, you will not be alone! If there is a boundary between these terms it is often very diffuse and seems more to depend on the role or job title of the person applying the term.) Such a blueprint cannot possibly contain detailed instructions on how to construct every element of the system. The useful function that it does fulfil is to inform early decisions. Given the increasing complexity of systems this is vital as the initial decisions are a long way – temporally and logically – from the final reality.

8.1.1 Features of an architecture

There are also some useful parallels to be drawn between some of the steps in arriving at a building's architecture and that of a distributed system.

Shape

An early and fundamental decision to be made in defining a system architecture is the overall 'shape' or 'style' of the system. For example one style might have an application distributed across a number of relatively autonomous mid-range systems. Another may employ a large number of client workstations clustered around a small number of closely coupled mainframe systems. Any number of options may be technically feasible but it is likely that only a few will suit the purpose of the application well.

There are a number of factors which will influence the shape of the architecture some of which are described further below. Just as aesthetics or dogma rather than practical considerations seem sometimes to define the architecture of buildings so it can be with systems architecture. Ultimately, however, it should be a matter of 'fitness for purpose' which drives the decisions.

Surroundings

A good architect designs buildings that are in harmony with their surroundings. This does not mean that old styles and conventions have to be slavishly followed but that the new draws on the best of and blends with the old. So it should be with systems architecture.

As we have already seen in Chapter 6, it is rare to be able to implement any application in the absence of an existing legacy of systems. A key element of any architecture must be to describe the relationships with such systems. The shape and style of a building may be severely constrained by its environment and so it is with system architecture. After addressing the fundamental purpose of the system its shape is likely to be most influenced by its surroundings.

Materials

The raw materials of a distributed system are the technology choices with which it will be constructed. So a system architecture should define whether, for example, messaging or RPC is to be used or if distributed TP is necessary. If a number of different technologies are needed it is the job of system architects to define in broad terms where each is appropriate. They must also ensure that the selected technologies will work successfully together and with the surroundings. They are also responsible for laying down the basic rules for interconnection and interworking.

It is easy for the choice of technology to have too great an influence on the overall system architecture. It can be very difficult to be objective about what is the best tool for the job at hand. One of the aims of this book is to provide a reasonably wide-ranging view of the technology options.

Critical elements

There may be some critical elements of design which need to be specified in some detail very early on in order to ensure that the system as a whole can be successfully built. An example of this might be key security mechanisms. It may be necessary to analyse and design some such elements in detail before the required level of assurance can be achieved. Those building the system will have to adhere rigidly to these initial decisions if security is not to be compromised.

It is often the 'non-functional' aspects of design – those topics covered in Chapter 7 – which will need special attention within the architecture. Poor decisions at the architectural stage will be very hard to correct as the construction of the system progresses.

Degrees of freedom

An architecture may contain a large number of rules and prescriptions which must be followed in building a system. However, it is just as important that the architecture recognizes what it does not need to specify. Unnecessarily strict regulations imposed early on may cause system developers great difficulties later.

8.1.2 Describing an architecture

Having said that you need an architecture, what does one look like in practice? There is no universal agreement or single answer. However, there are a number of aspects which are commonly covered such as those described above. These could be separately described and documented or all contained in a single unit. The right way will depend very much on the scope and purpose of the system and on the people who need to use the architecture. One thing is certain, however, if the architecture is too detailed, complex or obscure to be accessible to its intended audience then it will be useless – no matter how 'right' it may be.

Although this is by no means the only way of defining an architecture, one approach is to address the problem from three aspects: functional, technical and physical. These are not independent (they are very closely related) but they can provide convenient ways of 'cutting the cake'.

Functional architecture

The purpose of the functional architecture is to describe the overall structure of the system in terms of its major functions and data. This is largely independent of any technology which might be used to implement the system. In building a distributed system this architecture enables you to see where the main interfaces between components lie – and hence opportunities for splitting and distributing such components. If object-oriented techniques are used to describe the architecture the definition of interfaces forms a very natural part of the description process.

Although not directly concerned with technology, the functional architecture can influence technology choices. For example if the architecture indicates that there is a need to safeguard certain critical interactions between components then it might lead to a requirement for TP or reliable queueing facilities.

Technical architecture

If the functional architecture is concerned with what a system is intended to do then the technical architecture is about the tools, technologies and techniques that will be used to do it. It should show, in particular, how these should be used together to provide the requirements of the functional architecture. So it might propose RPC as the most suitable synchronous communication technology and identify a suitable candidate product. It might also recognize a need for TP technology on some machines to manage coordinated update. There then needs to be a strategy and guidance for how and when these two technologies need to work together.

A single technical architecture may meet the needs of a wide range of applications. However, it must always be validated against the needs of the functional architecture that it is supposed to support. If the functional architecture identifies a need to draw upon a central database of customer information, for example, then it is the job of the technical architecture to identify that necessary mechanisms are available to allow this. This will have to draw in turn upon the physical and functional architectures to identify which specific systems this database will reside on.

Physical architecture

The physical architecture is the place where the real physical constraints on the system are identified and documented. It might say, for example, that all communication between clients and server systems will have to happen over public networks. To meet the needs of the functional architecture this might imply that the technical architecture will have to specify the use of certain encryption technologies.

The physical architecture often has the last word in saying what is practical. There is no point in specifying that servers should be replicated for resilience and performance if the only hardware you have is two machines connected by a wet piece of string!

8.2 Rules of thumb

We now turn our attention away from the dizzy heights of architecture to look at some of the issues that trouble those at the coal-face. This is very much a section for application developers although interested consumers may benefit from understanding some of the problems that face their suppliers.

There are good and bad ways of doing things. As Fred Brooks once said: 'good judgement comes from experience – and experience comes from bad judgement.' Here are some crystallized experiences based on mistakes that we, and others, have made. This collection is by no means complete, definitive or rigidly structured. However, we hope that some of these will save you from one or two of the tar-pits of distributed systems.

8.2.1 General

One man's client is another man's server

One of the greatest potential advantages to be gained from distributed systems is the ability to access a 'sea' of software components. Services packaged up and made available on the network can be reused and composed in an ever-expanding variety of ways. Many companies are seeing the promise of opening up the services provided by existing standalone, 'stovepipe' systems to a range of new clients. But in the rush to do 'client/server' there is a danger that the old problems of useful services locked in inaccessible systems will be recreated – and worsened.

A new business application drawing on services from a number of 'backend' systems may be created to run on a client workstation. However, it is likely that this new slice of business logic is now locked into an inaccessible and not very robust desktop machine. If a new application wishes to draw on those services it may have to either copy and modify the code or reimplement it afresh.

To get the most benefit from a distributed system new 'client' components should also be able to provide their value-added services to other components.

You're never alone in a distributed system

The 'reversed assumptions' described at the beginning of Chapter 4 can be viewed as the loss of two basic comforts for an application developer: predictability and control.

When you build a standalone application you usually have a good idea as to how that application will be used. Tight coupling between modules means that some can be lax in, for example, enforcing security and validation because they can rely on other parts of the application to take care of those functions. Building components for distributed systems is different. The safest assumption is that 'out there' are a potentially hostile set of users who are likely to use and abuse your component in unwanted and unexpected ways. Healthy paranoia is the watchword!

Hide whatever complexity you can

Much of the theme of previous chapters (especially Chapter 5) has been about a wide range of technologies which hide the complexities of distribution. They achieve this to a greater or lesser extent. Each technology provides different kinds of 'magic' – but the price of this is some loss in another area such as degree of control, flexibility, security or performance.

As a general rule you should aim to employ a technology which hides the greatest amount of complexity without compromising critical qualities of the overall system. It can be hard to make judgements about the right trade-offs between different functional and non-functional aspects of a design. It requires a broad understanding of a wide range of technical and non-technical options and issues. On the other hand, this is one of the things that makes the task interesting and challenging – and gives hope for the future employment prospects of people with skills in distributed systems!

Remember what complexity is being hidden

Sometimes magic goes wrong – particularly when the wrong magic is used in the wrong situation. Part of the motivation for attempting to explain how the various technologies work is to give you an understanding of what is going on 'under the covers'. While we have jokingly equated technology with magic (and as Arthur C. Clarke said: 'any sufficiently advanced technology is indistinguishable from magic') sometimes you need to know what is going on and why some things may not work as you first expect.

An example of this is the problem of data shuttling. RPC systems can make it very easy to access remote data-structures in precisely the same way as local data. This might include traversing linked lists or manipulating large arrays. Unfortunately, if the data for these structures really resides on a remote server then it may have to be shunted backwards and forwards repeatedly across the network resulting in poor performance.

To give a concrete example, a remote procedure call may retrieve a 10 000 element array. The programmer modifies element 527 and then calls another procedure to store the array away again. The result will be that 9999 elements of the array will have made two trips across the network for no good reason. From a programmer's point of view a lot of complexity has been hidden but some fundamental properties of networks may have been forgotten.

8.2.2 Security

Security is like personal credibility – very hard to regain if you lose it

The old adage about the futility of locking the stable door after the horse has bolted is still applicable (if rather anachronistic) in the information age. Restoring the integrity of a system after it has been accidentally or maliciously compromised is extremely hard and may be impossible. As we described in Chapter 7 security is more than just a matter of preventing unauthorized intrusion. An often-quoted statistic is that about 80 per cent of companies which suffer a fire in their central computer room will go out of business within a few years. The inability to recover from disaster is probably far more serious than allowing the disaster to happen in the first place.

Security needs to be designed in from the start – and that includes considering how the system will be operated once it is deployed. It is easier to relax security that proves to be unnecessarily tight rather than try to impose a non-existent control mechanism later.

Security costs – do not overdo it

Security is not an absolute concept but a matter of degree. It is impossible for any system to provide complete guarantees. The amount and level of security which is appropriate to any given system is proportional to the value of the information or services provided by that system.

It can, however, be difficult to quantify the value of information. Some sorts of data are obviously sensitive – bank account details or medical records. But what about a library of digitized pictures? They may be of little or no value – but they might be irreplaceable if they represent, for example, scanned images of rapidly decaying manuscripts. It can be an instructive exercise to take an office PC and ask how much it would cost in time and effort to replace it (including all the information it holds) if it were to be destroyed. The answer may be disturbing, especially given the poor backup regime in many offices!

On the other hand, it is easy to get carried away with unnecessary and inappropriate security measures. There is probably little point in auditing accesses to the office telephone list or encrypting the church flower rota! It is also the case that where security mechanisms are unwieldy then they will get ignored, abused and ultimately devalued.

A common problem is the huge number of 'confidential' documents in existence in companies. Most of them have been unnecessarily categorized as such not because they are particularly sensitive but simply because people assume that too much protection is better than too little or they think it lends greater weight to the contents. In practice it just devalues the label and ultimately leads people to be careless with information which is truly sensitive.

8.2.3 State, locks and caches

Statelessness is good – there is nothing to worry about
Statefulness is good – because sometimes you need to worry

One of the debates that sometimes rages fiercely between developers of distributed systems is around the issue of statelessness versus statefulness. In a distributed system there is usually no hard, permanent link between components. So the question arises as to how much information a server should maintain about clients which are interacting with it. Does the server maintain 'state' or not?

With a stateless server every request from a client must carry sufficient information to allow the desired operation to be performed without prior knowledge of any interaction that may have gone before. From a server's point of view this is very easy to handle. No special identification of a client as previously known is needed. No information needs to be stored and maintained. If a client crashes and restarts the server has to take no action and does not even have to know – requests from a newly restarted client are indistinguishable from those from one that has been running for months.

From a client's point of view stateless servers are also very useful. If each request is effectively self-contained there is no need for successive requests to be serviced by the same server. If there is a pool of identical servers then requests can be handled by the next available server to optimize performance. Also, if a stateless server dies another can take its place without the client knowing or caring.

It may seem that stateless servers are the ideal. It is certainly a good aim to make distributed system components stateless wherever possible. However, there are times when a completely stateless model runs into difficulties.

The first problem is one of efficiency. If every request has to be serviced independently of every other then this may mean that a significant amount of information needs to be transferred with every call. Further, the scope for performance optimization can be severely reduced.

Take, for example, the case where a client asks a server to perform a complex database query which may retrieve thousands of rows of data. With a stateless model the client will either have to retrieve the whole dataset immediately or to ask for only a portion of it. If it takes the former course it may involve the transfer of a huge amount of data which could either clog the network or exceed the client's memory capacity. If it takes the latter course it will have to rerun the entire expensive query again each time it wants to retrieve the next portion. In this case it would be better for the server to keep the retrieved data around and supply the 'next' chunk when asked.

Another problem is that sometimes a server really does need to know when a client crashes. A client may perform a sequence of operations which could leave the system inconsistent if not properly completed. If a server knows which clients are active it can take action to clean up if it detects that one has crashed.

Finally there are some problems that just seem easiest to solve when the server maintains state. This is particularly the case when multiple clients can perform potentially conflicting actions on the same basic resource. It could be disastrous to have one client successfully request that data be deleted while another is still using it simply because the server held no information that the data was in use.

In summary both stateless and stateful components have their place and it is a major element of good system design to make the right choices for the right situations.

Do not throw it away if you might need it again soon

Even if a server is stateless that does not mean that it should not hold any data. Caching (keeping a temporary copy of recently requested data) is a very useful technique. For example, it might be that in a customer service application nine out of ten requests to a server for a customer's address are followed within a few minutes by a request for their latest invoice details. If both sets of data are supplied by the same server from the same database it might well be worth retrieving the invoice as well when the address information is requested. If the invoice is held in memory for 15 minutes then there is a good chance that a subsequent call will be saved the trouble and cost of a second database look-up.

Caching is also useful within clients. When data is obtained locally you can be fairly careless about regularly going back to get more information as and when it is needed. However, if the same information needs to come from a remote system then it will be far more efficient to ask for the majority of the information in one shot rather than making repeated calls for small amounts.

There are some caveats to this, however. One big request may be more efficient than several small ones but it can have an unpleasant effect on usability. We know of one customer service system that fetched a large amount of data about customers as soon as they were identified. To do this on the terminal-based system it replaced usually required going through about 10 screen transactions each of which took at least 2 seconds to process. The new system used a number of optimizations and reduced the end-to-end time from over 20 down to under 15 seconds. Unfortunately the users hated it – a succession of tolerable 2-second delays had turned into one long pause of 15 seconds.

If you ask again you might get a different answer

Probably the biggest difficulty with the use of caching is the consistency problem. The longer you hold on to a copy of a piece of data, the more likely it is to be out of date. For some applications the likelihood of this happening is very small. For example the results of a library catalogue search will probably be valid for days. Also, even if new books are added to the library, if your search was for 'books on distributed computing' then it is probably not important that a few may be missing from the list – unless this one is among them, of course!

There are other applications where consistency and accuracy of information is of paramount importance. A stock trading application operating on day-old information will probably be worse than useless. Sophisticated strategies for maintaining cache consistency have been developed but this is difficult territory. Once again there is a trade-off to be faced, this time between complexity, performance and accuracy.

Lock sparingly, briefly and optimistically

An issue closely related to problems of caching, consistency and performance is that of locking.

In a single-user standalone system you do not have to worry that much about things being altered unexpectedly. The only reason data should change is because you alter it. That is why, for instance, undeleting an accidentally erased file is usually easy on a PC and next to impossible on a multi-user system.

It is almost an axiom of distributed systems that you should expect somebody or something else to interfere with any server you may be accessing. As we have already mentioned when discussing transaction processing in Chapter 5 one way to guard against potential inconsistencies is to employ locking techniques.

In standard 'pessimistic' locking you place a lock on a resource until you have completely finished with it and only then do you release it. This technique can certainly be applied in a distributed system but there are several features that make it less attractive than in a standalone system. The first is that it requires a server to be stateful so that it can retain knowledge about locks between calls and can release them if clients die. It also impacts on clients – if a server dies a number of clients may be hung waiting for locks that will never be released. Finally, it is all too easy for a rogue client to bring every other member of a system to a halt by failing to release locks it holds.

For all of these reasons probably a more appropriate strategy for use in a distributed system is that of 'optimistic locking'. Optimistic locking is perhaps best explained by example. We will use the case of a customer service application again.

A customer calls a service centre and an operator retrieves his or her details from the database. The record is (pessimistically) locked while the data is fetched and then immediately unlocked. In addition to name, address and other details the database record also contains an update count. After a few minutes of conversation the operator may need to make a change to the customer's details. The updated information is sent back to the server along with the original update count. The record is locked again. If the current update count is unchanged then no one else has modified the data in the mean time so the update can go ahead. The record update count is incremented before the lock is released. If the update count does not match the one in the request then someone else has modified the record in the meantime and the update cannot proceed without risking inconsistency.

If pessimistic locking had been used then the record would have been locked for minutes or longer preventing any other user from accessing the data. This would have been the case even if no change was to be made at the end of that time. Optimistic locking does require clients to be able to handle the 'sorry, someone beat you to it' case but the potential for other deadlocks and bottlenecks is vastly reduced.

8.2.4 Synchronicity

Everything is synchronous – if you wait long enough

In Chapter 5 we covered some of the pros and cons of synchronous versus asynchronous interaction styles. In the end neither style is inherently better than the other and it is largely a question of what you are most comfortable with and what other facilities you need.

As we have already mentioned in Chapter 4, a series of asynchronous interactions can be turned into synchronous interactions with the aid of multiple threads of control. For a concrete example of this consider Figure 8.1. The message flows between the two large boxes are identical. The lower part shows how the set of apparently arbitrary message exchanges might be the result of three parallel pairs of threads.

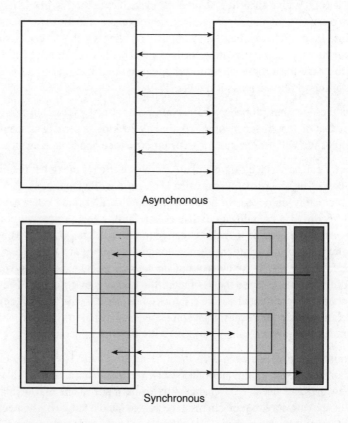

Asynchronous

Synchronous

Figure 8.1 Synchronous or asynchronous?

If you cannot do it now, queue it for later

There is at least one flavour of distributed processing that has asynchronicity as an absolute necessity. This is where there is no requirement that client and server should execute simultaneously. This distribution in time as well as space can only really be handled using some sort of queueing technology.

Queueing is almost a speciality of its own. It requires a different way of thinking, particularly about issues such as error handling. The originator of a queued request may have long since departed from the system. In such cases there may be no human to go back and figure out how to handle problems. There is no prospect of using pessimistic locking and clients and servers employing queueing must be prepared to handle potential consistency problems. Having said all this it is a very powerful tool for solving some tricky problems.

8.2.5 Error handling and debugging

If at first you do not succeed – try another server

We have touched on various issues of error handling throughout this chapter and elsewhere. Distributed TP and process groups provide very comprehensive solutions for coping with a range of failures and difficulties. However, even with less complex technologies there are still steps that can be taken to mask failure and provide automated recovery.

One of the fundamental characteristics of a distributed system is that components are not tightly welded together. This means that if one element fails there is often the opportunity to 'drop in' a replacement. It is relatively straightforward to implement a strategy within a client to handle this. When a client detects the failure of a server it can try to locate another similar server and then try again.

Of course, it is not quite this simple. The first problem is that it is not in general possible to know when a remote process crashed – or even if it has crashed. If I send off a command to pay my telephone bill and receive the message 'no response from remote system' did we lose communication before or after the funds were transferred from my account? A retry will also not work where a context is being maintained on the remote system which will be unknown to any other server.

The easiest approach is to reserve the automatic retry strategy only for those situations where it does not matter if an operation is run again. This covers most query type of operations and also many others whose sole function is to perform some form of transformation on their input data, for example a remote image processing server. In practice these categories cover a very large range of applications.

Peopleware sometimes beats software

The most capable and flexible error-handling technology available today is still the human brain. This may sound like something of an admission of failure but in truth it is very often more efficient and cost-effective to deploy people to resolve difficulties in distributed systems that any amount of technology.

People do need help, however. In particular it can be very difficult to trace end-·to-end problems through networks and distributed systems. For this reason it is sensible to develop an error-reporting strategy that places the right amount of information at a user's disposal. Defining the 'right amount' is hard but as a general rule every element in a system that detects a problem should report as much about it as it knows. A key facility that is then needed is to be able to correlate error reports from different sources.

For example, a client A might report that a call to server B for operation X failed at 9:32 a.m. Server B reports at 9:28 a.m. that it could not return the results of operation X to client A. Putting these together, and allowing for time skew, indicates that there was probably a network failure between A and B at around 9:30 a.m. It also indicates that if X was some form of update operation then it is likely that it was successful (as B had not crashed). If either report had been missing or had not contained full details then it might have been very hard to track down the real problem.

$2 \times 1 \neq 1 \times 2$

Two processors doing the same thing once is not the same as one processor doing the same thing twice. There are a number of difficult issues surrounding debugging in a distributed environment. One of the trickiest is the introduction of true concurrency.

On a single processor system multitasking is an illusion created by dividing up the processing time and allocating slices to different processes. So even if it appears that two processes are running at once the machine is only really doing one thing at a time. In the distributed environment simultaneous execution really does happen. This can often lead to subtle problems related to synchronization between such processes. Unfortunately many of the commonly used single-system tools cannot be used easily in a distributed environment. In addition, by their very nature synchronization problems tend to disappear when programs are being analysed and execution is slowed or single-stepped.

While there are a number of people trying to develop techniques for distributed debugging there are, as yet, few tools available. Probably the most helpful strategy is to instrument code to provide good diagnostic and tracing information when running in a live environment.

8.2.6 Location and naming

Never assume you know where anything is

One of the hardest aspects of distributed computing for some people to come to terms with is the fact that things move. The service that was provided on a machine in London yesterday may move to Paris tomorrow. There are great benefits to be had from the ability to construct an application dynamically from scattered components. But it is very easy to throw all of those benefits away by ossifying the assumed structure of a distributed system.

Ideally, the placement of components in a distributed system should be an issue that is left to those whose job it is to manage and optimize the performance of the system. As the needs of an application change, or entirely new consumers of services appear, the deployment of components may change radically. This can only happen, however, if the component designers have played their part and isolated themselves from dependence on particular structures.

Sometimes 'location' creeps in through the back door. When services are being implemented around existing systems or databases it is easy to express interfaces in terms of those systems rather than the services they really represent. So the interface to a billing system might reflect precisely the data-structures in the current database rather than the service it truly represents. This may lose the benefits of encapsulation – the ability to provide a different implementation while maintaining the same interface.

There are times when you need to know where something is

It is, as the saying goes, the exception that proves the rule. Sometimes you do need to know where some components are. Fixing the directory service server is hard if you need the directory service to locate it! Similarly, random selection from a sea of possible servers may not be the best policy – particularly if some servers are located on a completely different continent to your client.

Name spaces are precious – handle with care

Maintaining any form of shared global data in a distributed system is generally difficult and expensive. The systems that provide global name spaces work hard to maintain a reasonably consistent view. While all sorts of information can be shared via these mechanisms it is very easy to stress them beyond their limits.

A more important issue is one of management rather than technology. If a distributed system is to consist of hundreds if not thousands of services – each with its own demands for entries in the name space – then it can rapidly become difficult to find services in a chaotic jumble of names and hierarchies. This can be bad for normal users but a potential nightmare for operations staff who may have to understand and manage the spaghetti. Before any large-scale distributed system can be contemplated it is worth giving some thought to policies for managing and allocating portions of the global space.

8.2.7 Performance

Move the processing, not the data

Computers can usually process data faster than networks can ship it around. It is all too easy to get trapped into thinking that distributed processing is just about shuffling data between machines. It is perhaps a weakness of messaging technology that it encourages this sort of notion. RPC and ORB mechanisms force greater thought about the flow of application logic between components of a distributed system.

Much of the design of a distributed system is concerned with the correct balance between placing processing and data. It is a good general rule to aim to place the functions that will process data alongside it. In many ways this is easier with object-oriented systems where function and data are parcelled naturally.

A user very rarely wants a thousand answers to a question

Following on from the previous point, sensible interface design should also take account of how those services are really going to be used. It may be straightforward and in some respects easier to provide, for example, a service capable of returning an arbitrary amount of data. However, it is probably more sensible to design a service which returns limited amounts at a time. In many cases this will match the expected usage of the service. It will also guard against accidental or malicious abuse that could result in denial of service to others.

If you expose your service to the world, be prepared for the world to use it

While we have couched the previous discussion in terms of data being returned the same general principle applies to other aspects of a service. If it is to be shared between multiple clients it will do well to guard against excessive resource usage by any one client.

There are many mechanisms that might be used to do this. Too great a request rate from a single source may be throttled back or some form of quota of accesses imposed. (In fact you can see this done on some of the most heavily used WWW servers – particularly those serving large amounts of data such as images.) There may also be the need to bring up new instances of servers to support times of peak loads. One motivation for the use of TP systems is that they often have facilities to manage some of these issues.

Entities should not be needlessly replicated

Occam's Razor is this frequently quoted advice to reduce redundancy. From one point of view we want to exploit the benefits of replication of processes in a distributed system. These benefits may include increased reliability and performance. On the other hand replicating information so that it is consistent is hard.

Yet again there is a trade-off between the need to have data replicated for speedy local access, availability or reliability and the cost of maintaining the data. Where small amounts of largely static data are involved probably the most effective strategy is to have a central master from which data is pushed out to other users. (This can also work with large volumes of data, provided that the changes are not too frequent. In some circumstances – for example a product catalogue – the most efficient mechanism might be to make a CD ROM and send out copies to all recipients on a monthly basis.) If the data volumes are larger and more dynamic then almost certainly the only real option is to employ proprietary distributed database technology.

Computers type faster than humans

Chapter 6 discussed the issues surrounding integrating with legacy systems. One of the particular performance issues that arises in this context is the quality of the available interfaces. The only way in to many mainframe-based applications is through 'screen-scraping' the terminal interfaces originally intended for human consumption. However, computers can churn through far more screens of data at a considerably greater rate than any human operator. This can have an adverse effect on the performance of the whole system as it is stretched to its limits in handling such interactions.

For distributed systems to perform successfully they need to consider all the links in the chain and ensure that the end-to-end performance goals will not overstress any one of the links.

Do not prejudge the problems, measure them!

Even with the use of predictive modelling techniques it can be very hard to determine where likely performance bottlenecks will occur. This is especially true in a distributed system where the usage patterns of services and the physical characteristics of networks and platforms may alter radically over time. A performance model for a client/server pairing may fail utterly to describe the effect of a second, different client or server element.

The only real way to determine the performance characteristics of components is to measure them *in situ*. This means that attention needs to be given as to how those components will be instrumented to collect information. It also requires thought on how the data will later be analysed and used. Part of any template for component development should contain guidance as to how and what information will be recorded.

8.2.8 Manageability

It is no use if it cannot be managed

This is the solitary rule here not because there is little that can be said on this topic. Chapter 7 has already covered this topic in greater detail. Instead we just want to reiterate the importance of facing up to this issue throughout the development life-cycle. Effective management is probably the key to making distributed systems successful. Or, more starkly, ineffective management will mean almost certain disaster.

On a standalone system an application can get by with poor management because all the necessary components are in a single location and often delivered and deployed as a single 'lump'. A distributed application depends on potentially many other components which may be delivered, deployed and configured entirely separately. The task of knitting this mesh together and keeping it functioning will ultimately fall to system administration personnel.

A crucial part of deploying distributed systems ought to be a good management framework and infrastructure. New components need to be 'good citizens' and fit in with the requirements of this framework.

8.3 The people component

Much of this book has been about technology. But in the end technology is there not for its own sake but to serve human users. The means to implement large-scale distributed systems may now exist – but are people ready for them?

We have mentioned the 'reversed assumptions' of distributed computing several times. These primarily describe technical issues that undergo a transformation.

There are some softer aspects that suffer a similar reversal too. Leslie Lamport once characterized a distributed system along the lines of 'one where you cannot print your document on the printer next to you because a machine you've never even heard of has crashed.' The old assertion that you know where your program is running does not stand up in the distributed environment.

The World Wide Web has brought a distributed world to people's desktops. It has also illustrated some of the problems which need to be tackled to make the services of a distributed environment usable. A typical example is the case of the vanishing server. There are many Web servers that provide a useful or interesting service. Use of that service may grow until many users depend upon it. Then, for any one of a number of reasons, the service disappears. Sometimes there is a notice warning of the impending event, sometimes a redirection facility is provided but on many occasions the service just vanishes. The next time users try to access the service they are met with a frustrating error message.

In the free-wheeling anarchy of the Web, server owners are under no obligation to continue to provide services or to inform users if they wish to withdraw them. In fact, they probably do not even have sufficient information to do so even if they wanted to. Obviously in any kind of business-critical application such behaviour would be intolerable.

The impact of widely distributed systems on people is, at present, largely unknown. System designers have given far more thought to the technology than they have to its application. Chapter 9 looks at some of the open questions that should at least be thought about before moving into this brave new world.

8.4 Summary

In this chapter we have covered the role and scope of a good systems architecture. We have also tried to highlight some useful guidelines and notorious pitfalls for system designers and developers.

There are no references explicitly associated with this chapter for several reasons. The first it that it is largely a matter of consolidated, shared experience and opinion. In some cases there may be formally documented sources but often titbits, tips and tricks are passed on by word of mouth without attribution. Second, many of the references in other chapters will provide further reading on specific issues. Finally, we have tried to give some advice which we believe will be useful but many of the issues surrounding the widespread use of distributed computing are still at best only partly understood.

We hope we have some experience to share from which you can learn – the authors know that the problem of learning by your own mistakes is the sheer volume of knowledge generated!

CHAPTER 9

Metamorphosis

'It is often safer to be in chains than to be free' – Franz Kafka

This last chapter takes a step back from the detail to consider what it all means: partly an analysis of what we have already covered, partly an informed guess as to the shape of things to come.

From all that has been said in previous chapters, it would seem that we are destined to live in a world where technological change is the norm. Our everyday experience bears this out. We continually hear about some new idea or piece of equipment that promises to do something faster, more efficiently, cheaper, or just something different. Only a few of these things seem to have any direct or visible effect on our lives, at least on a day-to-day basis. But the cumulative effect on the way we live is considerable.

Our dependency on the computer is testament to this. It has permeated every aspect of modern life and there have been subtle advances in how they can cooperate over the past 10 years or so. These advances are now mature enough to allow yet another leap forward, one that is already evident in some places.

We have discussed and explained many of the central ideas, concepts and developments of cooperating computer systems. There is more that could be said and (in all likelihood) much more yet to happen. But what does this all mean and how is it likely to impact on our everyday lives.

Understanding the nature and driving force behind change is only a start. The technology of distributed computing is still largely the preserve of the specialist, although we hope that we have done our bit to demystify it. The way in which that technology actually changes our lives remains to be seen. Deploying technology, seeing if it lives up to its promise and taking the next step involves a much wider audience. This is the stage at which there is obvious, visible, day-to-day impact which, ideally, should be of choice rather than forced. As Walter Benjamin opined: 'technology is not the master of nature but of the relationship between nature and humanity.'

The final message in this book is that distributed computing permits a great deal of flexibility but that this is (or should not be) without bound. There is little doubt that computer systems that can respond to rapid flux will be important. If some limits, norms and ground rules are not placed on the level of flexibility, chaos (or worse) is possible.

Some of these ground rules will be founded on understanding and are down to local or internal discipline. Others are operational constraints imposed by legal and regulatory frameworks. If information is power then, as suggested in the quote that opens this chapter, some checks and balances need to placed on its availability and manipulation.

This chapter lays out a view of a future that contains distributed systems as an accepted way of doing things. It then asks some of the questions that surround this powerful new technology. Most of these are to do with the way that people are likely to adapt to a distributed world, and how this might impact the attendant systems. Others are concerned with the inevitable issues that arise when a society based on physical boundaries adopts a technology that transcends them. To close, we recap on the key elements that anyone aiming to distribute should bear in mind. An essential guide to success.

9.1 Great expectations

So, how will the technology of distributed systems impact on the society of the next millennium? To help answer this question, let us start by reviewing and consolidating some of the points already covered.

Here are some safe bets for the information industry, a few of the things that seem likely to happen:

- It will be distributed: by force of business changes. The rate of change seems likely to be even faster than that which drove computer dependency, as outlined in Chapter 2. It took some 30 years for us to become hooked on computers. The distribution of that addiction is set to take hold in a much shorter timescale, at least if the rapid spread of the likes of the World Wide Web is anything to go by. The initial fears of isolation as a consequence of distribution are subsiding as experience develops. In fact, there is evidence that people feel they have more choice when working with distributed systems (Sproull and Kiesler, 1991).

- It will divide as much as it unites. One fear gives way to another and those who exploit distributed systems seem set to leave others behind on the information highway. There may be millions of people who are hooked on networks but there are billions who do not have any sort of access – in danger of becoming an underclass. Just as there was a privileged class of scribes and readers in the middle ages, so there may emerge a similar group.

- It will draw on the concepts described here: people have built point solutions (stovepipes) and suffered; vendors have tried to market proprietary solutions and given up. At the same time, the adoption of a simple set of common principles has yielded the Internet, a demonstration of the power of cooperation. History teaches us that people tend to cooperate once they have exhausted all other alternatives.

- It will be technology intensive and will require informed application. Distribution is simple – but only in principle! At first glance, it consists of no more than establishing communications links between a network of resources and imposing some rules for their cooperation. The practicalities of finding and getting what you want quickly and reliably tend to become rather intrusive when the network of resources can be anywhere and can be supplied (more often, controlled) by anyone.

The concepts explained in Chapters 4 and 5 represent more than 10 years of concerted thought on how best to solve a complex reality. Distributed computing has challenged some of the best minds for long enough for the basic principles to be soundly established. This is undoubtedly a complex area but the fact that the key ideas can be articulated and an overall picture built in one slim volume is testament to its maturity. As with any technology, the successful early adopters are the ones who are well grounded in the established principles.

- It will, even more, require a change from traditional culture and organization to be best exploited. We have tried to emphasize the need to re-examine established common sense in a changed environment. This extends to the way in which people work as well as the way systems are organized, managed and maintained (Sproull and Kiesler, 1991). Nothing holds up the progress as much as the right ideas in the wrong environment.

To summarize, the technology of distributed computing has been a driven need for flexibility. Those who embrace both the technology to support it and its application will steal a march on the rest. But there is more to it than that. If people felt totally comfortable working completely online, with connections to all the resources they need, then there would be no need for books such as this. In fact, there would not be any books in this area because the prospective authors would not consider using such an antiquated format to convey information. Yet the traditional publishing industry continues to flourish! (It is remarkable to note the ever-growing range of magazines *about the Internet* on the stationers shelves, testament to most people's fondness for paper.)

There is clearly a need to think a little more about the absorption of distributed systems in the real world! Let us start by considering why and how printed matter relates to a modern world.

9.2 Sense and sensibility

Many people who work in the computing, network and software industries take pride in their mastery of computer-based facilities. The authors are no exception. We delight in exercising new applications, using remote resources to ease our work and culling data from many places. So why not publish electronically?

The answer to this question is not simple and has as much to do with the creativity of groups of people as it does the target format for some information. In looking at the main factors at play here we intend to discriminate the areas where distributed computing could and should contribute from those where most individuals would prefer that they did not.

Each of the following issues (based on the very limited experience of two people trying to assemble a single reference) is expanded on and generalized in the next section. For now, some key points:

- Ownership. You cannot copy a printed work, such as this book, anything like as convincingly as you can a computer file. What is more, the paper-based form is much more difficult to alter or misrepresent. The point here is that most people have a natural instinct to retain control and the closer, the better when it comes to their own data. Part of this is having physical copy to hand, as proof of ownership.

  In constructing the various chapters here, the authors quite happily posted portions of text for review – a fast and convenient mechanism for getting feedback. Posting the completed work, however, poses questions of ownership that do not arise if the final product is physical. Any online information (especially software) can be put into the public domain, for all to use (and abuse). There is no such thing as 'public domain hardware', however. Some of the implications of this are considered in the next section.

- Accessibility. For all the advances in computer interfaces, books are still faster to access and easier to mark up. Anyone who doubts this need only observe how people print their electronic mail!

  Much of this text was reviewed on trains, proofread in waiting rooms and edited on planes – very rarely on-screen, though. Only pen and paper offered the ease of access to use short periods of time effectively and all manner of surroundings. It is certainly the case that most of the fact checking and information retrieval took place via the Internet, the Web and various databases. Computer-presented information is surely superior in terms of searching, universal accessibility and so on, but, in practice, paper still has the edge when it comes to speed and flexibility of access. It is a cheap, universal medium that calls for no special training or equipment.

- Branding. A book has presence. It is visible in three dimensions. It has some degree of authority by virtue of its brand. In a purely electronic world, it can be difficult to differentiate the good from the rest. It is remarkably easy to set up a World Wide Web server and deliver attractively packaged information to a waiting world. The marque on the cover of this book indicates a known pedigree, some assurance of quality. It is all to easy to fake this online

So, there are some areas where established, low-technology solutions are preferred. This may be partly due to prejudice, partly due to a computing alternative or perhaps its users not being sufficiently mature, but it is not down to a lack of awareness. A final point of reflection from the authors' experience of their own (admittedly limited) distributed project is that some paperbound processes benefit greatly from computerization. The signing of contracts is a tortuous procedure when paper and mail is used. Intelligent agents, set up on target of clearing several copies of a document with several people, offer a much faster and easier solution.

9.3 A room with a view

Section 9.2 was somewhat parochial. Let us try to look beyond the authors' recent experience and consider some of the general points that will be encountered.

In the not very distant future, most of the important items that we use and work with will exist as a stream of bits. Many already do and the publication of books is a good example of that trend.

There will be increasing pressure to update the way we use and control computer systems as the logical assumes pre-eminence over the physical. Speed, access and cost all favour online production. The ease with which a document can be copied, cut and pasted into a new format using inputs and links from France, the U.S. and Japan begs a host of open questions, however.

For instance, the concepts of national boundaries and intellectual property based on ownership both require revision. When valuable items can be cloned perfectly (which is easy to do with bits) and exchanged (in seconds) between any locations in the world, new norms may have to be established.

By way of illustration, let us consider the traditional and brave new worlds of money. There is considerable appeal in using electronic tokens to trade instead of the existing physical tokens. Not only are transactions faster but also the storage and handling costs of the physical money are removed.

It is quite feasible to adopt electronic money. Automatic teller machines have been in use for some years now and are an accepted part of the fabric of modern society. With intelligent cards, such as Mondex, promising to remove the need for cash, one has to ask why hard currency has survived.

Well, this is where we need to re-examine the current situation. Electronic money has no intrinsic value (just like most banknotes), can be duplicated (just like most banknotes) and is accepted as 'legal tender' within a confined community (just like most banknotes).

To get to the bottom of this issue, we need to distinguish the two main functions of money. The first is that it is a medium of exchange and the second is that it is a store of value. It is at this stage that popular acceptance has an effect. Many people are happy to have a rapid means of settling bills and payments. Indeed most of the established electronic cash systems reside here (for instance, 1994 saw the opening of First Virtual Holdings, a bank operating purely to settle online transactions). They might be less happy to have their nest egg stored accessible only via their home computer with no physical evidence of ownership or obligation by creditors to accept it in exchange for food or shelter (in most countries, there is a legal obligation to accept hard cash).

The argument can be developed by assuming that electronic money was backed up with some tangible unit of exchange. This would lead to a world in which every cyberdollar caused a matching physical dollar to be held on account. The result would be that the electronic cash could earn no interest (as its backing cash was removed from the market) and so there would be a virtual economy with no concept of lending (at least, not for profit). This challenges the whole basis of the modern economy – and common sense has, yet again, to be revisited. Do the established principles of economics and banking dictate the limits of the exploitation of technology or does the new capability force a change to the *status quo*?

This is but one example of the complex interaction between a new way of doing business and a proven set of principles and norms. There is no prescriptive solution. The point of the above example is that knock-on effects, cultural acceptance and the like all have to be considered.

A second issue, another one very relevant to the authors, is that of royalties. If a work is available as a computer file, it can readily be copied and distributed. The question then arises of how the originator is reimbursed for his or her product. A book author might publish a table of contents along with a sample chapter on a public network and invite pledges. When they feel that they will be adequately rewarded for their efforts by a combination of pledges, they can push the relevant button and launch the fruits of their labours into the public domain. With this sort of arrangement there is no concept of royalty, as such. An alternative would be to implement pay per view access. Either way, the established way of doing things needs to be revised.

Now this sort of evolution may well grieve the publishing industry, but it is an issue that they are acutely aware of (see, for instance, the *Electronic Telegraph*, which resides on the World Wide Web and has a mechanism for recouping payment for its service). If plagiarism were to flourish, who would be responsible for controlling it? Within an organization, this may be taken care of with internal access control and external firewalls. In general, however, this is a more tricky issue, one of international law. The problem here is that not only do laws tend to be national (unlike most publishers), they also tend to be made by those with less exposure to and awareness of the potential (and perils) of electronic communication.

So what will the rules be when a file from a Canadian database is accessed by a Briton to be processed and stored on a French computer? Especially when the contents of that file contravenes French law and might result in a libel or defamation case in the U.S. Not only does open electronic exchange stretch existing law, but also the new forms of exchange (multimedia) have no precedence, so it is not clear where to start from! Standards in this area have yet to be established (the test case is a prosecution between Oklahoma and California).

Until these (and other) questions are answered, there may be blocks on the progress of distributed systems or at least some heavy influences on their deployment. So the vision of a connected and cooperating world may be spoiled, or at least deferred until such time as we have a workable electronic highway code (one of the worrying (hopefully not prophetic) anagrams of information superhighway is 'new Utopia, horrifying sham'!).

9.4 Paradise lost

New technology is as much a threat to some people as it is an opportunity and an enabler to others. There will doubtless be some casualties in the information age.

As with any migration, there are those who are lost or left behind. Some will not mind – they simply may not fancy the journey. Others will have been left by virtue of a lack of infrastructure, underinvestment or lack of foresight and/or planning.

Many will want to avoid being left behind. For these people, there are a few things that are going to happen that will have to be dealt with. For instance:

- Infosurge. With everything at your fingertips, the world is your oyster – you are empowered. The only problem with this is that nobody knows what the fully empowered individual or organization can do because there has never really been one. When you have all the information available, can distribute all design, manufacture and so on, and customize every product, what does this imply? When information is there at the touch of a button, how much of it is valued? When it comes from a remote server, how can you be sure that it is valid? It is so easy to make an attractive presentation from low-grade base material (in information terms, it is possible to make a silk purse from a sow's ear!), to pose as an authoritative source or to have your intentions subverted by a long forgotten (and once relevant or useful) system utility. The signal to noise ratio changes when local familiarity and trust is removed.

- Is the technology really following our thinking? We started this book explaining the pressures for distribution. The technology (at least ostensibly), follows this competitive business pressure. But when the 'knowledge is power' maxim is diluted through widespread access, what organizational effect will this have? Virtual teams already recognize the impact. Perhaps the traditional hierarchies will implode, if exposed to the information society. The spectre of censorship looms when established structures are threatened.

- How long will the user be in control. Most of the foregoing has placed users' views at the front and looked at the way that serving resources can best be deployed to meet their needs. If telecommunication networks are the nervous system and computers the brains, is there scope for independent thought and action? The nightmare of the thinking computer that dominates its creator (or, more likely, one that goes out of control) seems more viable as the complexity and diversity of the machine expands. Intelligent agents are already being deployed within networks. These allow you to invoke a series of actions (for example a transaction with a retailer to make a purchase plus another with a bank to pay for it), or to preselect what information you are interested in so that it reaches you selectively (for example your personalized newspaper). In this regime you never go offline – you simply let the system act on your behalf. Fine when it works!

- What happens to those political, economic and social layers that become obsolete when it can all be done online. Banking, publishing, teaching and so on may all be prone to significant revision. Just as old skills are affected by technology, so new skills will be required as information needs to be found, sorted and organized; processes need to be automated and maintained, and so on. Will technology lead the way to new structures of business or will the existing structures apply and lead to new technology?

- The traditional roles of author and publisher have become somewhat blurred. It used to be that there were many of the former but that they were filtered in their output by the selectivity of the latter. The World Wide Web has rapidly popularized the range of facilities on the Internet, making it easy to find information and to use it. The tools that have been developed in conjunction with the World Wide Web allow the author also to be the publisher. This has significant consequences in that the authenticity of source is no longer assured by visible brand.

None of the above are technical issues, but rather questions of how new technology will be integrated into 'business as usual'. Some of them have been raised in the previous sections – they are revisited and extended here to emphasize the importance of people in any system (Lipnack and Stamps, 1994). Once the above issues are accounted for, the mechanics of deployment begin. We now consider some guidelines for the implementor.

9.5 The master builder

So what is it that you need to have, to know and to do in the information age? Well, we introduced seven labours in Chapter 2 – some of the challenges to be tackled. Now, in the spirit of seven being a lucky number we give some pointers to the way ahead.

9.5.1 Principles

Given that the principles of distributed systems can be realized in a number of ways, there will be diversity in the options for building them. There are already a large number of competing products in the marketplace. Some complement each other, some do similar jobs. Making choices between them has been largely avoided here as this tends to be a case-by-case decision. It may transpire that one supplier will dominate but it is more likely that a set of popularly preferred components will emerge. The basic principles covered in Chapter 4 are enduring and provide a sound platform for structuring your system and selecting your components.

9.5.2 End-to-end

With the flexibility of distributed systems comes a need to be very clear in end-to-end operations. At present, many systems are driven by the nature of the distribution channels – the big supermarkets have enjoyed a dominant market position because they own the interface to the customer. Now the rules are changing. With distribution and distributed systems comes the potential of logical retail. It probably will not appeal to all (for instance, a well-known jeans company tried installing machines to scan customer's lower bodies and send the data to the factory so that their customized jeans could be made and be waiting for them by the time they returned home – an impressive use of technology but one rejected by shoppers who did not enjoy the experience) but there is another way of doing things and most choices promote exploitation – at least part of the traditional market has an alternative end point. One of the uses of distributed systems is to support transaction trading. (One car manufacturer in the UK has dispensed with traditional showrooms in favour of an automated customer ordering system that allows people to specify, online, the car of their dreams. The customer's specification is immediately relayed to the factory for construction. Shoppers *do* seem to enjoy this one.) This makes you less location-dependent in shopping or any other purchase for that matter. The system design should take into account the overall process, from initiation through to means of delivery.

9.5.3 Top to bottom

A specific set of suppliers play a key role in distribution – the telecommunications companies whose connections underpin all of this. With increasing amounts of data being exchanged between an increasingly diverse set of computers (and increasing expectations of speed of response), they play an important part in enabling effective distribution. It is thanks to technologies like asynchronous transfer mode (ATM) that the applications used in the local network can be extended into the wider area. This permits a fast multiservice network – an essential piece of infrastructure for supporting a wide range of traffic types. When combined with relevant standards for protocols and formats (such as MPEG for video clips) it becomes viable to carry (real-time) multimedia across a wide area. The availability of appropriate 'plumbing' cannot be assumed. It is a part of the overall picture and needs to be planned for.

9.5.4 (Virtual) teamwork

The one thing you can rely on is change. This is likely to accelerate the current trend for organizations to focus on core business and to encourage all types of non-core knowledge work to be contracted out to a growing number of self-employed knowledge workers and small consultancy businesses. The knowledge-intensive company, in this context, can readily be a geographically distributed 'virtual' organization (Gray *et al.*, 1993). Given that information has no weight or substance, yet is valuable and takes effort to assemble, it could form the basis of a truly global business. Early signs of this trend can already be seen as some Silicon Valley companies buy competitive programming skills from India (it is noteworthy that global communications are growing at three times the rate of national communications).

The overall result is likely to be an increasingly competitive market in which the slightest advantage (often in time) could prove crucial. Although large companies are likely to remain important, far fewer people will work directly for them, and the opportunities for individuals to engage their entrepreneurial skills will increase. The marshalling of such a fluid workforce will be key.

9.5.5 Think global

This applies both in terms of opportunity and competition. Suppliers can be sited anywhere, competition can come from anywhere (not just foreign shores but also different market sectors spreading their wings). By way of illustration about 5 per cent of the UK software market is supplied by teleworkers. The author's personal experience of having no fixed location gives plenty of conviction of the effectiveness of virtual working. There is evidence that some are being displaced and with a speed that makes the demise of the British motorbike industry look pedestrian. It will become increasingly important to be first in the market to win. Over time, quality of service and level of customization will become vital differentiators.

9.5.6 Think cooperative

As we have seen, it is not really that long since each computer was an isolated piece of equipment – useful but lonely. Advances in network technology and communication software have changed all that. The distinguishing feature of the information age is that it combines the (previously disparate) drives of the computing and the communications industries. This means that there are so many aspects to the design, build and operation of modern systems that you cannot do it all on your own. Involving others is vital; alliances and strategic supply relationships need to be forged.

9.5.7 Trade off

Today's new system is tomorrow's legacy – so it is very much in the interests of the user to plan how their needs can be met with minimal long-term effort and expense. Some needs are best served with well-established technology and it may be preferable to retain the *status quo* and plan how to integrate some information or service. This trade-off is one of many. Not only should one be aware of the pros and cons of replacement against integration, but also of:

- abstraction against specialization, where the more complexity that is hidden away, the less control you have;

- consistency against availability, as universal availability implies lots of local copies, whereas consistency dictates one controlled source;

- autonomy against uniformity, with more complexity being the result of allowing things to be done differently, according to individual preference;

- security against convenience, as illustrated in Chapter 6. A common problem is that the more secure a system is, the less easy it is to use.

Some of these balanced decisions are specific to local need and should be part of a broader planning process (Norris, 1995), others are informed judgements that require the technical background and detail contained in the preceding chapters. The main point is that an open framework and a range of alternative parts are key to constructing systems with the flexibility needed these days.

9.6 Never-ending story

Early on in this book, we considered the way in which computers have been absorbed into the fabric of everyday life. We used the term 'information age' to reflect the world as we now see it – one in which the information held on, and manipulated by, computers is a vital commodity.

We might have been a little more correct in referring to a 'second information age', the first one being the one where value was vested in the words and pictures copied into illuminated books produced by monks. The two ages may be 500 years apart but one general feature unites them – the fact that those who master the media have control.

So it goes full circle. The Benedictine monks at Holy Cross Abbey in Virginia have recently broken out from their long-established fruit cake business into the conversion of conventional library card catalogues to electronic format. The turnover of the Electronic Scriptorium is rising rapidly (*Telecommunications*

Policy Review, 1995) with demand easily outstripping supply. More brethren are being rallied to the new cause with every passing day.

The same is true elsewhere. Pace of change in business operations seems unlikely to slow. The operational support systems upon which they base so much of their business will need to adapt to remain in step. Change is inevitable and the only organizations that have the agility to respond in this environment will be those who anticipate this by building their systems to cope. That is what this book has focused on. We have explained the expectations and technologies for information-rich systems and outlined the principles and guidelines for building them. It may be uncomfortable to adapt to a new order but it seems that the penalty of not changing will shortly be greater.

As Charles Darwin said in his observations on natural selection: 'It is not the strongest of species that survive, nor the most intelligent, it is the one that is most adaptable to change.' The same is likely to be true of systems that support high-technology business.

APPENDIX A

Standards for distributed systems – who's who and who matters?

'*All government, indeed every human benefit and enjoyment, every virtue, and every prudent act is founded upon compromise and barter*' – Edmund Burke

For complex and disparate entities like distributed systems to work effectively, there needs to be some sort of agreement on how they should be constructed, deployed and operated. This means that some level of standardization is essential.

Many people spend a large part of their working lives defining, developing and harmonizing standards. In the broadest sense, this can entail anything from specifying the colour that a ripe banana should be to designing a precise sequence of events for two computers to exchange confidential data.

Given the breadth and detail of standards making, it is likely that the standards professionals are the only ones who truly understand the intricacies of the process. They are probably the only people who really know what the interrelation of the various standards bodies is, either in theory or in practice (even within the standards community, this is not universally known – a source of many problems in its own right). The last thing that someone struggling with the concepts of distributed computing needs is the added burden of having to understand this sort of detail.

To many of us, standards just happen and have to be suitably acknowledged, adhered to or coped with – rather like the weather. Usually they creep up on you and are quietly accepted. Occasionally, they come like a bolt out of the blue and cause a major headache. Some groups of people have the motivation or where-withal to make the weather.

A little awareness of what these people do and how they do it can be valuable. That is what this appendix covers. It is worth putting this in context, however.

The role of some of the main standards bodies that have something to say about distributed computing is explained here, along with an outline of what their main offerings are and how they work with each other. We also discuss some of the more useful deliverables from the various standards bodies – the specifications and, increasingly, products that help set a baseline for cooperation between systems.

Given the potential impact of new standards, be they *de jure* or *de facto*, we also briefly consider the various options and strategies for interacting with the standards makers.

The overall coverage here will, of necessity, be superficial. There are many issues that can only be resolved through commercial judgement, even intuition (for example whether to opt for the latest offering from one supplier in preference to that of another). What follows should allow some sort of positioning, however, and we at least introduce many of the more prominent players who determine the shape of distributed computing.

Before any of that, however, some background.

A.1 A little history

Standards that relate to distributed computing are fairly new on the scene. It is, therefore, quite useful (and valuable) to trace some of the main influences and developments in the area.

A lot of the early work came out of a variety of research initiatives in computer networking. Perhaps the two most relevant are the U.S. Department of Defense (DoD) experiments with computer network resilience and communication protocols that provided the basis for the Internet, and the development of remote procedure call (RPC) mechanisms at Xerox Park. In terms of technology, both of these were well established by the late 1970s. These, and other, investigations laid firm foundations for later development and provided many of the raw ideas that were later refined into standards for open systems. It was some time later that any concerted effort was made to codify the principles established by this work, however, with standardization starting in the mid-1980s.

After a few years (the late 1980s) it became obvious that there were two parallel groups developing relevant standards. Both were concerned with cooperation between systems but each was adopting a different focus. ISO is an organization known to most people (and the prime source of standards over an enormous number of areas). This is an agency of the UN in the UNESCO family. Each member country is represented by a single national body, for instance the UK has the British Standards Institution (BSI). In ISO, open systems interconnection (OSI) communications standards were well advanced, while in IEEE, the POSIX system services interface standards were being defined. POSIX is portable operating systems interface. It is part of the IEEE standards and is concerned with the standardization of the application programming interfaces (APIs) that allow applications that can be ported from one machine to another to be written. In essence, these reflected two communities with two preoccupations: communications experts wanted to allow systems to interconnect by defining open (that is, not proprietary) communications standards, and systems software experts wanted to make software more portable by defining open operating system standards.

The reaction of ISO to this was to take a broader view by establishing work on the reference model for open distributed processing (RM-ODP) with the goal of providing a basis for open and distributed systems. The RM-ODP (sometimes called 'OSI done properly') set the context for a new family of open systems standards whose objectives included system interconnection, software portability and applications interoperability.

Some of the initiatives explained here, such as ODP, have been kept within the formal standards communities, while others, such as X/Open are vendor driven. X/Open is an industry standard consortium that seeks to publish detailed system specifications for open standards. By way of illustration, X/Open exclusively licenses the UNIX trademark, thereby bringing focus to its various flavours (Ultrix, AIX, Solaris and so on). The overall aim, however, remains common – to define the standards and frameworks for interoperability of computer systems. This, in turn, fulfils the aim of allowing systems to be assembled with interchangeable hardware and the software components options to best suit the end users particular needs.

The quest for viable open systems has gained momentum since these initiatives were launched and there are now usable open system components that conform to well publicized standards.

For now, we give a brief overview of the main players. Some of those listed here provide standards in the normally accepted form of detailed guidance documents, mandated through committee discussion. Others are key influencers whose work has been widely adopted and is subsequently reflected in reference products or in published standards. In all cases, the consequence of ignoring the accepted norm(s) is a loss of market credibility or flexibility, rather than a matter of transgressing a mandate.

A.2 The key players

In this section we give a brief résumé of the main organizations that make and influence standards in the distributed computing marketplace. Their interrelation and impact on practical systems is covered later.

A.2.1 ANSA

Scope

ANSA stands for advanced network systems architecture. It is a UK-based industrial consortium that was established to define and demonstrate a practical architecture for distributed computer systems. It was set up under the aegis of the pre-competitive Alvey research scheme in the mid-1980s with support from UK-based companies such as GPT, ICL and BT. The consortium membership was expanded to include HP, DEC and other global suppliers.

The work of the ANSA consortium was initially aimed at defining a coherent architecture for distributed processing. This is presented in the ANSA reference manual, a comprehensive and detailed guide for the designer of distributed systems. A second objective of ANSA was to build the software elements and test harnesses that enable the architecture to be implemented, an objective realized with ANSAware. In many ways, ANSA can be viewed as pioneering the practical application of concepts such as object orientation.

In terms of coverage, a key ANSA aim has been to bring together the three disparate areas of computing:

1   desktop (that is the applications seen by the user);

2   databases (distributed, federated and other strategies for storage);

3   business systems (online transaction processing systems);

and to provide a common framework within which they can all be described.

Offerings

ANSA has produced a reference manual – a very detailed technical architecture to meet its aims – along with a number of the components that are required to build real systems to that architecture (ANSAware). The results that have come out are applicable to a wide range of applications, for instance:

- general computing, such as office automation, finance packages and so on;

- operational computing systems;

- integration of networks and computing – relevant to intelligent networks and in the work of TINA.

The results have influenced other industry organizations such as the OMG, and have also been taken up by individual vendors. For instance, Telcos, such as Bell Northern, have developed their own ANSA-based systems, principally for network management. ICL's DAIS is based on ANSAware.

Overall ANSA has made a strong impact on the distributed processing community as a whole. The consortium has a detailed workplan for several years ahead which aims to produce working systems as proof of concept. The step on from ANSAware, called ANSAweb, is intended to ease the distribution of applications.

In practice, the lifetime of the consortium is open-ended – they operate as a permanent team rather than an occasional gathering. The feed through into other activities is taking place (for example TINA and OMG) but this is not really measurable.

Links to other groups

ANSA has links with other organizations, both commercial and research and standards initiatives, specifically:

- The object management group – ANSA has direct participation and is generally regarded as providing much of the architectural input. It also influences the input of the individual vendor members.

- TINA – the work here focuses on telecommunications and can be regarded as complementary.

- ISO open distributed processing – ANSA have made direct contributions to the work and have also influenced the input of member companies (both nationally and internationally).

Overall, much of the ANSA output has been adopted by other standards bodies. This is not really surprising as the initial task within ANSA was to harvest seminal work by Xerox, DoD and so on. There is some background information available from ANSA via World Wide Web, via http://www.ansa.co.uk.

A.2.2 Object management group

Scope

The OMG is an international consortium of over 300 vendors and users. The OMG produces specifications for the components of an object-oriented distributed environment. These specifications are chosen from submissions by member companies rather than being developed wholly through the committee processes used in ISO and ITU. As such, OMG specifications are *de facto* rather than *de jure* standards.

Offerings

As an organization the OMG has two roles:

1   stimulating interest in the marketplace for object-oriented technologies;

2   producing specifications for product procurement.

Both of these are intended to be of benefit to end users of these technologies. Perhaps the best known output from OMG is the common object request broker architecture (CORBA).

Products are beginning to emerge that are claiming compliance to the OMG specifications, for example HP's ORBplus, IBM's System Object Model and others. These technologies have been identified as being particularly relevant not only to general distributed systems but also in specialist areas such as network management systems.

The OMG's process of adopting rather than developing specifications allows a timescale of around 18 months to standardize on any given technology. By way of illustration, for CORBA, the initial specification already existed. Revisions and extensions were added around this specification and other services were then developed.

Links to other groups

The OMG has ties with many organizations, most notably with X/Open and the OSF. X/Open will be responsible for handling conformance to OMG specifications and has also identified OMG specifications within its own work.

ANSA is directly involved in the OMG and also influences the input of its member companies. The OMG has identified the ISO open distributed processing standardization initiative as being of strategic architectural importance and requires statements of architectural conformance to ODP for all submissions (although it is not necessarily true that OMG specifications will actually be conformant).

It may seem that the OMG overlaps with the ISO open distributed processing initiative. In practice, however, the OMG's considerably shorter timescales mean that the activities are more complementary. As indicated above, it is anticipated by many users that ODP provides the architecture and OMG the detailed component specifications.

A.2.3 Open software foundation

Scope

The OSF is an international industry group of approximately 400 member companies delivering *de facto* system software and specifications. These technologies cover user interfaces, distributed environments and management frameworks.

Offerings

Most of OSF's technologies are of direct relevance to the production of operational systems. The OSF deliver software that is subsequently incorporated into commercial products. There is typically something like a six month lag between the release of software by OSF and its re-emergence in a product from a major vendor. The key OSF technologies are:

- Motif. This is a user interface toolkit and style for X/Windows-based applications. It has been widely available since 1992 and is in 'mainstream' use in many places as a means of providing an access interface between workstations and UNIX servers.

- Distributed computing environment (DCE). This is recognized as the strategic direction for distributed computing by many (and is covered in more detail in the main text).

- Distributed management environment (DME). The original vision for DME was of an all-encompassing framework together with applications. While this was widely regarded as being a fine and noble aim, it was subsequently found to be unachievable and led to the acronym DME being redefined by cynics as 'distributed management eventually'. Consequently, the scope of the DME has been refocused and is now being delivered in three phases, the first of which was completed during 1994.

  Phase 1.   Distribution services (for example print control, software distribution)

  Phase 2.   Network management options.

  Phase 3.   Object management framework (management request broker) – which is to be aligned with the OMG's CORBA.

The general intent in DME is to take vendor products on board as they begin to emerge.

Links to other groups

OSF has close working relations with the OMG, X/Open and network management forum (NMF). OSF and X/Open merged in 1996.

In terms of technologies, the DME management request broker will be compliant with the OMG's CORBA and the NMF have identified DME components in the OMNI*Point*™ specifications, (in particular, they use the OSF's instrumentation broker).

From an organizational perspective, it seems likely that there will be an ongoing relationship between X/Open and OSF, with X/Open providing the standards coordination and endorsement, OSF delivering the goods.

A.2.4 X/Open

Scope

X/Open is a worldwide, independent open systems organization dedicated to providing a unified path to open systems specification and implementation. This unification is achieved through the close cooperation and integration of input from users, vendors and standards organizations worldwide.

The X/Open specification, which covers both interoperability and applications portability, is based on *de facto* and international standards. X/Open operates a test and verification service for products developed in line with its specifications. It awards its brand as the mark of compliance.

X/Open operates requirements topic groups (RTGs) and technical working groups (TWGs) for generating detailed requirements and specifications in specific areas.

Offerings

X/Open is a route through which suppliers and users can deliver requirements for the development of standards for computing platforms (relevant to SPIRIT and procurement). It is also a forum for sharing information on the current IT industry trends and developments, a good basis for the formulation of IT technical strategy.

A large part of the value of X/Open lies in the benefits that are attained continuously through industry watching and networking. They can be regarded as the sprinklers of the industry holy water.

Links to other groups

X/Open can be regarded as the principal standards selection group. It is an independent, user-driven group that collates and endorses standards from *de facto*, formal or informal bodies, such as ISO, OMG, OSF and so on.

A.2.5 Network Management Forum

Scope

The work of the Network Management Forum (NMF) is considerably broader than its name suggests. The initial focus was on the interfaces and procedures needed to manage complex networks comprised of many different elements. The fact that many of the components of modern networks are computers has broadened the Forum's remit.

Its current direction, described in the OMNI*Point*™ strategic framework, is a service-based approach to the management of networks and systems. This covers the traditional concerns of both telecommunications networks and distributed computer systems

There are over 100 members of the Forum and there is a good balance between all the major trading regions and across the computing and telecommunications industry. The board members are, AT&T, BT, Bull, DEC, HP, IBM and STET (Italy).

Offerings

The NM Forum is the only industry consortia which is interested in covering the full scope of interoperable management systems. This means everything from requirements through to product delivery and testing. Results of note have been the delivery of:

- OMNI*Point*™ 0 and 1 specifications for management systems, drawn together from the 19 members of the OMNI*Point*™ roadmap programme. These introduced the CMIS/CMIP standard for interfacing network elements and management systems.

- OMNI*Point*™ 1+ extensions to cover TMN/OMNI*Point*™ implementations and SNMP/CMIS interworking.

- SPIRIT. An initiative to capture service provider requirements for computing platforms (jointly with X/Open).

- AIMS. A group of smaller vendors who have developed the open edge – a legacy system integration and migration technique.

The Forum holds a detailed workplan proposal which covers a two-year period and is based upon the strategic direction in the OMNI*Point*™ strategic framework (which covers a five year timescale).

Links to other groups

The Forum has positioned itself as the consortia of consortia for all matters concerned with service and network management. It has pro-actively sought to cooperate with all other interested groups who in the main have management on only a part of their agenda. This includes, for instance, the various broadband technology groups (ATM and Frame Relay Fora and so on) as well as the groups mentioned above.

The Forum has a long-standing and productive relationship with the regional workshops of X/Open, OSF, major procurement groups such as the U.S. NIST (GOSIP U.S.) and CCTA (GOSIP U.K.), and the regional testing organizations. It is also actively cooperating with the ITU (a long-standing international standards body, familiar to many in its former guise as the CCITT. In the past, this organization, which represents the world's public network operators, has focused very much on telecommunications issues. With the convergence of computing and communications, however, it has come to address similar areas to ISO and jointly publishes RM-ODP with ISO) and with the Internet engineering task force.

In the main, the Forum overlaps with just about all the other organizations which carry out some work on service and network management, but does aim to ensure that work programmes are aligned and that duplications are kept to a minimum.

A.2.6 SPIRIT

Scope

Service providers integrated requirements for information technology (SPIRIT) is an initiative that came from the Network Management Forum. It is a consortium of telcos, aided by their major IT suppliers, jointly specifying a general purpose computing platform. Rather than producing standards, SPIRIT's aim is to provide guidelines that help a buyer to select appropriate system components.

Offerings

The benefits from SPIRIT follow on from those associated with the deployment of open systems. They line up with the ideals of distributed systems – that they will prove cheaper, faster to deploy, have wider availability, be technologically innovative, scalable, easier to integrate and so on.

The fact of the matter (at least for the time being) is that the open systems movement has resulted in an enormous diversity of both standards and products. While increasing choice and reducing costs through greater competition, any potential benefits that may have been attained are offset from the additional cost of supporting this diversity and coping with the irritating interworking issues that come with it. As one salesman of proprietary computing equipment was heard to say: 'We do not want to get locked into open systems!'

SPIRIT is all about the specification of open systems platform components, the aims being to reduce the diversity of choice, to increase the chances of interoperability and portability and to decrease the breadth of skills required to develop and maintain such systems.

In effect, SPIRIT shares the cost of many organization's in-house activities and provides a partial (if not full) replacement of the company-specific guide. It also provides a coordinated statement to the IT supply industry from a large industry sector (that is telecommunications).

The SPIRIT documents have come into use as they have been produced and have been seen to deliver immediate benefit in reducing the diversity of open systems. At the time of writing, SPIRIT had largely completed its work.

Links to other groups

SPIRIT is 'harvesting' activity that has selected the most pragmatic standards from the most appropriate standards body or vendor. It is parented by the Network Management Forum and consequently any standards chosen specifically for management come from choices made in the NMF OMNI*Point*™ programme.

SPIRIT has met regularly in locations adjacent to the X/Open offices and it is intended to publish SPIRIT and X/Open specifications jointly.

A.2.7 TINA–C (Telecommunications information networking architecture – consortium)

Scope

The TINA–C comprises leading companies in telecommunications that have come together to address the convergence of computing and telecommunications. It aims to assess and assimilate some of the emerging methods and technologies from the computing sector which are expected to have an impact on the telecommunications industry.

A 'core team' has been established to develop architecture specifications for computing in telecommunications. In addition, a selection of the core team – BT, BNR, GPT, Stratus and ICL – are involved in an auxiliary project to develop multimedia virtual private services. The aim is to validate the TINA architecture specifications against an important application area for the future.

Offerings

TINA–C is concerned with precompetitive research and as such the benefits are primarily technical rather than business oriented. The main objectives of the planned work are:

- A better understanding of the interrelation between computing and communications elements in telecommunication systems.

- The study of object orientation and information modelling in telecommunications.

- The study of the role of distributed processing telecommunications.

The issues dealt with in the above include service construction, configuration and management; federation, naming and trading; and flexible service evolution.

Links to other groups

TINA is drawing on the efforts in ODP and OSI, and has direct input from ANSA.

A.2.8 IAB – Internet architecture board

Scope

The Internet activities board (IAB) is an influential panel that guides the technical standards adopted over the Internet. Linked to the IAB are two bodies that do much of the down-to-earth work to make the Internet a practical reality. The better known of the two is the Internet engineering task force (IETF), the source of the operational and technical standards on the net (captured in the widely used Requests for Comment, RFCs). The Internet research task force makes up the trinity. This body takes on the research questions for future development of the Internet.

A more recent extension to these established bodies is the Internet Society, which aims to provide a forum for disseminating information and discussing future directions. Internet information is also available from the Internet network information centre (InterNIC), a central repository for everything from how to connect through to directory services. Some of the relevant contact points are listed in the Electronic References section at the end of Chapter 3.

Offerings

The IAB is responsible for the widely accepted TCP/IP family of protocols. As such they are the focal point for the name and address space for the vast majority of the publicly networked computers across the world.

The IAB has also adopted SNMP as its approved network management protocol.

The most widely used of the IAB offerings are probably the RFCs, which define the various Internet standards.

Links to other groups

The IAB is interesting in that it is open to virtually anyone who wishes to contribute. It has traditionally comprised a mix of researchers, networkers and computer developers. Given its fairly pragmatic approach it has tended to work in parallel with the more formal standards bodies. It does have a direct link, though, in that Internet standards are offered for adoption by the likes of ISO.

There are other standards bodies that could have been included here – there always will be (for example DAVIC, the Digital Audio Visual Council is rapidly setting out how networked multimedia should be handled) – but the above are those that have set the pace to date in distributed systems. As stated at the beginning, understanding who the standards bodies are and what they are doing is only one part of the picture – politics, alliances and user preference all play their part in determining what is used in the field (not always usefully, either; for instance, there are several flavours of transaction processing procedure call – TXRPC for Encina, C-PIC for CICS and so on – to suit different vendors). In light of this limitation, we will now move on from looking at the visible players in the standards arena.

One final point in this section, however, is an observation: that it is two of the less heavily populated bodies that have made the biggest impact – ANSA and the IAB. This contrasts with, for instance, telecommunications, where the formal, consensus-oriented bodies – the ITU and ISO – have dominated. The reason for this lies, mostly, in the nature of the distributed computing market. It is a fast-moving area and driven by differentiation.

A.3 Standards strategy

In many ways, the nature and content of standards reflect the interests and opinions of the users and suppliers in that market. There are many drivers (an appropriate time, perhaps, to mention that standards making has been said to be 'as interesting as a Russian truck' by one eminent industrial leader!) and influencing factors that determine the courses of actions taken.

This section aims to put the activities of the various standards makers described above into some sort of overall context. In particular, we intend to characterize each of the key players and show why their recommendations have evolved as they have.

To do this, we identify three overlapping categories of primary reason for participating in standards organizations:

- Precompetitive. The contributors are concerned with collaborative research. The participants are seeking to share the cost and effort of exploring a new area.

- Cost reduction. The contributors participate as they wish to reduce the cost of their systems, primarily through reducing the diversity in the marketplace.

- Core business. The activities of the standards organization are directly relevant to contributors' core business, so they need to ensure that they protect, enhance or maintain their commercial interests.

Most of the standards players described in the previous section can be placed in one of these categories. Figure A.1 shows where they fall. Not surprisingly in an area where consensus and commonality are vital, the majority of the effort is on precompetitive work. So much so that the area of core business is not populated at all in Figure A.1. The way in which distributed systems are applied to particular business concerns is touched on in the likes of TINA–C and NMF but is not tackled directly.

We can understand a little more of the operation of the standards players by digging a little deeper into the way they work. So far we have discerned some overall focus for each of the players. In terms of how they arrive at their decisions, there is a less clear tale to tell. Most of the bodies described in the previous section are composed of a large number of delegates – each with their own agenda. To reach a consensus, there needs to be shared satisfaction with the courses of action taken.

There is no one reason for wanting to standardize, however, so we list below a whole set of the motivations that come into play in standards making. Any one contributor (and many organizations contribute to most or all of the bodies described in the previous section) will have a different set of motives for participating in each of the standards fora.

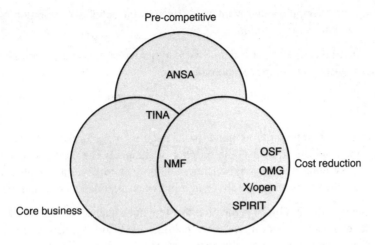

Figure A.1 Drivers for standards.

To understand really how each of the players work, it is necessary to have some idea of where each of the contributors places their emphasis.

Here is a list of 'reasons for participating' that covers most of the motivations :

- cost reduction – deliverables will reduce the procurement cost of distributed systems;

- investment protection – ensuring that the work does not adversely affect current technology investment;

- strategic – the work is of strategic importance;

- reducing options – a desire to have single solutions that reduce/eliminate the need to consider alternatives;

- withdrawal – withdrawing from the work would be embarrassing;

- world watch – a general interest in the area and a desire to see what others are up to;

- public relations – being involved earns points with others;

- precompetitive – the undertaking of precompetitive research on a collaborative basis (this may be for shared risk world watch or other reasons);

- influence – wish to ensure that the direction of the work is beneficial;

- shared risk – undertaking some activity of interest but doing it on a collaborative basis in order to share the risk;

- playing our part – need to be seen to be involved in the activity;

- knowledge of use – looking to acquire an understanding of how to use available technologies;

- company champion – involvement is driven by the belief of one or more persons within an organization;

- stimulating activity – wish to see work in particular areas or encourage the marketplace to consider technologies;

- spoiling – participation is in order to deliberately prevent the work meeting its objectives!

Many of these points apply as much to standards in the broadest sense (for example those advanced by a single supplier or alliance). The immaturity of the distributed systems market makes it more important to discern signals from noise, so it is worth bearing the above in mind where standards are concerned.

A final point in this is simply to mention that too much analysis of the behaviour and intent of standards bodies can be wasted time and effort. While it is true that there are a range of aims and motivations in standards making, a lot of what actually happens in the real world defies prediction. Chance, tiredness and misunderstanding all have their part to play. But it is worth being clear what aims are being followed by those who do participate!

Having outlined a (fairly cynical) view of the way in which consensus is reached, we close by looking at the standards 'life-cycle' – how the various bodies talked about earlier work together to move from concept to reality.

A.4 How they work together

The previous section indicated that a prime focus in the distributed computing standards organizations is cost reduction. If this is to be achieved then there needs to be some sort of working relationship between the various players. This is a particularly complex area with most of the organizations having declared strategic relations with the others. So the first point to note is that coordination is fairly loose, mostly effected through the transfer of ideas between the people involved. In general, however, the following holds true.

X/Open, NMF and SPIRIT can all be regarded as providing a standards selection process. They tailor the output of other standards bodies and, in the case of SPIRIT, some vendors' products, and produce integrated solutions that can be applied by an end user. X/Open, from an overall perspective, provides general purpose solutions in the form of its X/Open procurement guide – the XPG. The NMF and SPIRIT are more focused: NMF in terms of a specific application domain (that is network management); SPIRIT in terms of user group (that is telecommunications).

The OSF and OMG are both concerned with delivering technology. The OMG produces component specifications and the OSF produces component technologies in the form of reference implementations.

This may all seem convoluted and forbiddingly complex at first sight but, once seen in operation, is quite rational. Figure A.2 illustrates the flow of distributed computing solutions from their concept and specification (mostly the remit of formal standards) through to delivery of the product (the prime aim of the industry consortia). From the end user's point of view, there is a spectrum of standardized offerings from formal standards (useful for reference) through to conformant software components (essential for systems building).

Figure A.2 gives the general picture of cooperation between the various standards bodies. To understand how this actually translates into working practice, we can take an example – the OMG's common object request broker architecture (which also illustrates the potential influence gained through collaborative research).

The OMG specifications, which are submitted by vendors based on their products, have been influenced by the results of ANSA and also ISO's open distributed processing initiative. As well as being implemented directly by vendors (products are now beginning to become available), the CORBA specifications have been adopted as part of the OSF's DME (phase 3),which also includes the DCE. Following from that, both the NMF and X/Open are to adopt the DME as their management request broker. X/Open also endorses the CORBA specifications in their own right. This flow is illustrated in Figure A.3.

Finally, one caveat. The fact that industrial consortia play a major part in determining standards means that commercial pressures inevitably play a major part in what happens. There will inevitably be some diversity in the marketplace and some value judgements to be made by the users as to the best product for their needs. This contrasts with more regulated areas, such as telecommunications, where standards tend to be technical agreements that everyone expects adherence to.

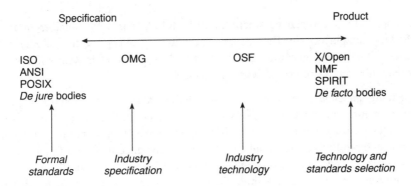

Figure A.2 The standards 'life-cycle' for distributed computing.

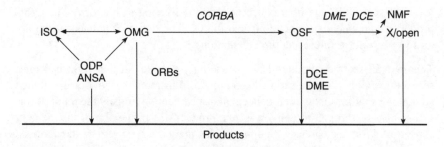

Figure A.3 The flow of ideas through the standards bodies.

A.5 Summary

An important part of distribution is to have shared ways of doing things. After all, when you are removed from a colleague, you need to have some preordained practices to guard against misunderstanding. In the world of distributed computing, the standards that embody this shared understanding are now becoming available.

There are a number of points that relate to standards for distributed computing:

- There is no one body to provide everything you need. This is not really surprising when you consider the diversity and complexity of the area. The main standards bodies have been described here.

- The standards that have been produced are not uniform in nature – some are technical (protocol definitions, architectural specifications), some are more oriented towards supply, management or operations.

- It should not be forgotten that standards are but one piece of the jigsaw. Market forces, vested interest and pure chance sometimes prevail over all manner of consensus.

This appendix has explained where the drive for standards has come from and who the main players are. The intent has been to give an appreciation of why the current situation exists and to impart some understanding of how it is likely to evolve – the motivators and drivers for change.

One thing that should be clear in this appendix is that standardization of computing elements (or anything else for that matter) is a complicated affair. Nonetheless, it is vital to effective distribution, as cooperation relies on mutual understanding. For all the complexity that is involved, some form of negotiated consensus is needed in a diverse world. To quote Darryl F Zanuck: 'If two men on the same job agree all the time, then one is useless. If they disagree all the time, then both are useless.' The latter scenario is the one to avoid!

Glossary

'*For the snark WAS a boojum, you see*' – Lewis Carroll, *The Hunting of the Snark*

With computing pervading more and more areas of modern business, its associated vocabulary has grown ever more difficult for the non-specialist to follow. In particular, the convergence of computing and telecommunications has led to a broad and often confusing set of terms that are assumed by many suppliers to be widely known. Here we list here many of the key terms, abbreviations, 'buzzwords' and concepts in common use these days. A number of the terms below have been covered in the main text, many are not. In either case the aim is to clarify the more complex ideas by giving some indication of their context and application. For a broader (and free) dictionary of computing terms see World Wide Web pages at http://wombat.doc.ic.ac.uk/.

0–9

3270   An IBM block mode terminal, once ubiquitous as the user interface to the mainframe. Many PCs have 3270 emulation capability.

2-tier	Two-tier client/server application consisting of a single client and server pairing. Frequently the server is a central database with most of the application code in the client. See Section 4.4.
3-tier	Three-tier client/server systems partition the application code according to the type of processing they perform. This may, but does not have to be, distributed across three different physical systems. See Section 4.4.
4GL	Fourth generation language. A term usually applied to languages such as SQL designed to allow databases to be interrogated.

A

ABI	Application binary interface. The interface by which an application program gains access to an operating system and other services. It enables the producers of application programs to write their code so that it runs on any system.
Abstraction	A representation of something that contains less information than the something. For example, a data abstraction provides information about some reference in the outside world without indicating how the data is represented in the computer.
Abstract	Containing less information than reality.
ACID	The ACID properties are atomicity, consistency, isolation and durability. See Transaction Processing and Section 4.3.2.
Address	A common term used both in computers and data communication designating the destination or origination of data or terminal equipment in the transmission of data. Types of address include hardware addresses (for example 0321.6B11.5643 for an Ethernet card), logical addresses (for example 132.146.6.11, an IP address for a workstation) or a personal address (M.Norris@axion.bt.co.uk, to reach an individual).
Agent	'Intelligent agent' is a general term sometimes used to describe a semi-autonomous program that is capable of roaming through a computing network collecting and processing data on behalf of its originator, sending back results as necessary. See Section 4.3.2
Agent	In systems and network management a term usually applied to a server specialized for performing management operations on the target system or network node. See Section 4.3.2 and Chapter 7.

Algorithm — A group of defined rules or processes for solving a problem. This might be a mathematical procedure enabling a problem to be solved in a definitive number of steps. A precise set of instructions for carrying out some computation (for example the algorithm for calculating an employee's take-home pay).

Alpha test — See Beta test.

Anonymous FTP See FTP.

Amdahl's law — A means of calculating the speed benefits of using processors in parallel. It states that if F is the fraction of a program that is sequential, $1-F$ the fraction that can be executed in parallel, then the speed benefit of using P processors is $1/(F+((1-F)/P))$. Put more simply, you cannot speed up a program by using multiple processors if the program will only use one of them at a time. See Section 4.6.1.

ANSA — Advanced networked systems architecture, a research group established in Cambridge, UK in 1984 that has had a major influence on the design of distributed processing systems. The ANSA reference manual is the closest thing to an engineers' handbook in this area. See Appendix A.

API — Application programming interface – software designed to make a computer's facilities accessible to an application program. It is the definition of the facilities offered to a programmer. All operating systems and network operating systems have APIs. In a networking environment it is essential that various machines' APIs are compatible, otherwise programs would be exclusive to the machines on which they reside.

APPC — Advanced program to program communication – an application program interface developed by IBM. Its original function was in mainframe environments enabling different programs on different machines to communicate. As the name suggests the two programs talk to each other as equals using APPC as an interface designed to ensure that different machines on the network talk to each other.

APPC/PC — A version of the advanced program to program communications (APPC) developed by IBM to run a PC-based Token Ring network.

Applet — A small software component of little use on its own but which may be 'plugged in' to form part of a larger application. Used mainly in the context Java-type mobile code environments. See Section 5.7.

AppleTalk	OSI-compliant protocols that are media independent and able to run on Ethernet, Token Ring and LocalTalk. LocalTalk is Apple Computers' proprietary cabling system for connecting PCs, Macintoshes and peripherals and uses CSMA/CA access method.
Application	The user task performed by a computer (such as making a hotel reservation, processing a company's accounts or analysing market research data). Often used as a synonym for the program that runs to support the application.
Application generators	High-level languages that allow rapid generation of executable code, sometimes referred to as 4GLs: Focus being a typical example.
Application program	A series of computer instructions or a program which, when executed, performs a task directly associated with an application such as spreadsheets, word processing or database management.
Applications software	The software used to carry out the applications task.
Archie	A network-based service that provides look-ups for packages in a database of the offerings from anonymous FTP sites (of which there are many).
Architecture	When applied to computer and communication systems, it denotes the logical structure or organization of the system and defines its functions, interfaces, data and procedures. In practice, architecture is not one thing but a set of views used to control or understand complex systems. A loose definition is that it is a set of components and some rules for assembling them.
Argument	See Parameter.
ASN.1	An ISO/CCITT standard language for the description of data. ASN.1 is defined in the ITU standard X.208 (which equates to ISO standard 8824). ASN.1, along with some standard basic encoding rules, is used to specify the exchange of structured data between application programs over networks. It allows data structures to be described in a way that is independent of machine architecture and implementation language. OSI application layer protocols such as X.400 MHS electronic mail, X.500 directory services and SNMP have all used ASN.1 to describe the protocol data units (PDUs) that they exchange. See p. 96.
Asynchronicity	See Section 4.6.2.

Asynchronous transmission	A data transmission in which receiver and transmission transmitter clocks are not synchronized, each character (word/data block) is preceded by a start bit and terminated by one or more stop bits, which are used at the receiver for synchronization.
ATM	Asynchronous transfer mode. A technology for transporting high-speed data over networks. Equally applicable to local and wide areas and heralded as the uniform fabric for carrying voice, video and data traffic. It is possible that ATM networks will provide the multiservice networks that underpin multimedia applications.
ATM	Automatic teller machines – 'through the wall' cash dispensers. Another example of well overloaded acronyms! And yes, networks of ATMs could use ATM networks ...
Automation	Systems that can operate with little or no human intervention. It is easiest to automate simple mechanical processes, hardest to automate those tasks needing common sense, creative ability, judgement or initiative in unprecedented situations.

B

Batch processing	In data processing or data communications, an operation where related items are grouped together and transmitted for common processing.
Beta test	Commonly used term to describe the state of a system that is believed to be mainly functional but not yet completely tested. Beta testing is often performed by a set of trusted users or customers who are willing to accept the existence of and report problems before the system is released for full field use. Beta testing is conventionally preceded by alpha testing, which generally indicates a system in a 'just about working, many known problems, use at your own risk' state.
Big endian	See Endianness.
Binding	The process whereby a procedure call is linked with a procedure address or a client is linked to a server. In traditional programming languages, procedure calls are assigned an address when the program is compiled and linked. This is static binding. With late, or dynamic, binding, the caller and the callee are matched at the time the program is executed. See Section 5.1.3.
Brooks' law	This is the maxim that adding programmers to a project that is late will cause it to be further delayed. Brooks explains the law

in his 1975 book *The Mythical Man-Month*, which draws on his experience of the IBM OS/360 project. The law is as true in the 1990s as it was in the 1970s.

Bug   An error in a program or fault in equipment. Origin of the term is disputed but the first use in a computing context is often attributed to Vice-Admiral Grace Murray Hopper of the U.S. Navy. In the early days of valve-based electronic computing she found that an error was caused by a genuine bug – a moth fluttering around inside the machine.

Byte-code   See Virtual machine.

C

C   A widely used programming language originally developed by Brian Kernighan and Dennis Ritchie at AT&T Bell Laboratories. C became most widely known as the language in which the UNIX operating system was written.

C++   A programming language based upon C but adding many enhancements particularly for object-oriented programming. It has probably now surpassed C in popularity. C++ provides the basis for Java.

CCITT   Consultative Committee of the International Telegraph and Telephone. The body responsible for many telecommunications standards. Now known as ITU – International Telecommunications Union.

CDS   Cell directory service. The local directory service provided by DCE. See Chapter 5.

CEN/CENELEC The two official European bodies responsible for standard setting, subsets of the members of the International Standards Organization (ISO). The main thrust of their work is functional standards for OSI-related technologies.

CEPT   The European Conference of Posts and Telecommunications. An association of European PTTs and network operators from 18 countries.

CERN   The European laboratories for particle physics. Home of the HTML and HTTP concepts that underpin the popular Mosaic and Netscape browsers.

Class   See Object and Section 4.5.

Client   A requester of a service. More precisely a client is an entity – for example a program, process or person – that is participating in an interaction with another entity and is taking the role of requesting (and receiving) the required service. See Section 4.3.1.

Client/server
The division of an application into (at least) two parts, where one acts as the 'client' (by requesting a service) and the other acts as the 'server' (by providing the service). The rationale behind client/server computing is to exploit the local desktop processing power leaving the server to govern the centrally held information. This should not be confused with PCs holding their own files on a LAN, as here the client or PC is carrying out its own application tasks.

Clipper
An integrated circuit for the encryption of telephone traffic. The U.S. government's preference for secure environments. Also, the name of a programming language. See Chapter7.

Cluster controller
A device such as an IBM 3x74 to which older terminal devices can be connected so that they can access network services built for modern, intelligent peripherals.

CMIP/CMIS
Common management information protocol/service. A standard developed by the OSI to allow systems to be remotely managed.

Code
A computer program expressed in the machine language of the computer on which it will be executed, that is the executable form of a program. More generally, a program expressed in representation that requires only trivial changes to make it ready for execution.

COM
Common object model. The expansion of the component object model (see below) to add support for distribution. Developed by Microsoft and Digital. See Chapter 5.

COM
Component object model. The non-distributed framework underlying Microsoft's OLE object technology. See Chapter 5.

Components
Parts of a larger entity – a program, a network or a computer system.

Computer
A piece of hardware that can store and execute instructions (that is interpret them and cause some action to occur). If you needed to look this one up you may have difficulties with the rest of the book!

Concurrency
Describes a situation where two things are happening at the same time. Usually taken as a synonym for parallelism. There is a difference, however. With parallelism the various strands of activity are related. This is not necessarily so with concurrency. See Section 4.3.2.

Configuration	A collection of items that bear a particular relation to each other (for example data configuration of a system in which classes of data and their relationships are defined).
Conway's law	This states that the organization used to produce a system and structure of the system are congruent. For example if you have three groups working on a compiler project, then they will produce a three-pass compiler.
Conversational	A conversational interaction is a dialogue between two parties where each 'speaks' alternately. See Section 4.3.2.
CORBA	Common object request broker architecture. Strictly, the name of a framework specification produced by the Object Management Group describing the main components of a distributed 'object environment'. More loosely, the name for any of a number of related specifications produced by the OMG. See Chapter 5 and Appendix A.
CPU	Central processing unit. The heart of a computer. Many CPUs are synonymous with the class of computer built around them. For instance, the 486 class of PC is based on an Intel 80486 processor.
Cyberspace	A term used to describe the world of computers and the society that gathers around them. First coined by William Gibson in his novel *Neuromancer*. A follow-on term (Cyberia) is sometimes used to denote an isolated existence where your screen is your main outlet.

D

Daemon	A program that lies dormant waking up at regular intervals or waiting for some predetermined condition to occur before performing its action. Supposedly an acronym rationalized from *d*isk *a*nd *e*xecution *mon*itor.
Data	Usually the same as information. Sometimes information is regarded as processed data.
Data compression	A method of reducing the amount of data to be transmitted by applying an algorithm to the basic data source. A decompression algorithm expands the data back to its original state at the other end of the link. Compression can be 'lossless' or 'lossy'. In the lossless case the compression–decompression process preserves all the original information. In the lossy case some information is sacrificed to gain greater compression. Lossy

compression is typically applied to data such as digitized photographic images where such losses are largely unimportant.

Database
A collection of interrelated data stored together with controlled redundancy to support one or more applications. On a network data files are organized so that users can access a pool of relevant information.

Database server
The machine that controls access to the database using client/server architecture. The server part of the program is responsible for updating records, ensuring that multiple access is available to authorized users, protecting the data and communicating with other servers holding relevant data.

Deadlock
A condition where two or more processes are waiting for one of the others to do something. In the meantime, nothing happens. A condition (undesirable) that needs to be guarded against, especially in the design of databases.

Derivation
In object orientation a relationship between classes. A subclass is derived from its superclass. See also Inheritance and Section 4.5.

Dongle
A security or copy protection device for commercial microprocessor programs. Programs query the dongle (a device that needs to be inserted in the external port of the computer) before they will run.

DBMS
Database management system. A set of software used to set up and maintain a database that will allow users to call up the records they require. In many cases, a DBMS will also offer report and application generating facilities.

DCE
Distributed computing environment. A set of definitions and software components for distributed computing developed by the Open Software Foundation, an industry-led consortium. It is primarily an RPC technology with integrated security and directory services. See Chapter 5.

Debugging
The detection, location and elimination of bugs.

Design
(n) A plan for a technical artefact.

Design
(v) To create a design; to plan and structure a technical artefact. In software engineering the phase that is often preceded by implementation ...

Directory
A directory provides a means of translating from one form of information to another. In a distributed system directory services are a key component. Examples include NIS, CDS and

	NDS. They often perform much the same function as a telephone directory – translating from a symbolic name to a network address. See Chapter5.
Distributed computing	A move away from having large centralized computers such as minicomputer and mainframes, and bringing processing power to the desktop. Often used as a synonym for distributed processing.
Distributed database	A database that allows users to gain access to records, as though they were held locally, through a database server on each of the machines holding part of the database. Every database server needs to be able to communicate with all the others as well as being accessible to multiple users.
Distributed processing	The distribution of information processing functions among several different locations in a distributed system.
DME	Distributed management environment. DME has been planned as the management adjunct to the distributed computing environment. See Chapter 5, Chapter 7 and Appendix A.
DNS	Domain name service. The method used to convert Internet textual addresses – for example, gatekeeper.dec.com – to their corresponding numerical addresses.
Domain	Part of a naming hierarchy. A domain name consists, for example, of a sequence of names or other words separated by dots.
DoD	The U.S. Department of Defense.
DOS	Disk operating system. Usually used as a shorthand for one particular disk operation system, MS-DOS.
DTP	Desktop publishing. DTP software provides the capability to produce documents using personal computers to professional quality. The quality achieved in practice is largely a function of the professional skill of the users.
DTP	Distributed transaction processing. See Transaction processing and Chapter 5.
Dumb terminal	See Intelligent terminal.

E

EBCDIC	Extended binary coded decimal interchange code.
ECMA	European Computer Manufacturers' Association. An association composed of members from computer manufacturers in

Europe, it produces its own standards and contributes to CCITT and ISO.

e-mail or email   Common shorthand for electronic mail.

Endianness   A term used to describe the packing of bytes into words within a computer processor. Processors are typically 'little endian' – least significant byte first – or 'big endian' – most significant first. Little endians are typified by Intel and DEC VAX and Alpha processors.

Enterprise   A term (usually used as a descriptor for 'network' or 'computing') to denote the resources deployed to suit the operating needs of particular organizations.

ESIOP   Environment-specific inter-ORB protocol. A protocol defined by the OMG for communication between ORBs. See pp. 131–6.

Ethernet   A local area network (LAN) characterized by 10 Mbit/second transmission using the CSMA/CD (collision sense multiple access with collision detection) access method. Ethernet was originally developed by and is a registered trademark of Xerox Corporation.

F

FAQ   Frequently asked questions. A set of files, available over the Internet, that provide a compendium of accumulated knowledge in a particular subject.

FDDI   Fibre distributed data interface. An American National Standards Institute (ANSI) LAN standard. It is intended to carry data between computers at speeds up to 100 Mbit/second via fibre optic links. It uses a counter-rotating Token Ring topology and is compatible with the first, physical level of the ISO seven-layer model.

Feature interaction   Term used to describe knock-on effects in system design. Most commonly experienced when an 'enhancement' to one feature causes another to cease working (a feature that allows access to more databases causes the system configuration records to over-write). In many ways, a fancy way of describing a design bug.

Federation   A union of otherwise largely independent systems to support some common purpose. Federated systems share some basic agreements or protocols to enable them to work together but are operated and managed autonomously. See Table 4.1, Section 4.7 and Chapter 5.

File server	A machine in a local area network dedicated to providing file and data storage to other machines on the network. See Section 4.3.1.
Firmware	Halfway between software and hardware Firmware is a term often used to describe the software within a device which has been permanently committed to ROM.
FLOPS	Stands for floating point operations – another measure of computer power. See MIPS.
Frame Relay	A packet-based data communications service standard that is often regarded as a lightweight version of X25. It transmits bursts of data over a wide area network in packets that vary in length from 7 to 1024 bytes. Frame relay is data oriented, and typically used for LAN-to-LAN connection.
FTAM	File transfer, access and manipulation. A protocol entity forming part of the application layer enabling users to manage and access a distributed file system.
FTP	File transfer protocol. The Internet standard (as defined in the RFC series) high-level protocol for transferring files from one computer to another. A widely used *de facto* standard (c.f. the sparingly used *de jure* standard FTP). Anonymous FTP is a common way of allowing limited access to publicly available files via an anonymous login.
FYI	For your information. These are Internet bulletins that answer common questions. See also FAQ and RFC.

G

Gateway	Hardware and software that connect incompatible networks, which enables data to be passed from one network to another. The gateway performs the necessary protocol conversions.
GIF	Graphics interchange format. An image file format widely used on the Internet. More compact than the alternative JPEG (.jpg) standard but lower quality pictures. GIF files are easily spotted by their .gif extension.
GIOP	General inter-ORB protocol. A protocol defined by the OMG for communication between ORBs. See p. 131.
Gopher	One of a number of Internet-based services that provide information search and retrieval facilities. See also FTP, HTTP, WAIS and WWW.

GOSIP	Government open systems interconnect profiles. Government initiatives to help users procure open systems. There are both UK and U.S. GOSIPs.
Groupware	A general term to denote software-based tools that can be used to support a distributed set of workers. This covers applications as disparate as Windows for Workgroups through to PC video-phones. More formally called computer supported cooperative working (CSCW). See Chapter 3.
GSM	Global system for mobile communications. The standard for digital cellular communications that has been widely adopted across Europe. The GSM standard operates in the 900 MHz and 1800 MHz bands and provides a host of services thanks to a sophisticated signalling system. Apart from better speech quality than the older analog mobile standards, GSM allows people to use e-mail and other similar facilities remotely.
GUI	Graphical user interface. An interface that enables a user to interact with a computer using graphical images and a pointing device rather than a character-based display and keyboard. Such interfaces are also known as 'WIMP' interfaces – WIMP standing for Windows, Icons, Menus and Pointers. The most common pointing device is that electronic rodent – the mouse.

H

Hardware	The physical equipment in a computer system. It is usually contrasted with software.
Heritage system	Another euphemism – synonymous with the Legacy system (see Chapter 6).
Hierarchical network	A network structure composed of layers. An example of this can be found in a telephone network. The lower layer is the local network followed by a trunk (long-distance) network up to the international exchange networks.
Heterogenous	Of mixed or different type.
Homogeneous	Of the same type.
Hostage data	Data which is generally useful but held by a system which makes external access to the data difficult or expensive.
HTTP	Hyper-text transfer protocol. The basic protocol underlying the World Wide Web system (see WWW). It is a simple, stateless request–response protocol. Its format and use is rather similar to SMTP. HTTP is defined as one of the Internet's RFC series.

HTML	Hyper-text markup language. HTML is the language used to describe the formatting in WWW documents. It is an SGML document-type definition. It is described in the RFC series of standards.

I

IAB	Internet Activities Board. The influential panel that guides the technical standards adopted over the Internet. Responsible for the widely accepted TCP/IP family of protocols. More recently, the IAB has accepted SNMP as its approved network management protocol.
IDL	Interface definition language. A notation that allows programs to be written for distribution. An IDL compiler generates stubs that provide a uniform interface to remote resources. Used in RPC systems. See Section 5.1.1.
IEEE	The Institute of Electrical and Electronic Engineers. U.S.-based professional body covering network and computing engineering.
IEE	Institute of Electrical Engineers. UK equivalent of the IEEE.
IETF	Internet engineering task force. A very active body parented on the IAB, responsible for many of the *de facto* standards used on the Internet.
IIOP	Internet inter-ORB protocol. A protocol defined by the OMG for communication between ORBs. See p. 131.
Information processor	A computer-based processor for data storage and/or manipulation services for the end user.
Information retrieval	Any method or procedure which is used for the recovery of information or data which has been stored in an electronic medium.
Inheritance	In object orientation a relationship between classes. A subclass inherits from its superclass. See also Derivation and Section 4.5.
Intelligent terminal	A terminal which contains a processor and memory with some level of programming facility. The opposite is a dumb terminal.
Interface	The boundary between two things: typically two programs, two pieces of hardware, a computer and its user or a project manager and the customer.

Internet	A concatenation of many individual TCP/IP sites into one single logical network all sharing a common addressing scheme and naming convention.
Interoperate	The ability of computers from different vendors to work together using a common set of protocols. Suns, Vaxen, IBMs, Macs, PCs and so on all work together allowing each to communicate with and use the resources of the other.
IPX	A proprietary protocol for local area networks, developed by Novell. IPX is very widely used.
ISDN	Integrated services digital network. An all digital network that allows transmission of simultaneous voice and data under the control of separate out-of-band signalling. The residential form of ISDN provides two 64 kbits/second channels for data and one 16 kbits/second channel for signalling.
ISO	International Organization for Standardization. Commonly believed to stand for International Standards Organization. In fact ISO is not an abbreviation – it is intended to signify commonality (derived from the Greek *iso* meaning 'same'). ISO is responsible for many standards including those for data communications and computing. A well-known standard produced by ISO is the seven-layer open systems interconnection (OSI) model.

J, K

Java	A programming language and environment for developing mobile code applications such as the HotJava browser. See Section 5.7.
JFDI	Just do it. An approach to managing software projects that spurns too much introspection in favour of action.
JPEG	Joint photographic experts group. An image file format used in files with a .jpg extension. See GIF. Viewers for JPEG encoded files (for example Lview) are readily available in the public domain.
JVM	Java virtual machine. See Section 5.7.
Kermit	A communications protocol developed to allow files to be transferred between otherwise incompatible computers. Generally regarded as a backstop, if all else fails.
Kernel	The level of an operating system that contains the system level commands – the functions hidden from the user. This program is always running on a processor.

Key	In encryption systems, this is the digital code used with a coding algorithm to render a data stream unique once it has been encrypted. Keys can be either public or private.

L

LAN	Local area network. A data communications network used to interconnect terminal equipment and peripherals distributed over a limited area (typically a building or site).
Language	An agreed upon set of symbols, rules for combining them and meanings attached to the symbols that is used to express something (for example the Pascal programming language, job-control language for an operating system and a graphical language for building models of a proposed piece of software).
LAN Manager	A network operation system developed by Microsoft for PCs running IBM's OS/2, based on Intel's 80X86 series of microprocessors.
Latency	The time it takes for a packet to cross a network connection, from sender to receiver or the period of time that a frame is held by a network device before it is forwarded. Two of the most important parameters of a communications channel are its latency and its bandwidth.
Legacy system	A system which has been custom-developed to satisfy a specific requirement and is, usually, difficult to substantially reconfigure without major re-engineering
Life-cycle	A defined set of stages through which a system development passes over time – from requirements' analysis to maintenance. Common examples are the waterfall (for sequential, staged developments) and the spiral (for iterative, incremental developments). Life-cycles do not map to reality too closely but do provide some basis for measurement and hence control.

M

Mainframe	The traditional, centralized, batch-processing computer, placed in a computer room, serving many users. Used to be virtually synonymous with large, powerful IBM machines (such as a 370). The distinction between the mainframe and any other computer has become less clear as workstations have become more powerful.

Maintenance	Changes to a system component after its initial development; also called evolution. In practice, it is the task of modifying (locating problems, correcting or updating and so on) a system software or configuration after it has been put into operation.
Marshalling	See p 95.
MBWA	Management by walking about. An approach taken by those who believe that you learn more about reality by talking to those at the coalface than by poring over project reports and so on. Projects that follow this approach tend to be more successful.
Messaging	Exchanging messages. Often refers, but is not limited, to the context of electronic mail. See Section 5.2.
Message passing	Communication through the exchange of messages. Although not a rigorously used term message-passing systems usually have the connotation of real-time immediate message exchange. See Section 4.2.
Message queueing	A message-passing technology augmented by a store-and-for ward capability. See Section 4.2.
Method	A way of doing something – a defined approach to achieving the various phases of the life-cycle. Methods are usually regarded as functionally similar to tools (for example a specific tool will support a particular method).
Methodology	Strictly, the science or study of methods. More frequently used as a more important sounding synonym for 'method'.
MHS	Message handling service. The protocol forming part of the applications layer and providing a generalized facility for exchanging messages between systems.
MIME	Multi-purpose Internet mail extensions. A method of file identification such that the first packet of information received by a client tells it about the type of file the server has sent (for example postscript, word document and so on). See Chapters 3 and 5.
MIPS	Millions of instructions per second. A crude measure of a computer's processing power is how many instructions per second it can handle. A similar measure applied to more numerically intensive computing is FLOPS or floating point operations per second – although the 'megaflop' (one million floating point operations per second) is the more often quoted derived unit.
Model	An abstraction of reality that bears enough resemblance to the object of the model that we can answer some questions about the object by consulting the model.

Mobile code
: Programs capable of being run on and moving between many different systems. See Section 5.7.

Modelling
: Simulation of a system by manipulating a number of interactive variables; can answer 'what if ...?' questions to predict the behaviour of the modelled system. A model of a system or subsystem is often called a prototype.

Modem
: MOdulator–DEModulator. Data communications equipment that performs necessary signal conversions to and from terminals to permit transmission of source data over telephone and/or data networks.

Modularization
: The splitting up of a software system into a number of sections (modules) to ease design, coding and so on. Only works if the interfaces between the modules are clearly and accurately specified.

MPEG
: Moving picture experts group. This group has set a number of standards for the encoding of video clips and other moving images. Players for MPEG encoded files (for example Sparkle) are readily available in the public domain.

MOM
: Message oriented middleware. A term used to describe commercial message-passing and message-queueing products.

MP
: Abbreviation used for both multiprocessing and message passing.

MQ
: See Message queueing.

MS-DOS
: Microsoft disk operating system. The operating system developed for the original IBM PC (when it was known as PC-DOS).

Multiplexing
: The sharing of common transmission medium for the simultaneous sending and receiving of independent information signals. There are two dominant types of multiplexing: frequency division multiplexing (FDM), in which separate carrier frequencies are used for different signals, and time division multiplexing (TDM), in which the signals are interleaved in discrete time slots.

Multiprocessing
: Running multiple processes or tasks simultaneously. This is possible when a machine has more than one processor or processing is shared among a network of uniprocessor machines. See also multitasking and multithreading.

Multiprocessor
: A single computer having more than one processor and capable of executing more than one program at once.

Multitasking
: Performing (or seeming to perform) more than one task at a time. Multitasking operating systems such as Windows, OS/2

or UNIX give the illusion to a user of running more than one program at once on a machine with a single processor. This is done by 'time-slicing', dividing a processor into small chunks which are allocated in turn to competing tasks. See Chapter 4.

Multithreading	Running multiple threads of execution within a single process. This is a lower level of granularity than multiprocessing or multitasking. Threads within a process share access to the process' memory and other resources. Threads may be 'time-sliced' on a uniprocessor system or execute in parallel on a multiprocessor system. See Sections 4.3.2 and 4.6.
MVS	An operating system developed by IBM for their mainframe systems.

N

Named pipes	Part of Microsoft's LAN Manager – an interface for interprocessing communications and distributed applications. An alternative to NetBIOS designed to extend the interprocess interfaces of OS/2 across a network.
NetBIOS	Network basic input/output system. An IBM-developed protocol. It enables IBM PCs to interface and have access to a network.
NetWare	A Novell, Inc. network operating system and associated products. Widely used to manage LANs.
Network	A general term used to describe the interconnection of computers and their peripheral devices by communications channels. For example public switched telephone network (PSTN), packet switched data network (PSDN), local area network (LAN), wide area network (WAN).
Network interface	The circuitry that connects a node to the network, usually in the form of a card fitted into one of the expansion slots in the back of the machine; it works with the network software and operating system to transmit and receive messages on the network.
Network management	A general term embracing all the functions and processes involved in managing a network, including configuration, fault diagnosis and correction. It also concerns itself with statistics gathering on network usage.
Network operating system	A network operating system (NOS) extends some of the facilities of a local operating system across a LAN. It commonly provides facilities such as access to shared file storage and printers. Examples include NetWare and LAN Manager.

Network topology	The geometry of the network describing the way the nodes are interconnected.
NDS	Netware directory service. The directory service that forms part of Novell's Netware system.
NDR	Network data representation. The 'on the wire' data format used by DCE. See p. 95.
NFS	Network file system. A method, developed by Sun Microsystems, that allows computers to share files across a network as if they were local. See Chapter 5.
NIC	The Network Information Centre. Source of much information on the Internet and related networking issues.
NIS	Network information services. Once known as 'Yellow Pages', a distributed directory service developed by Sun Microsystems. See Chapter 5.
NIS+	An enhanced version of NIS. It has influenced X/Open's federated naming standard (XFN).
NMF	Network Management Forum. See Appendix A for a description of this organization.
Non-proprietary	Software and hardware that is not bound to one manufacturer's platform. Equipment that is designed to specification that can accommodate other companies' products. The advantage of non-proprietary equipment is that a user has more freedom of choice. The disadvantage is when it does not work, you may have to do your own fault finding.
NOS	See Network operating system.
Notification	An unsolicited message sent out by a process to inform interested parties that some event has occurred. See Section 4.3.2 and Chapter 7.

O

Object	An abstract, encapsulated entity which provides a well-defined service via a well-defined interface. An object belongs to a particular class which defines its type and properties. See Section 4.5.
Object orientation	A philosophy that breaks a problem into a number of cooperating objects. Object-oriented design is becoming increasingly popular in both software engineering and related domains, for

example in the specification of network management systems. See Object and Section 4.5.

Object program   The translated versions of a program that has been assembled or compiled.

ODP   Open distributed processing. An attempt by the ISO to define a common architecture for distributed systems. See Appendix A for a description of the ISO.

OLE   Object linking and embedding. Microsoft's proprietary object 'component' technology. Often compared to CORBA. See Chapter 5.

OMG   Object Management Group. An industry consortium responsible for the CORBA specifications. See Appendix A.

OMNI   Open managed network interoperability. A set of standards for network management from the Network Management Forum (see Appendix A). The OMNI standards includes the CMIS and CMIP definitions for connection between network elements and network management systems.

OO   Common abbreviation for object orientation.

Open system   A term much abused by marketing departments. The usual meaning of an open system is one built to conform to published, standard specifications or interfaces, for example POSIX. Openness, like beauty, is often in the eye of the beholder. See also Non-proprietary.

Operating   Software such as MVS, OS/2, Windows, VMS, MS-DOS or
system   UNIX that manages the computer's hardware and software. Unless it intentionally hands over to another program, an operating system runs programs and controls system resources and peripheral devices.

OS/2   An operating system for PCs developed by IBM (originally in conjunction with Microsoft).

OSCA   Open systems cabling architecture. A flexible structured cabling system for local networks.

OSCA   Open systems communications architecture. An influential set of concepts to cope with the interoperability of large-scale software products. OCSA was developed by Bellcore in the 1980s, and many of the ideas it contained have found their way into modern thinking on how distributed systems should be built.

OSF   Open Software Foundation. An industry consortium that specifies and develops a number of software technologies. One of

| | these is OSF DCE. See Chapter 5 for more technical detail on DCE and Appendix A for a description of OSF as an organization. |
| OSI | Open systems interconnection. The ISO reference model consisting of seven protocol layers. These are the application, presentation, session, transport, network, link and physical layers. The concept of the protocols is to provide manufacturers and suppliers of communications equipment with a standard that will provide reliable communications across a broad range of equipment types. Also more broadly applied to a range of related computing and network standards. |

P

Packet	A unit of data sent across a network.
Parallel processing	Performing more than one process in parallel. Usually associated with computer-intensive tasks which can be split up into a large number of small chunks which can be processed independently on an array of relatively inexpensive machines. Many engineering and scientific problems can be solved in this way. It is also frequently used in high-quality computer graphics. See also multiprocessing and Chapter 4.
Parameter	A variable whose value may change the operation but not the structure of some activity (for example an important parameter in the productivity of a program is the language used). Also commonly used to describe the inputs to and outputs from functions in programming languages. In this context they may also be known as 'arguments'.
Pathological testing	Use of a dataset that is at (and beyond) the extremes of the typical. Pathological data is frequently used to test a system's response to exceptional conditions.
PC-DOS	See MS-DOS.
Peer-to-peer	Communications between two devices on an equal footing, as opposed to host/terminal, or master/slave. In peer-to-peer communications both machines have and use processing power. See Section 4.3.
Pipe	A feature of many operating systems, a pipe is a method used by processes to communicate with each other. When a program sends data to a pipe, it is transmitted directly to the other process without ever being written onto a file.

Polling	Process of interrogating terminals in a multipoint network in turn in a prearranged sequence by controlling the computer to determine whether the terminals are ready to transmit or receive. If so, the polling sequence is temporarily interrupted while the terminal transmits or receives.
Port	(n). A device which acts as an input/output connection. Serial port or parallel port are examples.
	(v). To transport software from one system to another different system and make the necessary changes so that the software runs correctly.
POSIX	Portable operating system interfaces. A set of international standards defining APIs based upon the UNIX operating system. See Appendix A.
Process	The usual term for a program currently being run by an operating system. A process is assigned resources such as memory and processor time in the operating system. The term 'task' is sometimes used as a synonym. See also multiprocessing, multitasking and multithreading.
Processor	That part of a computer capable of executing instructions. More generally, any active agent capable of carrying out a set of instructions (for example a transaction processor for modifying a database).
Proprietary	Any item of technology that is designed to work with only one manufacturer's equipment. The opposite of the principle behind open systems interconnection (OSI).
Protocol	A set of rules and procedures that are used to formulate standards for information transfer between devices. Protocols can be low level (for example the order in which bits and bytes are sent across a wire) or high level (for example the way in which two programs transfer a file over the Internet).
Prototype	A scaled-down version of something, built before the complete item is built, in order to assess the feasibility or utility of the full version.
Proxy	See Section 7.1
PSTN	Public switched telephone network – the public telephone system providing local, long-distance and international telephone service. In addition, widely used (with modems) for many other data services.

PTT

Postal, Telegraph and Telephone – the administrative authority in a country that controls all postal and public telecommunication services in that country. Same as PNO – public network operator

Q

Quality assessment

A systematic and independent examination to determine whether quality activities and related results comply with planned arrangements and whether these arrangements are implemented effectively and are suitable to achieve objectives.

Quality system

The organizational structure, responsibilities, procedures, processes and resources for implementing quality management.

Quality system standards

A quality system standard is a document specifying the elements of a quality system. The ISO 9001 standard (which is generally used to control software development) is a widely known and used quality standard.

R

Remote procedure call

An RPC provides a distributed programming mechanism where an apparently local procedure call in a client causes an implementation of the procedure provided by a server to be invoked. See Section 5.1.

Resolve

Translate an Internet name into its equivalent IP address or other DNS information.

RFC

Request for comment. A long-established series of Internet 'standards' documents widely followed by commercial software developers. As well as defining common Internet protocols RFCs often provide the implementation detail to supplement the more general guidance of ISO and other formal standards. The main vehicle for the publication of Internet standards, such as SNMP.

Routers

A router operates at level 3 (the network layer) of the OSI model. Routers are protocol specific and act on routing information carried out by the communications protocol in the network layer. A router is able to use the information it has obtained about the network topology and can choose the best route for a packet to follow.   Routers are independent of the physical level (layer 1) and can be used to link a number of different network types together.

Routing	The selection of a communications path for the transmission of information from source to destination.
RPC	See Remote procedure call.
RSA	A well-known and widely used software-based, public key encryption method. It is named after its inventors – Rivest, Shamir and Adleman.

S

SATAN	Security administration tool for analysing networks. This probes networked systems to see if services such as FTP are correctly set up, if well-known security flaws are present and so on. The results of a SATAN analysis are stored in a database for subsequent viewing with a standard HTML browser. A script called 'repent' is included with the system to revise its name to SANTA.
SCP	Service control point. A concept developed primarily in the telecommunications community to describe the place where 'intelligent' network functions are carried out. In practice, an SCP is one of a set of distributed processors that respond to user service requests.
Screen-scraping	A method of accessing a server where the client presents itself as being a direct interface to a human user. The client 'reads' information from the 'screen' presented by the server and 'sends' information as 'keystrokes' from the pretend user.
SCSI	Small computer system interface. A bus-independent standard for system-level interfacing between a computer and an intelligent device (for example an external disk). Pronounced 'scuzzy'.
Serializing	Another name for marshalling.
Server	An object which is participating in an interaction with another object, and is taking the role of providing the required service. See also Client and Section 4.3.1.
Session	The connection of two nodes on a network for the exchange of data – any live link between any two data devices.
SGML	Standard graphical markup language. An international standard encoding scheme for linked textual information. HTML is a subset.
Signalling	The passing of information and instructions from one point to another for the setting up or supervision of a telephone call or message transmission.

Smalltalk   An object-oriented programming language and environment originally developed by Xerox in the 1980s.

SMP   Symmetrical multiprocessing. The use of a balanced set of computing elements to give high performance processing.

SMTP   Simple mail transfer protocol. The Internet standard for the transfer of mail messages from one processor to another. The protocol details the format and control of messages. It is defined in Internet RFC 822. See Chapter 4.

SNA   Systems network architecture – a set of layered communications protocols for sending data between IBM hardware and software.

SNMP   Simple network management protocol – consists of three parts: structure of management information (SMI), management information base (MIB) and the protocol itself. The SMI and MIB define and store the set of managed entities. SNMP transports information to and from these entities.

SOM   This is IBM's object-oriented development environment that allows users to put together class libraries and programs. Associated with SOM is an OMG CORBA conformant object request broker (known as DSOM) for building distributed applications. See also COM, the Microsoft equivalent of SOM.

SQL   Structured query language. A widely used means of accessing the information held in a database. SQL enables a user to build reports using the data held.

Stateful   When applied to a server, this term implies that the server maintains knowledge about and context for its clients between requests. See Sections 4.3.2 and 8.2.3.

Stateless   When applied to a server, this term implies that a server maintains no knowledge about its clients between requests – each request is handled in isolation from all preceding and following requests. See Sections 4.3.2 and 8.2.3.

Stub   See Section 5.1.2.

Subclass   See Object and Section 4.5.

Superclass   See Object and Section 4.5.

Switching   Process by which transmissions between terminals are interconnected, effected at exchange at nodal point exchanges in the network.

Synchronicity See Section 4.6.2.

Synchronization   The actions of maintaining the correct timing sequences for the operation of a system.

Synchronous transmission   Transmission between terminals where data is normally transmitted in blocks of binary digit streams and transmitter and receiver clocks are maintained in synchronism.

Syntax   The set of rules for combining the elements of a language (for example words) into permitted constructions (for example phrases and sentences). The set of rules does not define meaning, nor does it depend on the use made of the final construction.

System   A collection of independently useful objects which happen to have been developed at the same time.

A collection of elements that work together, forming a coherent whole (for example a computer system consisting of processors, printers, disks and so on).

System design   The process of establishing the overall architecture of a system.

T

Task   See Process.

TCP/IP   Transmission Control Protocol/Internet Protocol – a set of protocols that have become a *de facto* networking standard. They were devised within the Internet community and issued by the IETF. Commonly used over LAN and public networks; they can be viewed as one of the few protocols available that are really universal. TCP/IP operates around the third and fourth layers of the OSI model (network and transport respectively).

Telecommunications   The general name given to the means of communicating information over a distance by electrical and electromagnetic methods. The transmission and reception of information by any kind of electromagnetic system.

Teleworking   Using computing and communication technology to work away from an office.

Telnet   An TCP/IP-based application that allows connection to a remote computer as if connected directly to the remote host.

Terminal   Usually, the end-user device used to access a computer network. Can be anything from a 'dumb terminal' giving no more than display and keyboard input to a powerful workstation. See Chapter 2 for the evolution of terminals.

TINA	Telecommunications intelligent network architecture. This organization, which is applying distributed systems technology to telecommunications, is described in Appendix A.
Topology	A description of the shape of a network, for example star, bus and ring. It can also be a template or pattern for the possible logical connections onto a network.
TP	See Transaction processing.
Trading	Matching requests for services to appropriate suppliers of those services, based on some constraints. See Chapter 5.
Transaction	A single, atomic unit of processing. Usually a single, small 'parcel' of work which should either succeed entirely or fail entirely. See Chapter 5.
Transaction processing	Originally a term that mainly applied to technology concerned with controlling the rate of enquiries to a database. Specialist software – known as a TP monitor – allowed potential bottlenecks to be managed. Now more widely applied to systems supporting the 'ACID' properties. See Chapter 5.
Transparency	Distribution transparencies provide the ability for some of the distributed aspects of a system to be hidden from users. For example location transparency may allow a user to access remote resources in exactly the same way as local ones. See Section 4.1.

U, V

UDP	User Datagram Protocol. A connectionless protocol which, like TCP, is used with IP. Defined in RFC 768, UDP is well suited to carrying the more basic Internet services. It is efficient but not as reliable as TCP.
Uniprocessor	A computer having only a single main processor.
UNO	Universal network objects. A standard defined by the OMG for communication between ORBs. See p. 131.
URL	Uniform resource locator. Essentially, this is the form of address for reaching pages on the World Wide Web. A typical URL takes the form http://www.myname.com/.
Usenet	A distributed bulletin board system supported mainly by UNIX machines. Probably the largest decentralized information utility in the world. It encompasses government agencies, universities, schools, businesses and hobbyists. Hosts well over 1200 news

groups and incorporates the equivalent of several thousand paper pages of new technical articles, news, discussion, opinion and so on every day. To join in you need a news reader such as xrn.

UUCP
UNIX–UNIX communication protocol or UNIX–UNIX copy. A basic and now largely obsolete mechanism that allow computers running the UNIX operating system to interoperate. Was once one of the primary means for exchanging mail and news within Usenet.

UUID
Universally unique identifier. See Section 5.1.1.

VAX
A minicomputer developed by the Digital Equipment Corporation that was once the mainstay of many academic and commercial computing environments.

Vaxen
The attractive and whimsical, if incorrect, plural of 'VAX'.

Vendor independent
Hardware or software that will work with hardware and software manufactured by different vendors – the opposite of proprietary.

Virtual device
A module allocated to an application by an operating system or network operating system instead of a real or physical device. The user can then use a facility (keyboard or memory or disk or port) as though it was really present. In fact, only the operating system has access to the real device.

Virtual machine
An assumed resource that exists as a definition rather than as a real machine. The concept of a virtual machine is useful in that it gives developers a target for their applications. They can write for the virtual machine and reasonably expect the translations and additions required by a range of real machines to be available.

Virtual team
A group of people working together on the same project, who are physically separate, their only link being via a network and computer screen plus (hopefully) some application software that helps them to work together.

Virus
A program, passed over networks, that has potentially destructive effects once it arrives. Packages such as Virus Guard are in common use to prevent infection from hostile visitors.

VMS
An operating system developed by DEC originally for their VAX computers.

VRML
Virtual reality markup language. An extension of the HTML concept into virtual reality. VRML provides a language for coding virtual reality images that can be accessed over a network by anyone with a compatible browser.

W

W3	Common abbreviation for World Wide Web.
WAN	Wide area network. A network (usually one provided by a national public operator) that spans a long distance (for example several miles, beyond the reach of an Ethernet)
Waterfall	The name for the 'classical' system development cycle, so named because each activity leads neatly into the next so the chart used to portray it suggests a waterfall.
Window	A flow control mechanism the size of which determines the number of packets that can be sent before an acknowledgement of receipt is needed, and before more can be transmitted.
Windows	A way of displaying information on a screen so that users can do the equivalent of looking at several pieces of paper at once. Each window can be manipulated for closer examination or amendment. This technique allows the user to look at two files at once or even to run more than one program simultaneously.
Windows	The generic name (though not a registered trademark) for Microsoft's family of operating systems, including Windows 3.1, Windows for Workgroups®, Windows 95® and Windows NT®.
Workstation	A networked personal computing device with more power than a typical PC. Often a UNIX machine capable of running several tasks at the same time.
Worm	A computer program which replicates itself – a form of virus. The so-called 'Internet worm' of 1988 was probably the most famous. It successfully duplicated itself across thousands of machines.

X, Y, Z

X.400	A store-and-forward message-handling system (MHS) standard that allows for the electronic exchange of text as well as other electronic data such as graphics and fax. It enables suppliers to interwork between different electronic mail systems. X.400 has several protocols, defined to allow the reliable transfer of information between user agents and message transfer agents.
X.500	A directory services standard that permits applications such as electronic mail to access information, which can either be central or distributed.

X/Open   An industry standards consortium that develops detailed sys-
                tem specifications drawing on available standards. It has pro-
                duced standards for a number of distributed computing tech-
                nologies. X/Open also licenses the UNIX trademark and there-
                by brings focus to its various flavours (for example HP-UX,
                AIX from IBM, Solaris from SUN and so on). See Appendix
                A.

XDR   External data representation. The 'on the wire' data format
                used by Sun RPC. See p. 95.

XFN   X/Open federated naming standard. See Chapter 5.

Yahoo   Yet another hierarchically organized oracle. One of the many
                search utilities that can be used to trawl and crawl the informa-
                tion held on the World Wide Web. Others include Lycos, Alta
                Vista and Excite. See Chapter 3.

Zip   A compression program, from PKWare, to reduce files to be
                sent over a network to a more reasonable size. This was origi-
                nally popularized on MS-DOS but has now spread to other
                operating systems.

References

Atkins J. and Norris M. (1995). *Total Area Networking – ATM, SMDS and Frame Relay Explained*. Chichester: John Wiley and Sons.

Atkins J., Norris M. and Pretty S. (1996). *The Corporate Internet – Practical Design for Enterprise Networks*. Wokingham: Addison-Wesley.

ANSA (1988). *ANSA reference manual*. Cambridge: ANSA Consortium.

Bangemann M. (1994). *Report of the Bangemann High Level Group*. ETSI Collective Letter 968. Brussels; ETSI.

Barnes I. (1991). Post Fordist People. *Futures*, November.

Berners-Lee T., Fielding R. and Frystyk H. (1995). *Hypertext Transfer Protocol–HTTP/1.0*. INTERNET-DRAFT 0.4. (Latest draft available via http://www.w3.org/pub/WWW/Protocols/HTTP/1.0)

Birman K.P. (1993). The process group approach to reliable distributed computing. *Comm. ACM*, **36**(12), 37–54.

Birrell A.D. and Nelson B.J. (1984). Implementing Remote Procedure Calls. *ACM Transactions on Computing Systems*, **2**, 39–59.

Borenstein N. and Freed N. (1993). *MIME (Multipurpose Internet Mail Extensions): Mechanisms for Specifying and Describing the Format of Internet Message Bodies*. RFC 1341.

Cheswick W.R. and Bellovin S.M. (1994). *Firewalls and Internet Security: Repelling the Wily Hacker*. Wokingham: Addison-Wesley.

Clarke K. and Norris M. (1994). Data and Information Highways. In *Proc. Geographic Information Systems Conference,* October. London: Elsevier.

Cooke P., Moulaert F., Swyngedouw E., Weinstein O. and Wells P. (1993) *Towards Local Globalisation.* London: UCL Press.

Coulouris G., Dollimore J. and Kindberg T. (1994). *Distributed Systems – Concept and Design.* Wokingham: Addison-Wesley.

Crocker D. (1982). *Standard for the Format of ARPA Internet Text Messages.* RFC 822.

Datamation. (1991*a*). *Enterprise Networks: One step at a time.* 60–66.

Datamation. (1991*b*). *Connecting the Enterprise.* 26–31.

Davies D., Hilsom C. and Rudge A. (1993). *Telecommunications after AD2000. London:* Chapman and Hall.

Dennis J. and Van Horn E. (1966). Programming semantics for multipro-grammed computation. *Comm. ACM,* **9**(3), 143–155.

Drucker P. (1993). *Post Capitalist Society.* Oxford: Butterworth Heineman.

Federal Information Processing Standards. (1993). *Secure Hash Standard.* FIPS PUB 180–1.

Frenke K. A. (1990). The European Community and Information Technology. *Comm.* ACM, **33** (4), 23–31.

Gilder G. (1993). When bandwidth is Free. *Wired,* Sept/Oct.

Goldberg A. (1984). *Smalltalk-80: The Interactive Programming Environment.* Wokingham: Addison-Wesley.

Gore A. (1995). Infrastructure for the global village. *Scientific American* (special issue), 156–9.

Gray M., Hodson N. and Gordon G. (1993). *Teleworking Explained.* Chichester: John Wiley and Sons.

Hague A. (1991). *Beyond Universities. A New Republic of the Intellect.* London: Institute of Economic Affairs.

Handy C. (1990). *The Age of Unreason.* London: Arrow.

IEEE Journal - Selected Areas In Communications. (1992). Strategic impact of broadband communications in insurance, publishing and healthcare. *IEEE Journal,* 10 (9).

INMOS Ltd. (1987). *Occam 2 Reference Manual.* Hemel Hempstead: Prentice-Hall.

ISO/IEC (1990) 7498-4, 10040, 10164, 10165, 9595, 9596.

ISO/IEC. (1990*a*). *Information Technology – Open Systems Interconnection –
Specification of Basic Encoding Rules for Abstract Syntax Notation One
(ASN.1)*, ISO/IEC 8825. ISO.

ISO/IEC. (1990*b*). *Information Technology – Open Systems Interconnection –
The Directory – Part 1: Overview of Concepts, Models and Services.*
ISO/IEC 9594–1. ISO.

ISO/IEC. (1995). *Information Technology–Abstract Syntax Notation One
(ASN.1)*, ISO/IEC 8824, Parts 1–4, ISO.

ISO/IEC. *Information Technology – Open Systems Interconnection – Remote
Procedure Call*, ISO/IEC DIS 11578. ISO.

Johansen R. (1988). *Groupware*. New York: Free Press.

Kostner J. and Books W. (1994). *Knights of the Tele-Round Table*. New York:
Warner Books.

Lamport L. (1978). Time, clocks, and the ordering of events in a distributed
system. *Comm. ACM*, **21**(7), 58–565.

Linn J. (1993). *Generic Security Services Application Program Interface*. New
York: O'Reilley and Associates.

Lipnack J. and Stamps J. (1994). *The Age of the Network: Organizing principles for the 21st Century*. New York: Oliver Wight Publications.

Lu M. and Farrell C. (1989). Software development – an international perspective. *Systems & Software*, **9**, 88–97.

Meyer B. (1988). *Object-Oriented Software Construction*. Hemel Hempstead:
Prentice-Hall International.

Mills D.L. (1992). *Network Time Protocol (Version 3) Specification and
Implementation*. RFC 1305.

Mockapetris P.V. (1987*a*). *Domain Names – Concepts and Facilities*.
RFC 1034.

Mockapetris P.V. (1987*b*). *Domain Names – Implementation and Specification*.
RFC 1035.

Morton M. (1991). *The Corporation of the 1990s. Information Technology and
Organization Transformation*. New York: Oxford University Press.

Muffet A. (1992). *Crack Version 4.1: A Sensible Password Cracker for UNIX*.
Aberystwyth: University of Wales.

Mullender S.J., van Rossum G., Tannebaum A.S., van Renesse R. and van
Staveren H. (1990). Amoeba – A Distributed Operating System for the
1990s. *IEEE Computer*, **23**(5), 44–53.

Naisbitt J. (1994). *Global Paradox*. Nicholas Brealey Publishing.

Negroponte N. (1995). Products and services for computer networks. *Scientific American* (special issue), 102–9.

Norris M. (1995). *Survival in the software jungle*. Boston, USA: Artech House.

Norris M. and Rigby P. (1992) *Software Engineering Explained*. Chichester: John Wiley & Sons.

Norris M., Rigby P. and Payne M. (1993) *The Healthy Software Project*. Chichester: John Wiley & Sons.

Object Management Group. (1992). *Object Management Architecture Guide*, Revision 2.0. 2nd Edn. Object Management Group.

Ohmae K. (1990). *The Borderless World*. HarperCollins.

Ousterhout J.K. (1994). *Tcl and the Tk Toolkit*. Wokingham: Addison-Wesley.

Porter M. E. (1986). *Competition in Global Industries*. Harvard, USA: Harvard Business School Press.

Posch R. (1991). Forum column. *Software Magazine*. July.

Quarterman J. (1989). *The Matrix: Competitive Networks and Conferencing*

Quarterman J. and Smoot C-M. (1993). *The Internet Connection – Systems Connectivity and Configuration*. Wokingham: Addison-Wesley.

Reich R. (1991). *The Work of Nations*. Simon and Schuster.

Rivest R.L. (1990). *MD4 Message Digest Algorithm*. RFC 1186.

Rivest R.L. (1992). *MD5 Message Digest Algorithm*. RFC 1321.

Schiller J.I. (1994). Secure Distributed Computing. *Scientific American*, 54–58.

Sellar W.C. andYeatman R.J. (1993). *1066 and All That: A Memorable History of England*. London: Alan Sutton Publishing Ltd.

Silberschatz A. and Galvin P. (1994). *Operating System Concepts*, 4th Edn. Wokingham: Addison-Wesley.

Simon A. (1993). *Enterprise Computing*. Random Australia.

Sloman M. (1994). *Distributed Systems Management*. Wokingham: Addison-Wesley.

SNMP Version 1: RFC1155, RFC1157, RFC1212.

SNMP Version 2: RFC1441–1452.

Softwares Chronic Crisis, *Scientific American*, September 1994.

Spafford E.H. (1988). *The Internet Worm Program: An Analysis*. Purdue Technical Report CDS-TR-823.

Sproull L. and Kiesler S. (1991). Computers, networks and work. *Scientific American* (special issue), 128–40.

Stallings W. (1993). *Networking Standards – a Guide to OSI, ISDN, LAN and MAN Standards*. Wokingham: Addison-Wesley.

Steiner J.G., Neuman B.C. and Schiller J.I. (1988). *Kerberos: An Authentication Service for Open Network Systems*. Usenix Conference Proceedings, Dallas, Texas, 191–202, February.

Stoll C. (1989). *The Cuckoo's Egg*. Doubleday Books.

Sun Microsystems Inc. *XDR: External Data Representation Standard*. RFC-1014. Sun Microsystems, Inc.

Systems Integration. (1990). Ten of the leading architecture proposals for Enterprise Computing. *Systems Integration*. July.

Systems Worldwide. Digital Press.

Telecommunications Policy Review, January 1995.

Ward J., Griffiths P. and Whitmore P. (1993). *Strategic Systems Planning*. Chichester: John Wiley & Sons.

X/Open CAE Specification C193. (1992). *Distributed TP: The XA Specification*. X/Open Co. Ltd.

X/Open CAE Specification C309. (1994). *X/Open DCE: Remote Procedure Call*. X/Open Co., Ltd.

X/Open CAE Specification C403. (1995). *Federated Naming: The XFN Specification*. X/Open Co. Ltd.

X/Open CAE Specification C419. (1995). *Distributed TP: The XCPI-C Specification, Version 2*. X/Open Co. Ltd.

X/Open CAE Specification C505. (1995). *Distributed TP: The TxRPC Specification*. X/Open Co. Ltd.

X/Open CAE Specification C506. (1995). *Distributed TP: The XATMI Specification*. X/Open Co. Ltd.

X/Open Guide G307. (1993). *Distributed TP: Reference Model, Version 2*. X/Open Co. Ltd.

X/Open Guide. (1993). *Systems Management: Reference Model*. X/Open Company Ltd.

X/Open Ltd. (1991). *The Common Object Request Broker: Architecture and Specification*. X/Open Ltd. Object Management Group.

And finally, for a whole raft of references on many aspects of distributed systems, try – ftp://ftp.ira.uka.de/pub/bibliography/distributed/index.htm.

INDEX

Note: In addition to this index, references to particular subjects within the main text can be traced via the glossary.

Abstract Syntax Notation (ASN.1) 96
Access control 175
    lists 149
ACID properties 115, 121
Agents 202
Agile companies 14, 247
Amdahl's Law 82, 206
Andrew file system 153
ANSA 144, 152, 182, 252
Applets 128, 155
Architecture 182, 215
    enterprise 32
    functional 218
    physical 219
    technical 218
    three tier 68, 73, 182
    two tier 72
Asynchronicity 113
ATM 29
Atomicity 115
Authorisation 191
Authentication 147, 191
    tickets 147, 150, 173
Availability 171, 192, 208

Binding 96
Broadband 6, 7, 29
Business process re-engineering 163
Byte code 156

Caching 224
Cairo 137, 140
Causality 126
Cedar 89
Cell Directory Service (CDS) 144
Client/Server 64, 71
Communication 98
    networks 2

Complexity 36, 195
    hiding 220
Component Object Model (COM) 128, 137
Computer bureaux 21
Configuration control 200
Consistency 116, 224
CORBA 131, 135, 254
Cyberspace 2

Data communication 4
Data diversity 168
Data Encryption Standard (DES) 145, 198
Database 25, 49
    federated 155
    hierarchical 50
    object oriented 50
    relational 25, 50
Deadlock – *see* Deadly Embrace
Deadly Embrace – *see* Deadlock
Digests 146
Distributed Computing Environment 32, 89,
    91, 120, 136, 149, 153, 255
Distributed File System 153
Distributed Management Environment 198,
    205, 255
Distributed SOM (DSOM) 136
Distributed Time Service (DTS) 150
Distributed Transaction Processing 115, 119
Directories 143
Domain Name Service (DNS) 142
Durability 116
Dynamic Invocation Interface (DII) 134
Dynamic linking 92, 96
Dynamic Skeleton Interface (DSI) 134

Electronic mail 42, 109
Electronic scriptorium 246
Encina 120

Encryption 145, 196
End to end 199, 244
ESIOP 136
Evolution 79
External Data Representation (XDR) 95

FAQ 43
Feature interaction 213
Fingerprints 146
Firewalls 196
Fordism 13, 213
Forgery 35, 194
FTP 25, 44, 97
FYI 58

GDMO 205
GIOP 136
Global business 5
Global Standard for Mobiles (GSM) 28
Good Things 33, 92

Hashes 146
High Level Design 216
HotJava 155
HTTP 152

IDEA 145
IIOP 136
Information
    age 1, 3, 27, 221
    branding 239
    highway 2, 16
    management 34, 200
    ownership 238
Intelligent agents 168
Integration strategy 184, 257
Integrity 190
Interface Definition Language (IDL) 89,
    131
Interface strategy 180
Internet 22, 35, 41, 47
    activities board 260
    addressing 42
    applications 43
    history 41
Internet Protocol (IP) 41, 97
Internet Worm 194
InterNIC 91
IRDA 28
ISDN 28
ISIS 126, 140
Isolation 116

Java 47, 156
Journalling 116

Kerberos 36, 147, 173
Keys 145
    distribution 147

Legacy 165, 231
List server 43
Local Area Network 24, 28
Location 229
Locking 120
    mutual exclusion (mutex) 207
    optimistic 225
    pessimistic 225

Mainframes 22
Management Information Base (MIB) 202
Marshalling 95
Mbone 46
Message Oriented Middleware (MOM) 104
Message managers 105, 108
Messaging 63, 103
    dequeuing 111
    format 106
    forwarding 108
    queuing 108, 110
    reliability 113
    types 107
MIME 43
Mobile Code 155
Monikers 138
Multimedia 29, 54
Multiservice networks 7, 49
Multithreading 66, 83
Mutex – see Locking

Name Services 141
Naming 229
Networks 4, 6, 48
    enterprise 13, 31
    computer 22, 58
    multiservice 49
    protocols 101, 105
    virtual 12
Network Data Representation (NDR) 95
Network File System (NFS) 153
Network Operating System 25, 153
Network Information Service (NIS) 142
NIS+ 144
Network Time Protocol (NTP) 150

Object 52, 73
    distributed 127
    identifiers 91
    managed 202
    orientation 27, 74
    repositories 134
    services 131
Object Adaptor 133
Object Linking & Embedding (OLE) 28, 51,
    97, 128, 139
Object Management Group (OMG) 128,
    254
Object Request Broker (ORB) 129, 134
Occam 82

Occams Razor 231
OMNIPoint 256, 257
Open Database Connectivity (ODBC) 155
Open Distributed Processing (ODP) 251
OpenDoc 28, 51, 128, 139
Open Software Foundation (OSF) 255
Open Systems 32
Operating Systems 22, 24
Organisational disciplines 13

Parallel processing 61, 82
Partitioning 79
Peopleware 186, 228
Personal computer 23, 27
Plug and play 55
Polling 203
Pretty Good Privacy (PGP) 146
Privacy 190
Private key 145
Process Groups 122
  consistency 124
  ISIS 126
  synchronization 125
Product differentiation 14, 164
Proxy servers 179, 196
Public key 145

Queuing 227

Remote procedure call (RPC) 88, 251
  efficiency 101
  reliability 102
  security 99
  semantics 99
  strengths/weaknesses 100
Reversed assumptions 12, 60
RSA encryption 145

Secure Sockets Layer (SSL) 146
Security costs 222
Signatures 146
Smalltalk 73, 128, 156
SNMP 201
SMTP 42, 152
Spirit 183, 258

Standards 249
  strategies 263
  interworking 264
State 67, 222
Stovepipes 166, 220, 237
Stub code 89, 93, 96
SuperJanet 46
Synchronicity 101, 226
Synchronization 149
System management 35, 199, 232

Technology evolution 19
Telnet 25, 97
Threads 83, 102
Three tier model 68
Timestamps 150
Trading 92, 144
Transaction management 117
Transaction processing 115, 119
Transaction trading 10
Transmission Control Protocol (TCP) 41
Transparency 62
Tuxedo 119, 141
Two phase commit 118, 154

Unforeseen use 168, 194
Universally Unique Identifier (UUID) 91
Uniform resource locator (URL) 46
Usenet 43
User Datagram Protocol (UDP) 41

Virtual teams 7, 9, 33, 244
Virtual Machine 156

Well known end points 97
World Wide Web 28, 34, 45, 53, 233
  application 47
  browsers 45

X.500 143
XA 118
X/Open 116, 256
XFN 144

Yellow Pages 142